Julius M. (Julius Mendes) Price

From the Arctic Ocean to the Yellow Sea. The narrative of a journey, in 1890 and 1891, across Siberia, Mongolia, the Gobi Desert, and North China

Julius M. (Julius Mendes) Price

**From the Arctic Ocean to the Yellow Sea. The narrative of a journey, in 1890 and 1891, across Siberia, Mongolia, the Gobi Desert, and North China**

ISBN/EAN: 9783743314924

Manufactured in Europe, USA, Canada, Australia, Japa

Cover: Foto ©Andreas Hilbeck / pixelio.de

Manufactured and distributed by brebook publishing software (www.brebook.com)

Julius M. (Julius Mendes) Price

**From the Arctic Ocean to the Yellow Sea. The narrative of a journey, in 1890 and 1891, across Siberia, Mongolia, the Gobi Desert, and North China**

# CONTENTS.

## CHAPTER I.

### FROM BLACKWALL TO SIBERIA.

The object of the expedition—The steamer *Biscaya* and its passengers and cargo—Across the North Sea—Uncomfortable experiences—First glimpse of Norway—Aalesund—The Lofoden Islands—The midnight sun—A foretaste of the Arctic regions—"Cape Flyaway"—Our ice-master, Captain Crowther—We sight the coast of Siberia—The village of Kharbarova—The entrance to the Kara Sea ... ... 1

## CHAPTER II.

### THE KARA SEA.

In the midst of the ice-floes—Tedious work—Weird effects at twilight—A strange meeting—We pay a visit to the home of the walrus-hunter—Curio-hunting—A summer morning in the ice—Delightful experience—The Arctic mirage—We part from our new friends—An uncertain post-office—Ice-bound—Novel experiences—Seal-hunting ... ... 16

## CHAPTER III.

### THE KARA SEA—*continued*.

Further impressions of the Arctic regions—The awful silence—Average thickness of the ice—On the move once more—A fresh danger—A funny practical joke—The estuary of the River Yenisei—Golchika—A visit from its inhabitants—From Golchika to Karaoul   27

## CHAPTER IV.

### THE PORT OF KARAOUL AND ITS INHABITANTS.

The tundras of Northern Siberia—The Samoyedes—Arrival of the *Phœnix*—My first Russian meal—Vodka and tea—Our departure for Kasanskoi   36

## CHAPTER V.

### KASANSKOI.

Our Russian customs officer—A shooting-excursion—Visit to the settlement of Kasanskoi—The house of a Siberian trader—Interesting people—First experience of Russian hospitality—The return of the *Phœnix*—Departure of the *Biscaya*   48

## CHAPTER VI.

### THE RIVER VOYAGE OF THE *PHŒNIX* UP TO YENISEISK.

The Yenisei river—Its noble proportions—Scenery along the banks—The first tree—Our first mishap—The return of the tug—An exciting incident   60

## CHAPTER VII.

### THE RIVER VOYAGE—*continued*.

An awful fatality—Misfortune follows misfortune—M. Sotnikoff—Sellivanaka, the settlement of the Skopti—A visit from the village "elder"   70

## CHAPTER VIII.

### TURUCHANSK.

Visit to the monastery—Werchneimbackskoi—Our first visit from official Russia—The police officer of the district—The village priest ... 80

## CHAPTER IX.

### THE KAMIN RAPIDS.

A whole chapter of accidents—First touch of winter—Arrival at Yeniseisk ... ... ... 88

## CHAPTER X.

### THE CITY OF YENISEISK.

Custom-house officials—Novel sights in market-place and streets—My lodgings—Siberian idea of "board and lodging" — Society in Yeniseisk — A gentleman criminal exile ... ... ... 97

## CHAPTER XI.

### THE CITY OF YENISEISK—*continued*.

A visit to the prison—First impressions of the Siberian system ... ... ... 107

## CHAPTER XII.

### YENISEISK—*continued*.

The hospital — Siberian houses — Their comfort — The streets of the city ... ... 117

## CHAPTER XIII.

### FROM YENISEISK TO KRASNOIARSK.

My first experience of sledging—A delightful adventure—Krasnoiarsk—The market-place—The High Street ... 123

## CHAPTER XIV.

### KRASNOIARSK—*continued*.

Privileged criminal exiles — Ordinary criminals — A marching convoy on the road—Convoy soldiers—The convoy—Proceedings on arrival at the Perasilny of Krasnoiarsk—The staroster of the gang—A stroll round the Perasilny—The married prisoners' quarters—A "privileged" prisoner in his cell—Scene outside the prison—Prison labour—I give it a trial—Details as to outside employment of prisoners ... 134

## CHAPTER XV.

### MY JOURNEY FROM KRASNOIARSK TO IRKUTSK.

My servant Matwieff—The Great Post Road—The post-houses—Tea caravans—Curious effect of road—Siberian lynch law—Runaway convicts—A curious incident—The post courier—An awkward accident—Arrival at Irkutsk ... ... ... 156

## CHAPTER XVI.

### IRKUTSK.

Unpleasant experiences at hotel—Hospitality of Mr. Charles Lee—First impressions of the city ... 180

## CHAPTER XVII.

### PRISON LIFE IN SIBERIA—*continued.*

The Irkutsk prison—Comparative liberty of prisoners—Incongruities of prison life—The "shops"—Prison artists ... ... ... ... ... 192

## CHAPTER XVIII.

### PRISON LIFE IN SIBERIA—*continued.*

Outdoor employment of prisoners—A chat with an employer of convict labour—The "convict's word"—An interview with a celebrated murderess—The criminal madhouse—Political prisoners in solitary confinement—I get permission to paint a picture in one of the cells—End of my visits to the prison ... 198

## CHAPTER XIX.

### IRKUTSK—*continued.*

A gold-caravan—Particulars as to the gold-mining industry of Siberia—The Foundling Hospital—The fire-brigade—Celebration of the Czar's birthday—Living in Irkutsk ... ... ... ... 208

## CHAPTER XX.

### FROM IRKUTSK TO THE MONGOL CHINESE FRONTIER.

My journey to Kiakhta, the city of the tea princes—Across Lake Baikal on the ice—Interesting experiences ... ... ... ... ... 221

## CHAPTER XXI.

### FROM IRKUTSK TO THE MONGOL CHINESE FRONTIER—continued.

The road from Lake Baikal to Kiakhta—The "Kupetski track"—Incidents on the way—I change my sledge for a tarantass—Exciting adventures—Arrival at Troitzkosavsk, the business suburb of Kiakhta ... 235

## CHAPTER XXII.

### ACROSS MONGOLIA.

The Russo-Chinese frontier—Maimachin—The Mongols of to-day—Curious customs—Hair-dressing extraordinary—A pestilent farmyard—Exciting incidents—A forced encampment—An awful night's experiences—The Manhati Pass—Magnificent scenery—I pull off a successful "bluff"—"Angliski Boxe" in the wilds of Mongolia—Arrival at Ourga ... 249

## CHAPTER XXIII.

### THE SACRED CITY OF OURGA.

The Russian consul, M. Feodroff—Hospitality of the Consulate—The "lions" of Ourga—The colossal statue of the "Maidha"—The "Bogdor of Kurene"—An impromptu interview—Prayer-wheels—Praying-boards—Religious fervour of the Mongols ... 272

## CHAPTER XXIV.

### FROM OURGA TO THE GREAT WALL.

My preparations for the journey across the Gobi Desert—The Russian Heavy Mail—My camel-cart—Good-bye to Ourga—The first few days out—Discomforts of the journey—The homeward-bound mail—The desert settlement of Tcho-lyr ... 301

## CHAPTER XXV.

### THE GOBI DESERT—*continued.*

Sport in the desert—The "post-station" at Oud-en—The last of the desert—Saham-Balhousar—First impressions of China—Chinese women—Returning to sea-level—Curious experience—The eclipse of the moon—Arrival at Kalgan ... ... ... 318

## CHAPTER XXVI.

### KALGAN TO PEKING.

A hearty welcome—Yambooshan—The Great Wall of China—American missionaries—My mule-litter—From Kalgan to Peking—Scenery on the road—Chinese inn—First experience of a Chinese dinner—Amusing *rencontre*—The Nankaou Pass—The Second Parallel of the Great Wall—First impressions of Peking—The entrance to the city ... 331

## CHAPTER XXVII.

### PEKING.

Exciting times—A chat with Sir John Walsham—The Chinese city—Horrible scenes—Social life at the Legations in Peking—Lady Walsham's "At homes"—The hardest-worked man in the East—Interesting evening with Sir Robert Hart—His account of his life 353

## CHAPTER XXVIII.

### PEKING (*continued*)—AND HOME.

Difficulty of sketching in the streets—My journey from Peking to Tientsin—A Chinese house-boat—The Peiho River—Tientsin—From Tientsin to Shanghai—And home ... ... ... 371

# LIST OF ILLUSTRATIONS.

|  | PAGE |
|---|---|
| The "Biscaya" leaving Blackwall | 1 |
| Preparations for the Arctic Regions ... *To face* | 8 |
| A "Dead Reckoning" in the Kara Sea | 10 |
| Our Ice-master, Captain Crowther | 13 |
| Clearing the Drift Ice from the Propeller | 16 |
| The Home of the Walrus-hunter | 20 |
| The "Biscaya" Ice-bound in the Kara Sea ... *To face* | 24 |
| After Seals | 25 |
| "One Speck of Life in the Ice-bound Waste" | 27 |
| The Handsomest Member of his Family | 33 |
| Samoyede Boatmen ... *To face* | 34 |
| Karaoul | 36 |
| The Samoyede's Grave | 39 |
| A Samoyede Lady | 40 |
| Transhipment of our Cargo to the "Phœnix" | 43 |
| Our Custom-House Officer | 48 |
| Kasanskoi | 50 |
| Trader's House at Kasanskoi | 50 |
| Mine Host at Kasanskoi | 51 |
| Sweet Seventeen | 53 |
| A Home in Northern Siberia: The Morning Meal *To face* | 54 |
| Materfamilias | 55 |
| Temporary Farmyard on one of the Barges ... *To face* | 57 |
| Tea-time at the Men's Quarters on Shore | 57 |
| Cossacks | 58 |
| A House-boat | 60 |
| The "Phœnix" ... *To face* | 61 |
| Loading Wood for the "Phœnix" ,, | 66 |
| Difficult Navigation | 70 |
| Sellivanaka ... *To face* | 78 |
| The Principal Thoroughfare, Turuchansk | 80 |
| Our First Visit from Official Russia ... *To face* | 83 |
| Werchneimbackskoi ,, | 83 |
| Interested Observers | 83 |
| The Russian Police Officer *To face* | 84 |
| The Village Priest | 85 |
| A Village Boat | 88 |

|  | PAGE |
|---|---|
| A River Pilot ... ... ... | 89 |
| The River Yenisei at Worogovo ... To face | 90 |
| Storing the Winter Forage: A Village Scene on the Yenisei ... To face | 96 |
| Yeniseisk ... | 97 |
| Peasant Woman ... ... ... | 101 |
| In the Market-place, Yeniseisk To face | 101 |
| A Prison Beauty ... ... ... ... ... | 107 |
| The Governor visiting the Men's Prison, Yeniseisk To face | 109 |
| The Murderers' Department, Yeniseisk Prison ... | 111 |
| The Governor visiting the Women's Prison, Yeniseisk To face | 112 |
| Criminal Prisoners waiting at Yeniseisk for Convoy to start for Krasnoiarsk ... To face | 113 |
| Street Scene, Yeniseisk | 117 |
| A Water-carrier ... ... ... ... ... | 118 |
| Getting Water from the Frozen River Yenisei To face | 118 |
| The High Street, Yeniseisk ,, | 118 |
| A Swell ... ... ... ... | 119 |
| The Two Collegiate Schools, Yeniseisk ... To face | 120 |
| Life in Siberia: An Afternoon Drive in Yeniseisk ,, | 121 |
| Ready to Start ... | 123 |
| "Good-bye" ... ... ... | 126 |
| In the Meat Market, Krasnoiarsk ... | 131 |
| A Typical Siberian Interior, Krasnoiarsk ... | 132 |
| Snow Scavenger, Krasnoiarsk To face | 133 |
| The Cathedral, Krasnoiarsk ... ... ... | 134 |
| A Convoy of Prisoners on the March (Enlargement from an Instantaneous Kodak Photo) To face | 138 |
| Prisoners unloading Sledges on Arrival at Perasilny, Krasnoiarsk ... ... ... ... To face | 140 |
| Verification of Prisoners on Arrival at Perasilny, Krasnoiarsk ... To face | 141 |
| The Starostee of the Gang ... | 142 |
| Group of Prisoners (from a Government Photo) ... | 144 |
| A "Privilighee," or Privileged Prisoner ... | 148 |
| Peasant Women selling Provisions to Prisoners | 149 |
| Watchman on Duty in Fire Tower, Krasnoiarsk To face | 155 |
| My Servant ... ... | 156 |
| Arrival at a Post Station ... ... | 164 |
| Interior of a Post-house. To face | 166 |
| The Imperial Mail .. | 173 |

|  | PAGE |
|---|---|
| IRKUTSK | 180 |
| THE MOSKOVSKAIA PODVORIÉ, IRKUTSK ... *To face* | 180 |
| AN IRKUTSK BEAUTY | 185 |
| ENTRANCE HALL OF MILLIONAIRE GOLD-MINE OWNER'S HOUSE, IRKUTSK | 186 |
| STREET SCENE, IRKUTSK | 188 |
| A COSSACK ... *To face* | 190 |
| AN IRKUTSK POLICEMAN ... ,, | 191 |
| THE MUSEUM, IRKUTSK | 191 |
| THE RECREATION GROUND, IRKUTSK PRISON | 192 |
| MARRIED PRISONERS WAITING TO BE SERVED WITH NEW CLOTHES ON ARRIVAL AT PRISON, IRKUTSK *To face* | 193 |
| THE PRISON ARTIST ,, | 196 |
| THE BARONESS | 201 |
| A "POLITICAL" (FROM A GOVERNMENT PHOTO) *To face* | 205 |
| "SWEETHEARTS AND WIVES;" VISITING-DAY IN THE IRKUTSK PRISON ... *To face* | 206 |
| AUTOGRAPH LETTER FROM THE BARONESS ,, | 207 |
| THE HIGH STREET, IRKUTSK | 208 |
| IN THE COURTYARD OF A FIRE STATION, IRKUTSK | 215 |
| THE GOVERNOR-GENERAL'S HOUSE, IRKUTSK | 218 |
| STREET SCENE, IRKUTSK | 220 |
| A BIT ON THE ROAD TO LAKE BAIKAL | 221 |
| THE RIVER ANGARA NEAR LAKE BAIKAL | 225 |
| LIESTVINITZ, ON LAKE BAIKAL | 229 |
| A LAKE BAIKAL STEAMER | 231 |
| CROSSING LAKE BAIKAL | 233 |
| THE KUPETSKI TRACK | 235 |
| A POST-HOUSE ON THE KUPETSKI TRACK | 238 |
| A TEA CART | 240 |
| DAY-DREAMS: A SKETCH IN THE TRANS-BAIKAL *To face* | 242 |
| THE HIGH STREET, TROITZKOSAVSK ,, | 245 |
| MY FIRST GLIMPSE OF MONGOLIA ,, | 246 |
| A BOURRIATE LADY | 247 |
| SKETCH BY A POLITICAL PRISONER, MADE WHILST ON THE MARCH ACROSS SIBERIA (THE ORIGINAL IS IN SEPIA AND WHITE) ... *To face* | 248 |
| ON THE ROAD TO OURGA | 249 |
| A MONGOL YOURT | 253 |
| A MONGOL | 254 |
| OUR MIDDAY HALT | 260 |
| A STREET MUSICIAN, OURGA | 272 |
| THE PRINCIPAL THOROUGHFARE, OURGA *To face* | 273 |

# LIST OF ILLUSTRATIONS.

|  | PAGE |
|---|---|
| A PILGRIM FROM THIBET ... | 277 |
| A LAMA ... ... | 281 |
| A PRAYER-WHEEL, OURGA ... ... | 283 |
| PRAYER-BOARDS, OURGA ... ... ... | 284 |
| "THE OLD, OLD STORY ALL THE WORLD OVER" *To face* | 286 |
| IN THE CAMEL AND PONY BAZAAR, OURGA ... ,, | 293 |
| IN THE BAZAAR, OURGA ... ... ,, | 294 |
| THE PUNISHMENT OF THE "CARGUE:" A SKETCH OUTSIDE THE PRISON, OURGA ... ... *To face* | 295 |
| AN OURGA BEAUTY ... ,, | 299 |
| IN THE GOBI DESERT ... ... | 301 |
| MY CAMEL-CART ... ... .. ... *To face* | 303 |
| MONGOL CONVEYING THE RUSSIAN LIGHT MAIL ACROSS THE GOBI DESERT ... ... *To face* | 306 |
| THE MIDDAY HALT IN THE DESERT ... ... | 309 |
| MY CARAVAN IN THE DESERT (FROM A KODAK PHOTO) ... | 313 |
| WE MEET THE HOMEWARD-BOUND MAIL ... ... | 314 |
| THE LAMA SETTLEMENT OF TCHO-IYR IN THE GOBI DESERT | 315 |
| I TAKE TEA WITH A LAMA IN THE GOBI DESERT *To face* | 316 |
| THE RUSSIAN POST-STATION IN MID-DESERT ... ... | 318 |
| IN THE GOBI DESERT: A TEA CARAVAN ON ITS WAY TO SIBERIA (FROM A KODAK PHOTO) ... ... | 320 |
| IN THE GOBI DESERT: LADY VISITORS TO OUR ENCAMPMENT ... ... ... ... ... *To face* | 323 |
| "YE GENTLE SHEPHERDESS OF YE STEPPE" ,, | 324 |
| STREET SCENE, YAMBOOSHAN (SHOWING THE "GREAT WALL" ON MOUNTAIN IN BACKGROUND) ... ... *To face* | 332 |
| MY MULE-LITTER ... ... ... ,, | 338 |
| THE COURTYARD OF A CHINESE INN | 341 |
| A "ROOM" IN A CHINESE INN ... ... | 343 |
| A NASTY BIT OF ROAD ... ... ... *To face* | 346 |
| THE GREAT WALL OF CHINA AT THE ENTRANCE TO NANKAOU PASS ... ... ... ... *To face* | 348 |
| CHINESE REVENUE CRUISERS IN HONGKONG ROADSTEAD (FROM A PHOTO GIVEN BY SIR ROBERT HART) *To face* | 363 |
| STREET SCENE, TARTAR CITY, PEKING ... ... | 356 |
| SIR ROBERT HART, G.C.M.G., IN HIS "DEN" AT PEKING *To face* | 366 |
| MY HOUSE-BOAT ... ... | 375 |
| SHANGHAI ... ... .. | 380 |

THE "BISCAYA" LEAVING BLACKWALL.

# FROM THE ARCTIC OCEAN TO THE YELLOW SEA.

## CHAPTER I.

### FROM BLACKWALL TO SIBERIA.

The object of the expedition—The steamer *Biscaya* and its passengers and cargo—Across the North Sea—Uncomfortable experiences—First glimpse of Norway—Aalesund—The Lofoden Islands—The midnight sun—A foretaste of the Arctic regions—"Cape Flyaway"—Our ice-master, Captain Crowther—We sight the coast of Siberia—The village of Kharbarova—The entrance to the Kara Sea.

In these prosaic days of the nineteenth century one hardly expects a revival of the adventurous expeditions which made the fame of England in the days of Frobisher and Drake. As a matter of fact, the world is almost too well known now for such adventures to be possible, even were the leaders forthcoming, and the "good old buccaneering days" are long past. Still, I could not help thinking, on the day we left Gravesend for the far North-East, bound for a region but little known, and with the uncertainty of ever reaching our destination, that it must have been under somewhat similar conditions that the adventurers of old started on their perilous journeys; with, however, this very great difference —ours was not a filibustering expedition, but a commonplace commercial enterprise, backed up by several well-to-do Englishmen, with absolutely nothing of the romantic about it beyond the fact of its having to traverse these wild and comparatively unknown regions before it could be successfully achieved.

We started from the Thames on Friday, July 18, 1890, in the chartered Norwegian steamer *Biscaya*, eight hundred tons gross, bound for the Yenisei River with a nondescript tentative sort of cargo, consisting of a mixture of all sorts, from a steam saw-mill down to the latest toy for children, our ultimate destination being the town of Yeniseisk, which is situated some fifteen hundred miles from the mouth of this mighty river. The object of the expedition was to endeavour to open a trade route between

England and Siberia by means of the Kara Sea passage, which was discovered by Nordenskiold in 1875.

Nothing of particular interest occurred during the first few days after we left the Thames. We were so closely packed that it required some careful arrangement to get us all comfortably stowed, so to speak. Imagine seven men jammed into a cabin just about large enough to accommodate four, and each man with the usual amount of superfluous luggage without which Englishmen could not possibly travel, this baggage also stowed in the cabin, and you will guess that we were packed like sardines. As, however, no doubt even sardines get used to being packed, after a time so did we ; and, although the passage across the North Sea was about as uncomfortable a one as I ever experienced, we somehow managed to settle into our respective grooves long before we sighted the coast of Norway. Our party consisted of two representatives of the London Syndicate, two engineers, a master stevedore (to unload the ship on arrival), an experienced ice-master, who knew the Kara Sea thoroughly, the captain of the *Biscaya*, and your humble servant. I don't think I ever was on board a more crowded ship. Even the decks were packed with all sorts of paraphernalia, including a large steam-launch and several pens of live stock ; and, so as to obviate any fear of running short of coal in the outlandish parts we were going to, the fore and upper decks had over seventy tons of loose coal on them. We had a head wind and a heavy sea nearly the whole way after passing Harwich, where we dropped our pilot, thus bidding a last farewell to Old England. Off the Dogger Bank we went right through the fishing fleet which congregates there, and took advantage of the opportunity to get some fresh fish—a matter of no small difficulty, as the men had a preposterous idea of its value: they would not take money for it, but actually had the effrontery to want to swop a couple of small cod, a ling, and a pair of soles for two bottles of whiskey and a pound of tobacco! Fish is evidently dearer on the fishing-ground itself than in London. Whiskey, however, was far more valuable to us than fish, so, when the men saw we were not buyers on their terms, they eventually came down to $1\frac{1}{2}$ lb. of ship tobacco (value 2s. 4d.) for the lot, which was reasonable enough. After passing the Dogger Bank the wind freshened very considerably towards evening, and added much to the discomfort of the crowded ship; in fact, so badly did she roll about that not only was all our party busy "feeding the fishes" most of the time, but our cook was also so ill that he could not attend to his duties, and we all had to lend a hand in the galley as well as we could. I had never been a long voyage in a wooden ship before, so could hardly sleep a wink all night, owing to the (to me) unusual noise caused by the groaning of her timbers as she pitched and tossed about. It sounded not unlike what I should imagine it would be sleeping near a lot of new leather portmanteaus which were being continually shifted. During the whole of the following day it was blowing big guns, and the sea was so heavy that the cabin was almost dangerous to remain in, owing to the sort of cannonade of packages from all sides, many things being damaged. There was absolutely nothing to do but sit down and wait events, and, meanwhile, make one's self as comfortable as one could under the circumstances. By the next day the gale had moderated considerably, and during the morning we got our first glimpse of Norway—a high, rock-bound coast, with a dim vista of mountains in the background. Shortly after, a small pilot-boat hove in sight, evidently on the chance of a job, probably taking the *Biscaya* for a tourist steamer wishing to pass inside the islands, which is the most picturesque route, though somewhat longer. We had no time, however, to waste on scenery, so, although one of our party, who was suffering from an attack of dysentery, offered to pay the pilotage (about £15) out of his own pocket if the calm-water channel was followed, it was at once decided to keep outside the whole way up the coast, and thus get on as fast as possible, more especially as the weather showed signs of clearing up.

On the Norway coast we anchored for a short

time off the quaint little village of Aalesund, with its pretty wooden houses nestling under the high snow-clad mountains which encircle the beautiful fiord on which it is situated. I was disappointed on a nearer inspection of the village, which looked so quaint as seen from the sea: the houses all appeared to be almost new, doubtless owing to the fact that they are all built entirely of wood. The effect is thoroughly characteristic of Norway, the smell pervading the place especially so, being, as far as I could guess, a mixture of paraffin and pickled fish, with just a *soupçon* of burnt wood thrown in here and there. Everything looked as clean as a new pin, but, as each house is exactly like its neighbour, the effect is certainly monotonous. Nevertheless, there were several pretty bits which I should have liked to sketch had I had time. What, if anything, struck me most was the entire absence of any national or picturesque costume, which gives such local colour to most Continental villages. At Aalesund the inhabitants looked for all the world like English people, and their fair hair and blue eyes added to this resemblance. I was told, however, that on *fête* days there are some quaint costumes to be seen here and there.

No time was lost in getting away, and shortly after we had lost sight of the quiet little village, where we had spent a few lazy hours, and were heading it once more for the far-distant Arctic regions. The days after this date began to lengthen considerably, and, although we had hardly noticed it at first, it astonished us very much when we suddenly found that it was eleven o'clock at night, and yet the sun was shining as brightly as during the afternoon. When the novelty had worn off, as it naturally did after a few days, the amount of daylight almost palled on one. It seemed too absurd turning in while the sun was up; still, like everything else, one gets used to it after a time. The next few days were uneventful, as we were out of sight of land, and the usual monotony of shipboard life was only broken by the usual skylarking, without which no sea voyage would be complete.

On July 28 we sighted the Lofoden Islands, about fourteen miles off on our starboard quarter. It was a lovely morning, and the lofty snow-capped mountains towering against the calm eastern sky presented a grand and impressive sight. The effect was almost that of a colossal painting, so still was everything in the bright sunshine. I was so impressed by the quiet grandeur of the scene that I got out my paint-box and started a sketch, but only succeeded in making a sort of caricature of my impressions. Late the next evening we came across a fleet of small fishing-boats—about the quaintest lot of craft I ever saw: they looked as if they had been copied from the frontispiece of the *Argosy*. We got some coarse sort of fish from them in exchange for tobacco, biscuits, and the inevitable rum. The men were a very fine-looking set of fellows, very much like Englishmen (as, in fact, most Norwegians are), and seemed quite comfortable in their ramshackle-looking boats. After leaving them we saw for the first time the curious phenomenon of the sun above the horizon at midnight. It was so bright, and the atmosphere so clear, that I took an instantaneous photograph of a group on deck, and it came out very well.

The next morning we arrived off the North Cape, and passed it close in to the shore. We were now well inside the Arctic Circle, but perceived no difference whatever in the temperature, except that perhaps it was warmer than it had been previously. As a matter of fact, we had out the hose and took a most enjoyable bath on deck in the warm sunshine. In the afternoon, however, we had our first taste of the Arctic regions, as a dense fog came on, and lasted till late in the evening. Everything seemed saturated with moisture; the very rigging was dripping as under a heavy shower.

For the next few days nothing of interest occurred, when suddenly one morning, as we were nearing Kolguier Island, we were aroused by the news that there was a steamer in sight, and soon we were all on deck eagerly scanning the horizon. Considering how far we were from the ordinary track of vessels, our excitement was natural; for what was a ship

PREPARATIONS FOR THE ARCTIC REGIONS.

[*To face p.* 8.

doing in these outlandish parts? We soon made out that it was a large steamer, coming from due north straight towards us. She was coming at such a spanking rate that very soon we could see she was flying the Russian flag; and shortly after she passed round our stern, and we dipped our colours to each other as she did so. She then brought up, and stopped not far from us, while our captain hailed her in English, and asked if they would take some letters ashore for us. With difficulty, we understood their reply to be "Yes." When, however, in their turn, they asked us where we were bound for, and got the reply "Siberia," they seemed somewhat astonished, as well they might, for "Siberia" is vague. We then lowered a boat, and sent them our packet of letters; after which, bidding each other farewell by means of our fog-horns, we continued our way. We subsequently learnt from the mate, who had been in the boat, that it was a steamer which had been sent to Nova Zemla to try and discover a Russian ship, which had been lost there some months back.

During the remainder of that day our course was again obscured by thick fog, which prevented us from sighting Kolguier Island in the afternoon as we had expected. When, however, we came on deck after tea, a curious incident occurred. Our ice-master, who had been intently looking through his glasses at something which had attracted his attention, suddenly declared that he saw land on the horizon behind us. We were all naturally somewhat startled at this intelligence, as we hardly expected to see it in so distant a quarter, for even had we passed

A "DEAD RECKONING" IN THE KARA SEA.

Kolguier in the fog, at the rate we were going it could not possibly have been so far away from us in the time. But what land was it, then? for on looking through our glasses we certainly did see high mountains capped here and there with snow, their base lost in the surrounding mist. On consulting the chart we were not a bit the wiser, for it seemed as doubtful as ourselves. I give, as a proof, the following "caution," which is printed on the "Map of the Coast of Russia included between Cape Kanin and Waygatch Island" (Imray, 1883): "As the sea comprised within the limits of this chart is very imperfectly known, no survey of any portion of it having been made, it should be navigated with more than ordinary care. The geographical positions of headlands and islands are all, without exception, uncertain, and their general delineation is only approximately accurate." (This is from the map we were then consulting.) After a while, however, the mysterious land gradually disappeared in the distance; and, as we shortly after sighted the looked-for Kolguier Island ahead of us, there can be very little doubt that the mountains we thought we saw were part of what the sailors call "Cape Flyaway." It was a most realistic effect, and, even seen through powerful glasses, was exactly like land.

The sunset that evening was magnificent; in fact, I never remember seeing such glorious sky effects anywhere else as I have observed in these latitudes, the most wonderful part of them being their extraordinary stillness. For at least an hour I have frequently noticed masses of cumuli absolutely unchanged either in shape or position.

The days were now beginning to get shorter again, although it was still broad daylight all night (if such an expression is English), the sun remaining below the horizon a few minutes longer every day. By the way, I believe we were fortunate in getting in the neighbourhood of the North Cape exactly on the last day in the year, when the sun is visible above the horizon at midnight. All of us were now anxiously looking forward to getting a glimpse of the coast of Siberia, and yet the weather was so warm and the sea so calm and blue that it was more like yachting in the Mediterranean than a voyage through the dreary Arctic regions; in fact, on August 4, when we at length sighted the land, the sun was simply broiling. Lovely, however, as the day was, it seemed to have very little effect on the dreary-looking coast-line, for a more dismal and uninviting country I never saw, flat and uninteresting right down to the very water's edge, and with a striking absence of any colour, except a dingy muddy brown. This, of course, is easily accounted for, as it is only for two or three short months that the ground is free from snow, and there is no vegetation in these regions.

Captain Crowther, our ice-master, a veteran Arctic traveller, who was out with the *Eira* expedition in 1881-2, and is the only man on board who knows these parts, now assumed the command of the ship, and took up his position on the bridge. We were about to enter the Kara Sea by the Waygatch Straits, and it was uncertain as yet if the navigation was open, as this remote sea is never entirely free

OUR ICE-MASTER, CAPTAIN CROWTHER.

from ice. It was to be an exciting time for the next hour or so, for, if our passage through the Straits was blocked, we should have to return and try and get round by the coast of Nova Zemla, a much longer and still more doubtful route. Sailing as we were, on a summer sea and in the warm sunshine, one could hardly realize that, perhaps a mile or so ahead, we might find our passage blocked by impenetrable ice ; it seemed so utterly improbable as to be hardly worth the thought. But we did not know the Arctic regions yet.

We soon reached the entrance to the Straits, which are formed by the Island of Waygatch on one side and Siberia on the other, and are only about one and a half mile across, passing so close to the shore that we could plainly distinguish the battered wreck of a small vessel lying on the beach near a primitive sort of wooden beacon, which seemed strangely out of place in so melancholy a spot. Some distance farther, on the Siberian side, we could see the small hamlet of Khabarova, consisting of about a dozen wooden huts or cottages clustered round a little church, with a few fishing-coracles drawn up on the shingle in front, while a short distance away were several Polar bear skins hanging up to dry. It looked unutterably sad, this poor little outpost of humanity so far away from the busy world. One could not help wondering what inducement this dreary Arctic waste could possibly offer for any one to wish to dwell in it. I hear, however, that a few Russian merchants live there, carrying on a sort of trade with the Samoyede natives in return for furs, walrus tusks, etc.

Up till now we had been having real summer weather, with rippling waves sparkling in the brilliant sunshine. Suddenly the scene changed, and, with barely any warning, a drenching shower came down, and with it the wind veered round to the north-east, dark clouds obscured the sky, and as we entered the Kara Sea the effect was indescribably weird. It was like going from daylight into a horrid, uncanny sort of twilight. Behind us we could still see the lovely sunshine we had just left, while ahead the scene was Arctic in the extreme, and thoroughly realized my wildest expectations. All was cold and wretched, with a wintry sky overhead. Under the low cliffs which encircled the dreary shore one could see huge drifts of snow which the sunshine of the short Arctic summer had been powerless to disperse, while for miles round the sea simply bristled with drift ice in all sorts of uncouth shapes. I felt that it would require the pencil of a Doré or the pen of a Jules Verne to convey any adequate idea of the weird scene in all its desolate grandeur.

CLEARING THE DRIFT ICE FROM THE PROPELLER.

## CHAPTER II.

### THE KARA SEA.

In the midst of the ice-floes—Tedious work—Weird effects at twilight—A strange meeting—We pay a visit to the home of the walrus-hunter—Curio-hunting—A summer morning in the ice—Delightful experience—The Arctic mirage—We part from our new friends—An uncertain post-office—Ice-bound—Novel experiences—Seal-hunting.

NOTWITHSTANDING its unpromising aspect, our plucky ice-master put the *Biscaya* straight for the icy obstacles, and soon we were surrounded on all sides by ghostly shapes, which appeared to be hurrying past us like so many uneasy spirits under the leaden sky. Although the ship was well and skillfully handled, in a very short time we were actually blocked in on all sides by huge masses of ice, and remained so for several hours. Then the floes drifted sufficiently to allow of our gradually wedging our way through, which we did with considerable difficulty and not without several severe bumps; in fact, it was a wonder to me how we managed to get through at all, still more without serious damage. Curiously enough, all the ice for the moment seemed to be gathered in one spot, for the sea beyond was clear for several miles ahead after this; then more drifts appeared, and during the night we were again hemmed in on all sides.

The next morning the sun was shining in a cloudless sky once more, a great contrast to our previous evening's experience, and the effect of the snow-white drift-ice floating on the blue sea was very beautiful and novel. This time the water was sufficiently clear ahead to allow of our passage without much difficulty, and we proceeded without any special incident for several hours. Towards the afternoon, however, we observed a curious effect on the horizon before us: it was a sort of white reflection in the sky. Our experienced ice-master, who had been up to the mast-head with his glasses, however, did not look at it in the same light as we did; to him it was neither novel nor interesting. He told us that it was the reflection in the sky of enormous fields of ice, which it would be impossible to get through, unless we found a passage in some part of it. For the moment he could see nothing for it but to turn back and try another course, as the sea ahead was blocked on either side as far as he could see. This did not sound cheerful, as it immediately raised visions of wintering in the Arctic regions, if, indeed, our ship was not smashed up before then. Without any delay the *Biscaya's* head was immediately turned right round to the southeast, in the hope of finding a clear passage, and creeping north again under the shelter of the land. It was wearisome work going right back again over the old ground, but this was but a forerunner of what we had to do for some time afterwards, and by the time we had done with the Kara Sea we had all learnt a good lesson in patience. So as to economize the coal, we only steamed half-speed ahead all the time. After several hours on this course, it was decided once more to try our luck and get northward again, and all that night we went steadily on without meeting with any ice.

The next morning, when we got up on deck, a most provoking sight awaited us. We were steaming very slowly, for a few miles ahead of us was the wall of ice we had been trying in vain to avoid. There it lay, stretched out as far as the eyes could reach on either side in the bright sunshine, a ghostly barrier between us and our route. Our ice-master was pacing the deck in a very restless manner, and evidently did not like the look of affairs at all. At last he told us that it was no good humbugging about it: we were fairly in for it. As far as he could judge, the Kara

Sea was full of ice to the north, so that the only thing we could do was to dodge about on the chance of finding a weak spot to try and get through. If we did not succeed in finding a passage, he thought "it would be a very long job before we got out of the ice." His language was forcible enough to carry weight with it, even if his experience had not, so once more the ship's course was altered, and we started on a fresh voyage of discovery, westward this time. All that day we were pounding along the fringe of the interminable fields of ice, when, towards evening, it was decided to try what appeared to be a sort of opening some few miles ahead, although it did not look a very hopeful undertaking. For an hour or so, however, before making the attempt, the engines were slowed down as much as possible, in order to give our captains an opportunity of taking a little rest, as they knew that, once inside the ice, there would be no time for sleeping. At eight o'clock the ship's head was turned due north again, and in a very short time we were entirely surrounded by ice, which seemed to get more and more compact as we advanced, if advance it could be called; for at times we barely moved at the rate of a mile an hour, with continual stoppages to enable the men to clear away the drift-ice from the propeller. Round us was an extraordinary scene, and one which I hardly know how to describe. There was not a breath of air stirring; in the growing twilight the sea looked like polished glass, and on it the floating ice, which was rapidly melting, took all sorts of weird and grotesque shapes, conjuring up visions of low tide on some immense shore in antediluvian days, with uncouth monsters disporting themselves in the shallow water. We were so much impressed by our surroundings that we remained on deck watching the slowly moving panorama all night, or, rather, during the hours which are usually night, for it was but a sort of mysterious twilight all the time, which considerably added to the effect.

THE HOME OF THE WALRUS-HUNTER.

Towards morning we got into somewhat clearer water, when, to our great surprise, we sighted some vessels ahead of us in the ice. They turned out to be walrus-hunters, and, on our getting up to the nearest one, a sort of sloop with a crow's-nest at the mast-head, with a man in it on the look-out, they sent a boat over to us, and we then learnt that they were all in the same fix as ourselves, and had been blocked in for some days past, as they also wanted to get north. They hailed from Hammerfest, and had been in the Kara Sea since April, but hoped to be able to get out and on their way back to Norway towards the end of August. One of our party, an enthusiastic curio-hunter (without which no party could be complete), immediately "scented" his prey, and on inquiry found that the men had on board a Polar bear's skin they could sell him, also some seal-skins and walrus tusks; so we jumped into their boat, and they took us across to have a look at them while their captain and ours hobnobbed together and talked Norwegian to their heart's content in the *Biscaya's* cabin. On nearer inspection, the sloop proved larger than we had imagined it, and certainly dirtier. In a few minutes a cask was hauled up out of the hold, and a large yellowy-brown bundle, covered thickly with wet salt, pulled out of it and spread on the greasy deck. This was the Polar bear's skin we had come to see. Our curio-hunter's enthusiasm went down to zero at once, for it was as unlike the snowy-white rugs one sees in London drawing-rooms as chalk is to cheese; still, they actually asked the modest sum of £5 for it in this dirty state. The sealskins were also very disappointing, and we were about to return to the boat, when one of the crew produced a lot of Samoyede costumes and walrus tusks, which we all made a rush for, as, at any rate, they were interesting—and clean. Of such there were enough to satisfy us all, and they were soon bought up. I got off cheapest, as I managed to get some very curious articles in return for my Waterbury watch, which took the man's fancy. On returning to the *Biscaya* we found that it had been arranged to tow the sloop a short distance, as its captain said he knew the coast, and thought he could pilot us through the ice part of the way. The ships therefore got under way in company, and most of us then turned in for a few hours, after a most fatiguing day.

In the morning we were at a standstill, fairly blocked in on all sides by the ice, which glistened and sparkled round us till one's eyes ached from the glare. The sea was as calm as a mill-pond, the sun was shining in a cloudless sky, and it was so warm that had it not been for the ice around I should have suggested having the hose out and a bath on deck, for the thermometer marked fifty degrees in the shade. It was simply delightful, and made one feel quite pleased to be alive, so to speak. I could not help thinking, as I breathed the exhilarating air, how few Londoners have ever experienced such delight, as inhaling this sort of air seems to impart to one a kind of desire to jump about and give vent to one's animal spirits in quite a schoolboyish fashion, reminding one of one's youthful days before the cares of manhood were upon us, when on the weekly half-holiday the rush was made for the cricket-ground. Owing to the purity of the atmosphere, the refraction or mirage along the horizon was so great that the ice seemed to be literally standing straight up, thus producing the impression of our being surrounded by a high white wall or cliff—an almost indescribable effect, and which, when seen through the glasses, reminded one of a transformation scene at a theatre, when the background is formed of painted gauze which is gradually lifted to disclose further surprises behind. A long and wearisome delay now occurred, as it was manifestly absurd even to try and advance any farther in the direction we were in. At last it was decided that the *Biscaya* should get out again into the open sea as soon as possible, as our ice-master did not like the look of the huge masses of ice which were pressing tightly on her sides. The walrus-hunter expressed his intention of remaining where he was for a few days, to try and get some seals. Before parting company we entrusted to his care a packet of letters which he promised to post at the first port he touched at—rather a vague promise on his part, as he was uncertain when he would return to civilization. However, it was worth chancing, as he might possibly get back before we reached the end of our long journey. I could not help wondering how long my letter would take to reach the Strand, and felt certain I should never find a more uncertain post-office than this one.

For the next few days we were dodging the ice in all directions. North, south, east, and west, everywhere it seemed to be closing in on us, till at last, during a futile effort to break through, we got so hemmed in that it was deemed advisable to anchor to a floe for a time, and see if there was any chance of the drifts breaking up with the advancing season. So we brought up at a huge field of hummocky ice, and some men were sent down with the ice-anchor. Most of us then enjoyed our first bit of exercise for a fortnight. It was a novel experience being on one of these floating islands. Though not very slippery, one had to be careful. Along the edges the water deepened gradually, as upon a shore, for a couple of yards or so, till where the ice 'ended, when it suddenly went off into hundreds of fathoms, which looked like a black abyss beneath us. There was very little to see, however, and, although we took our rifles with us, we did not meet with a single living object, still less a bear or a walrus, as we had fondly hoped we might.

The next few days passed quietly. I managed to do a little sketching, although it was chilly work for one's feet on the ice. Then the weather changed, and it came on to rain, with a thick fog accompanying it, so we found the close and stuffy cabin very cosy after being in the bleak wind outside, and, if singing (or, rather, making an infernal row) could help to pass away the time, we certainly

THE "BISCAYA" ICE-BOUND IN THE KARA SEA. [*To face p.* 24.

did our best to lose no opportunity, our only drawback being that we had not a single musical instrument among us. However, as it generally only was a question who could invent the most unearthly noise to accompany the "songs," the result can be more easily imagined than described. Sometimes we managed to get a shot at a stray seal which was

AFTER SEALS.

rash enough to come within range, but, as they invariably dived down immediately we had fired, we could never tell if they had been hit or not, still less get them. One brute, with a face like that of an old man, was particularly "cheeky." He would come up alongside and almost stand up in the water and have a good look at us, as much as to say,

"Here I am, you fellows! Why don't you try and get me? But you know you can't!" Then, by the time we had got our rifles and ammunition ready, he would disappear suddenly, and a few seconds after come up on the other side of the ship. After a little of this sort of thing we simply got mad, and at last there was quite a battery waiting for him when he did appear. The ice-master, who was up at the mast-head, and could, from that elevated position, see him quite plainly under the water, directed our movements, and when at last we got a shot at him grew awfully excited, yelling out, "That's it! Hit him again in the same place, and you'll get him!" We did not get him, however, for the poor brute dived down, leaving a track of blood in the water, and did not reappear. We then got out a boat, and went on a sort of hunting-expedition round about, but without finding anything; in fact, we came to the conclusion, after paddling about for half an hour, that there was nothing to find, so we gave it up as a bad job.

At last it was decided to up anchor and once more try our luck, as our captains, and, in fact, all of us, were getting impatient at the delay, unavoidable though it was. The rain appeared to have loosened the floes considerably, so we were a bit more hopeful.

"ONE SPECK OF LIFE IN THE ICE-BOUND WASTE."

## CHAPTER III.

### THE KARA SEA—*continued*.

Further impressions of the Arctic regions—The awful silence—Average thickness of the ice—On the move once more—A fresh danger—A funny practical joke—The estuary of the River Yenisei—Golchika—A visit from its inhabitants—From Golchika to Karaoul.

THE novelty of being blocked in on all sides by fields of ice soon wears off. Even the chance of a shot at a seal now and again fails to enliven one. The silence of the surroundings is too oppressive; all seems dead, and it seems like some hideous dream to row about on these motionless waters, with the ghostly frozen monstrosities floating around. It reminded one of Doré's illustrations to Dante's "Inferno." One can realize how awful it must be to be forced to pass a winter in the far North, where continual night is added to the horrors of the death-like surroundings. The silence of the great forest Stanley tells us of in his book must be almost noisy (if one can use the expression) compared with it; at any rate, he had living nature around him, whereas in the Arctic regions all is gloom and eternal silence, without even vegetation to enliven it. Before leaving the floe to which we had been anchored, out of curiosity I ascertained the thickness of the ice, and to my astonishment I found it averaged seventeen feet, some pieces being even as much as *twenty-five feet* in thickness, and this after several weeks of continuous thaw.

It would take too long to describe the wearisome attempts we made during the next few days while trying to break through the immense barrier which lay between us and the mouth of the Yenisei River, and during all this time we experienced every variety of Arctic climate, from hot sunshine to sudden and icy cold fogs. This delay was trying to our patience, for time was precious, as we had to get up the river, discharge cargo, and get the ship off again on her return journey to England before the winter ice set in, otherwise it meant her being fixed in the Kara Sea till the late spring of next year. At length from the mast-head one evening came the long-expected and joyful intelligence that there was clear water visible ahead, and our ice-master reported having discovered what he thought looked like a passage to it. This was good news indeed, as the monotony of the last few days was beginning to pall on us, and we were none of us grieved when, after a few more hours of slow steaming, the intelligence proved correct, and we at last saw a clear horizon before us. Even then a new and unexpected danger presented itself. A gale had been blowing, and, although inside the ice-floes all was calm as in a lagoon, outside a heavy sea was running, and the enormous masses of loose ice were being tossed about like corks. It was an awful sight, and one of the utmost danger to the *Biscaya*, as it was most difficult to steer clear of the huge heaving masses which threatened at any moment to smash into us. Fortunately, however, we managed to pass through them without the slightest injury to the ship, and we gave a hearty cheer for our skipper when we found ourselves once more out in the open sea, and the order was given, for the first time for many days, "Full speed ahead!"

Before quite leaving the ice behind, I must tell you of a very funny practical joke our captain played on us while we were at anchor. One morning, at about three o'clock, when we were all fast asleep, we were aroused by the captain rushing into our cabin in a state of great excitement, and calling out

to us that there was a bear on the ice close by. To
jump out of one's bunk and make for one's rifle
was the work of a moment, while the captain, who
appeared to be in a frantic state of excitement at
the chance of such capital sport, was rushing about
looking for his ammunition. In a few seconds, and
without waiting to put on coat or slippers, I was
out on the deck, with nothing on but my pyjamas,
in order to get the first shot if possible. I found
all the crew looking over the bulwarks. It was
broad daylight, a cold, raw sort of morning, with a
dense fog enveloping everything a few yards ahead.
About a hundred yards away, on a huge piece of
ice which was slowly drifting towards us, was a large
animal looming out through the mist. It was too
far away to be distinctly made out, but there it was
undoubtedly—a Polar bear. It would make for the
water before I could get a shot, so without the
slightest hesitation I commenced blazing away. It
was so cold standing out in the frosty air, with
scarcely anything on and coming straight from one's
warm bed, that I could scarcely hold my rifle, still
less distinguish the dim outline in the distance at
which I fired four rounds in rapid succession, as I
expected every minute the other fellows would turn
up before I could hit it. All at once, the mass of
ice having by this time drifted nearer, the animal
turned slowly round towards us, and started a
plaintive bleating. "Why, it's only a sheep!" I

fairly yelled, as I now made out its form quite distinctly. Immediately there rose from all sides such shrieks of laughter as were never heard before in the Arctic regions, I imagine; the crew simply rolled about the deck in convulsions. As to the captain and the others, they nearly went into fits. To my astonishment, I then saw one of the ship's boats which had been waiting on the other side put off to fetch back the pseudo-bear—which was only one of our own sheep, after all, and which the captain, as a joke, had himself put on the ice, rightly guessing that in our half-awakened state none of us would hit it. The others, however, did not turn out quickly enough, so I was the sole beneficiary of what was one of the funniest practical jokes I ever heard of, and I laughed as heartily as any of them when I "twigged" it all. It was no use going back to bed again directly, so, to show I could appreciate a good bit of fun, and to keep out the cold, we opened a bottle of whiskey, and spent a pleasant hour, while laughing again and again at the description of how I looked, rushing out on deck in my pyjamas, half asleep, and firing wildly over the side of the ship. The sheep (which had been condemned for mutton), in recognition of its valour while under fire, was reserved as our very last victim for the flesh-pot.

We were once more fairly on our way towards the Yenisei, and, although we sighted a great deal more ice, we encountered none which formed any serious obstacle; we evidently had passed the worst. On August 11 we got as far north as it was necessary for us to go (our position being at the time 75 deg. north), and probably very few of us will ever get so near the North Pole again. It was a real Arctic day, as I take it, wretchedly cold, with heavy rain and a dense fog, so there was nothing for it but to remain in the cabin all day. In the afternoon we crossed the estuary to the river Ob, and—curious phenomenon—passed through fresh water for some hours. We got some on deck, and found it drinkable though brackish.

It was now only a question of making up for lost time, as it had been arranged that the river steamer, the *Phœnix*, should come from Yeniseisk and meet us at the mouth of the river about August 12, which would give us ample time to get out from England, allowing for delays. We reached our place of rendezvous on the 13th— wonderful time, all things considered—and brought up opposite the little station of Golchika, without seeing anything of the ship which ought to have been waiting for us. The river here was about ten miles wide, and the coast on either side was as bare and desolate as that we had seen when passing through the Waygatch Straits. It was profanely though graphically described by one of our party, who remarked that it looked as if it were "the last place God had made, and He had forgotten to finish it!"

In reply to our gun, which we fired as a signal, a boatful of men put off from the land, and soon

THE HANDSOMEST MEMBER OF HIS FAMILY.

reached the ship, and then we had before us our first visitors from the kingdom of the White Czar. There were six of them—two Russians, and the rest Samoyede natives. Good specimens of the Mongolian race, they were dressed in what looked like undressed sheep-skin of great age, judging from its colour, the fur being worn inside next their bodies. The two Russians were dressed in the usual peasant costume of the country. We could none of us make ourselves understood, although I got out my guide-book and vainly tried to pronounce some jaw-dislocating words; so we stood grinning at each other for several minutes, till some one thought of offering them a cigarette. This time no interpreter was necessary. What we wanted to find out from them was whether they had seen anything of the *Phœnix*, but could not make them understand; in fact, our difficulty now was to get rid of them—to let them know we were pleased to have had the pleasure of meeting them, but that "enough was as good as a feast." As they did not understand a hint, we simply pointed down to their boat, waving our hands to them as a sign for them to depart; this they acted on, but not before they had insisted on shaking hands with us all round—rather a trying ordeal. After their departure, it was decided to anchor in mid-stream and wait a few hours for the *Phœnix* before we attempted reaching the next station without a pilot.

In the mean time, the steam-launch we had on board was got out and put in readiness. The following day, there still being no signs of the *Phœnix*, it was decided to attempt to reach the next station,

SAMOYEDE BOATMEN.

[To face p. 34.

Karaoul, a distance of about a hundred and sixty miles, without her, as it was thought she might have met with an accident on her way down with so many lighters in tow; so, with the launch a few hundred yards ahead taking soundings, the *Biscaya* left Golchika, and started up the river in the hope of seeing the missing ship. We made slow but sure progress, considering we had no pilot, and how imperfect our only chart was, and it certainly was a bit of luck that we got on so well as we did, as the river is full of sandbanks. No incident worthy of note occurred. It was blowing a nasty head wind all the time, so those in the launch had a rough and wet time of it, as the river averaged three miles wide the whole way, and there was no shelter whatever; yet they stuck to their work manfully, although they were nearly swamped several times by the heavy seas. Towards evening the next day we came in sight of a solitary log-cabin on the dreary shore, with a dilapidated sort of storehouse next to it; close to the water's edge stood a Samoyede tent with a lot of native dogs lying round it; all about were empty casks and other miscellaneous rubbish. Not a human being was in sight. We had safely accomplished the risky voyage from Golchika without a pilot; for this wretched little station off which we dropped anchor, with all our colours flying, was Karaoul, the goal of the *Biscaya's* voyage.

KARAOUL.

## CHAPTER IV.

### THE PORT OF KARAOUL AND ITS INHABITANTS.

The tundras of Northern Siberia—The Samoyedes—Arrival of the *Phœnix*—My first Russian meal—Vodka and tea—Our departure for Kasanskoi.

In my last chapter I told you how we had safely reached Karaoul, the destination of the *Biscaya*, and that, to our great disappointment, the ship which ought to have been there to meet us was not at the rendezvous. What could have happened to her? Naturally, the first idea that suggested itself was that she had run aground and was unable to get off, encumbered as she was with the heavy barges that she was towing down from Yeniseisk to take back our cargo in. It was manifestly out of the question attempting to proceed any farther without a pilot, so it was decided to wait where we were, in the hope of the *Phœnix* turning up during the next day or two.

In the evening we all went ashore to have a look round, and were received on landing by quite a pack of native dogs, which, however, only offered a mild protest against an invasion by barking at us from a distance. A limp-looking individual, dressed in the usual Russian costume, with the inevitable top-boots, strolled listlessly down towards the beach with his hands in his pockets, and stared at us in an aimless sort of fashion. The dismal loneliness of the surroundings had evidently had their effect on him, and he was incapable of arousing himself to anything requiring a mental effort, for he did not evince the slightest interest in our arrival, strange and unusual though it certainly must have been to him in this out-of-the-way sort of place. We found, however, that he still retained the use of his tongue, and my slight knowledge of German then proved very useful, as it turned out he was not a Russian, but hailed from the "Vaterland." He informed us that he was the only white man in the place (which, by the way, only contained as many inhabitants as there are letters in its name), and usually spent the summer months there looking after the Samoyede fishermen who were working for the merchant who owned the dilapidated wooden buildings. In the winter he was employed as a butcher at Yeniseisk, and very glad he was to get back again there, as he said he had a fearfully dull time of it here, with not a soul to speak to except the Samoyedes, and very little work to do even when fish was brought in to salt. One could not help pitying a man who was so down on his luck as to be obliged to bury himself alive so far from his native land in order to earn his daily bread.

There was not much to see on the beach, so we started for a walk over the hills, and had a very pleasant ramble through country which reminded one not a little of the Scottish Highlands. Everywhere we were knee-deep in luxuriant grasses and moss, while all around flowers were growing in wild profusion—it was almost like being in a huge deserted garden. I noticed no end of old friends, such as the wild thyme, campanella, and mountain daisy. It was hard to realize that the ground is eternally frost-bound a foot or so beneath the surface, and that all this wonderful vegetation only comes up during the few months when the ground is not covered with snow; for during the greater part of the year there is absolutely nothing to relieve the white vista of the endless rolling plains, which are then deserted by even the aborigines themselves. We came across a solitary Samoyede grave on the hillside, the spot being marked by two sledges standing ready packed as for a journey. The Samoyedes thus leave their dead, and the custom is almost touching in its simplicity. All the earthly belongings of the deceased are placed on the sledges, covered with a reindeer skin, and abandoned to the mercy of the elements, with no other protection than a rudely carved forked stick stuck in the ground close by to frighten away evil spirits. They have no fear of robbers, as they know that their own people would not desecrate a grave, and to strangers the few primitive articles on the sledges would not offer much temptation; still, I must confess, it rather

THE SAMOYEDE'S GRAVE.

made my mouth water to see such a lot of tempting curiosities thus abandoned.

On our way back to the ship we had a look in at the loghouse, and one look was almost enough for most of us, as the heat inside was simply stifling; for, although it was quite a warm summer evening, all the windows appeared to be hermetically closed, and the large stove was in full blaze. There was nothing particularly striking about the interior, which was but a poor Russian home. I could not help remarking the extreme order in which the place was kept; everything seemed to have its place, to which it was scrupulously returned when moved.

We then paid a visit *en passant* to the Samoyede

A SAMOYEDE LADY.

hut, or tent, or whatever they call the bundle of dirty rags that serves them for a sort of shelter. Inside we saw an old man, two women, and four or five half-naked children huddled together, in an indescribable state of filth, round a few smoking embers which were intended to represent a fire. The stench was so great that it seemed more like looking at a den of wild beasts than at human beings. The river might have been ten miles away, instead of only as many yards, for all the use they ever made of it.

It had been decided that the next day our steam launch should be sent on a voyage of discovery up the unknown reaches of the mighty river, in search of the missing *Phœnix*. The launch had already been thoroughly overhauled, so without delay a supply of provisions, sufficient to last at least three months, was put on board of her, and three of our party told off for the expedition. At eight o'clock the next morning all was in readiness, and the little launch, packed absolutely to the gunwale and towing a boat full of coal for her engine, started on her venturesome journey, her crew looking very uncomfortable in their cramped quarters: still, as it was a lovely day, the sun shining brilliantly, it almost made one envy them their trip, if they had such weather all the time. There was just a slight mist on the river, so they were not long getting out of sight, blowing us a final good-bye with their steam whistle, to which we replied by firing a volley with our rifles. Our now reduced party then returned to the cabin to finish breakfast, wondering how long we were doomed to wait at Karaoul in glorious inactivity.

At the end of the meal, as we were getting up from table, we were startled by hearing the launch's whistle blowing with great vigour close at hand. We all rushed on deck, fearing some accident had befallen her, when, to our astonishment, we saw her returning at full speed, while close behind her, towering above the mist and with all her colours flying, was the ship she had gone in search of. We were simply dumbfounded, as the situation was almost too absurd; for, had the mist only lifted, or the launch been detained only a quarter of an hour, we must have seen her before her pursuer could have started, and thus saved ourselves a lot of trouble. As may be imagined, the gallant crew of the launch came in for a lot of good-humoured chaff, and we were able to congratulate them on the successful result of their mission and their safe return. In a very short time the *Phœnix* was alongside, and we then learnt that she had been delayed by the number of barges she had had to tow—so much so, in fact, that, in order to save time, it had been decided to leave most of them some twenty miles behind, at a convenient spot, and come on with only one, so as to commence the transhipment without any more unnecessary delay, and then return for the rest. No time was lost, therefore; and in less than an hour after we had shaken hands with those on board the steamer, our hatches were off, the steam winches going merrily, and the cargo being rapidly taken out of the hold, under the supervision of a stately Russian custom-house officer, who was attended by two Cossacks.

The *Phœnix* appeared to be crowded with men, as compared with our small crew of twelve. I learnt afterwards that no less than forty-five men had been brought down from Yeniseisk to work the barges and get in the cargo, and that among this

TRANSHIPMENT OF OUR CARGO TO THE "PHŒNIX."

big crowd there was a baker, a butcher, and a man specially told off to attend to the live stock, of which they had quite a farmyard, on one of the barges. They evidently knew how to make themselves comfortable while they were about it. I spent an hour in watching the men working at the cargo, and could not help coming to the conclusion that with a little less talk a good deal more work could have been accomplished in the time; there seemed to be too many foremen, and all seemed to differ in their orders at any critical moment, and so helped to increase the confusion which was already caused by the jabbering of the men. It was, however, a picturesque and interesting sight, this crowd of rough, unkempt men, with their coloured blouses and their loose trousers, tucked into high boots, reminding one not a little of bold buccaneers in the good old Adelphi dramas; and although, perhaps, they did not put quite as much energy into their movements as they might have done, they made up for it in "effect," from an artistic point of view—an effect which was heightened by a quaint sort of chorus they sang at intervals. They struck me as being a much better-looking lot of men than an average crowd of the same class in England, and looked well fed and contented with their lot. A few among them, I was informed, were exiles who have served their time, but who prefer to continue living in Siberia, where, from what I can gather, the general opinion is that one is better off as an exile than as a free man in Russia itself.

We had our first taste of Russian cooking that morning, as we all lunched on board the *Phœnix*— and a very good lunch it was, although it certainly was very trying to have to eat without drinking, as is the Russian custom, and I mentally decided to live *à la Française* while in Holy Russia. At the end of the meal a hissing samovar was brought in, tea was brewed, and a decanter of vodka passed round, and we all agreed that vodka makes a very good substitute for whiskey, but that weak tea without milk, drunk boiling hot out of tumblers, would take some getting used to, as it evidently is an acquired taste, and wants educating up to by a prolonged stay in Russia. The cabin of the *Phœnix*, though small, was so clean and cosy that it seemed quite a treat to have a decently served meal after all the "pigging" we had had to put up with on the *Biscaya*; it made us almost wish for the time to come when we should transfer our quarters to her for the river journey. Everything looked as prim as on a yacht, from the white paint on the deck-house to the deck itself, which was kept perfectly clean. I feel sure that were the *Phœnix* to return once more to her native port of Newcastle, her old owners would not recognize, in the smart-looking river boat, their quondam steamer, so thoroughly has she been altered and Russianized. The next day it was decided to go back to where the other barges had been left by the *Phœnix*, so our anchors were weighed, and both vessels started.

It took only a few hours to reach Kasanskoi, the next "station," which was destined to be our *pied à terre* for some little time. The scenery on the way up was tame, and varied but slightly from what I have previously described; in fact, so flat and uninteresting was it at times that one could see

rolling plains of green for miles and miles ahead
without even a bush to break their monotony. The
effect called "mirage" is very peculiar in these
regions. At times distant headlands appear to go
right away up into the sky, and one sees clouds
and river underneath them; sometimes great holes
appear, as it were, in the sides of the hills, and daylight thus seen through them; even on the darkest
and greyest days these effects are noticeable. As the
time was now fully occupied in getting the *Biscaya's*
cargo safely transferred to the barges, and as during
these operations the *Phœnix* could be of no service
to us, it was arranged that she should proceed down
to the mouth of the river and wait for the other ship
and the tug, which were to have followed us out
from England, and, in the event of their turning up,
to pilot them back to where we were. So we were
to have Kasanskoi all to ourselves for a few days.
There being now little of interest to me in the well-
known ship, I decided to explore the neighbouring
hills, so would go ashore by myself in the early
morning with my gun and my sketch-book, and
wander about to my heart's content. There was
very little to shoot, and still less to sketch; nevertheless it was very delightful, after being cooped up
for so many weeks, to find one's self once more alone
and free as the air on these boundless plains. The
bright sunshine, the familiar flowers, the birds
chirping merrily as they flitted from bush to bush—

in fact, the whole scene was the very antithesis of what one would have expected to see on the bleak tundras of Northern Siberia. It was almost with a feeling of sadness that one reflected how changed all would be in a few short weeks hence—for in these high latitudes the seasons change without any perceptible prelude. At a certain moment of each year, generally about the end of May, the snow melts away under the influence of the almost tropical heat of the sun, which now ceases to set; the earth wakes from her long sleep during the dark months of the Arctic winter, luxuriant grasses spring up, the flowers appear as if by magic, hundreds and thousands of migratory birds arrive, the air resounds with the buzzing of insect life;—it is summer. For about three short months this wonderful transformation lasts; then gradually the sun disappears, the long nights return, the piercing north wind commences to blow, and in a very short time—sometimes in a single night—the ice-king resumes his sway, the frost-bound earth disappears under a thick pall of snow, and all is darkness and desolation in the awful silence of the Arctic winter.

OUR CUSTOM-HOUSE OFFICER.

## CHAPTER V.

### KASANSKOI.

Our Russian customs officer—A shooting-excursion—Visit to the settlement of Kasanskoi—The house of a Siberian trader—Interesting people—First experience of Russian hospitality—The return of the *Phœnix*—Departure of the *Biscaya*.

WE had the Russian custom-house officer quartered on us during the absence of the *Phœnix*, and a very nice unassuming fellow we all found him, although we hardly understood a word he said. He was a typical specimen of a Russian—a great big chap with broad shoulders and long fair beard. I had heard he was an ardent sportsman, though he had no gun with him on board; so one evening after supper I thought he might like to come and have some shooting with me. But how was I to make him understand? for although I pointed to my guns, he did not seem to comprehend. At last an idea struck me. I got a piece of paper and drew a duck on it, at the same time making a sign of shooting with my gun. He guessed at once what it meant, and agreed to join me. Unfortunately, however, I had only one fowling-piece with me, and my Winchester was hardly the thing for wild duck, as he seemed to wish to tell me; but, to his great amusement, I drew a bear on the paper, and so made an excuse for taking the rifle also. As may be imagined, we had no occasion to use it. For a wonder, in a country like this teeming with birds, we only had poor sport in return for a long and fatiguing walk across miles of swampy ground.

After I had thoroughly explored the adjoining country, one morning I got out a small steam-launch belonging to the *Phœnix*, and, with a Russian who spoke a little German as fireman and interpreter, went down the river as far as the four or five log-houses and huts which constituted the settlement of Kasanskoi. As at Karaoul, the dogs gave us a hearty welcome, though, fortunately, they were all chained up this time, as they looked anything but gentle creatures, and tried hard to get at us. The

E

largest of the houses was really not a bad-looking sort of place, certainly far better than one would have expected to find. The proprietor came out and politely invited us to enter. We accepted his

KASANSKOI.

invitation, and, following him in, found ourselves in a large kind of kitchen, in which several members of the family were busily engaged in various household duties. But for the quaint costume of the man, and the fact that the women were smoking cigarettes,

TRADER'S HOUSE AT KASANSKOI.

there was nothing particularly striking about the place. I could not, however, help immediately noticing how wonderfully clean it was: the walls rivalled the boards of the floor in whiteness, the table shone like a looking-glass, and everything showed the handiwork of a careful housewife. The

MINE HOST AT KASANSKOI.

stove was alight, and the heat was excessive, yet, curiously, there was not the slightest feeling of ill ventilation. Immediately on entering I noticed (as my "Murray" told me I should in all Russian dwellings) the inevitable sacred picture in a corner of the room, and, in accordance with the advice he gives, I immediately took off my hat, so as to be quite *en règle*. The Russians, or rather the Northern Siberians, are certainly a most phlegmatic race, if they are all like the few I have already met. One would have thought that in this remote place the entrance of a stranger would have excited just the least little show of interest—but no, they hardly uttered a word; they just looked up for a second from their work, and then resumed it without the slightest comment, as if I had been an ordinary everyday visitor from a neighbouring house. Since they paid so little attention, I was equally cool, and walked round about the room, looking at everything as though I had been in a museum; and then got out my sketch-book, and, sitting down, started a portrait of my host. He seemed to understand what I wanted of him, and kept as rigid as a statue while I was doing it.

Even when it was finished, no one evinced the slightest curiosity to see the result. In any other part of the world one would have been pestered by people crowding round and all wanting to finger one's sketch-book; but here, in this far-away Siberian home, where, to say the least of it, sketching is not an everyday sight, stolid indifference was stronger than idle curiosity. I determined to take advantage of it, and, since my being there did not seem to disturb them a little bit, I got out the launch, and returned there the next day with my paint-box and largest sketching-block.

All the people I had seen on the previous afternoon were in the house, having what evidently was their morning meal. It was a simple and homely sight, this family gathering round the brightly polished table, with the glittering samovar towering in the centre. It struck me as being so interesting that I got a couple of chairs, one to sit on and the other as an easel, and commenced sketching in the group as rapidly as possible. Fancy what would have happened if such an event occurred in an English homestead! Imagine, for instance, a bearded Russian walking coolly in while breakfast was going on and the whole family present, and, without saying a word, taking possession of part of the room and commencing to paint the occupants without even

SWEET SEVENTEEN.

asking permission! In my case, however, all went as merrily as a wedding-bell : no one interfered with me, and they were so long discussing their weak tea that, by the time they had finished, I had managed to get a very fair idea of the *mise en scène*.

With the exception of an hour, when I went down and had my lunch in the launch, I worked there the whole day as comfortably as if I had been in my own studio. In spite of their natural indifference, the people, in their quiet sort of way, evidently wished to help me, and to show me some little politeness. I noticed that the children were forbidden to talk loud or even to come anywhere near me, and any one who has had any experience of sketching in strange places, where, as a rule, the children worry one even more than the flies, will understand what a boon that was; while, to cap my adventure with this unique family, during the afternoon my host came up to me, hat in hand, and, bowing very low, pointed to an adjoining room. Out of curiosity, I got up to see what was there, when, to my astonishment, I saw the samovar hissing away, and tea and cakes waiting for me. This was hospitality indeed, and my only regret was not being able to express my thanks in Russian ; but I fancy they must have pretty well guessed the meaning of the few bluff words I said to that effect in English as I drank to the health of my host's wife in boiling tea, and very nearly

A HOME IN NORTHERN SIBERIA: THE MORNING MEAL.

scalded myself. The ice was broken, and they all laughed very much, for fun is probably very much the same all over the world. We now became quite

MATERFAMILIAS.

friendly, considering I did not understand a word they said; and I made myself quite at home among them till I had finished my picture. Before leaving I presented my host with a pencil sketch of his wife as a souvenir of my visit, and he evidently prized it very much, for I fancy he intended fixing it up over the religious picture in the corner.

The *Phœnix* returned in about ten days, and, to our great satisfaction, was accompanied by the two vessels she had gone in search of—the *Thule*, a small steamer of 400 tons, and the small tug she had towed out from England. Never before had such a flotilla been seen on the river Yenisei; the only pity was that there was no one but ourselves to see it. So far the expedition, with the exception of a few unavoidable delays, had gone without a hitch. It was quite a treat getting something in the shape of news, such as it was, and all the papers brought by the *Thule* were devoured as eagerly as though they were of the previous day instead of seven weeks old. The only thing now was to get the cargoes transferred to the barges as quickly as possible, for the season showed unmistakable signs of being but a short one this year, and it was imperative that the two ships should get out of the Kara Sea on their way back to England before the winter came on. As if to emphasize the admonition the thermometer had given us, the lovely weather suddenly broke up, and, to our great astonishment, one morning we woke up to find a couple of inches of snow on the ground, and everything already looking very winterly, although it was only September 2. Every one, therefore, set to work with

almost feverish haste, so great a fear does the awful Arctic winter inspire.

The scene during this work of transhipping our cargo was one of surprising novelty. The barges intended for the reception of cattle, pigs, and poultry were temporarily turned into a sort of floating farmyard. The Siberians evidently did not intend to forget provision for the wants of the inner man during their long voyage up the river. In stowing the

TEA-TIME AT THE MEN'S QUARTERS ON SHORE.

cargo, all had to work against time, for every hour of summer in these regions is of the utmost importance. Here, too, was already present the inevitable Russian official, personified by one of the most charming men I ever met, with his two attendant Cossacks, prompt to scrutinize each package of the

*Biscaya's* cargo. Indeed, for this purpose they had been expressly sent down some 1500 miles, on board the river steamer *Phœnix*, to meet us; such is the vigilance of the Czar's officials, even at this remote distance from the central seat of government.

COSSACKS.

For us, meantime, who were spectators of the operations, the days were so much like each other that it was at times difficult to remember what day of the week it was. It was too cold and wretched to even think of going ashore, so there was nothing for it but to while away the time as best we could, and wait events. Every morning the question was asked, " When shall we get out of this ? " for we were all getting heartily sick of our prolonged inactivity —eight weeks since we left London, and still a month of dreary river journey before us ere we reach our destination, Yeniseisk. However, *tout vient à point à qui sait attendre*, and at last came the welcome news that the ships were at length ready to start for England, and that we were to transfer ourselves and luggage to the *Phœnix* in readiness for the river journey. Still, there was a mingled feeling of regret as we bid farewell to the good ship *Biscaya*, which had carried us through so many miles of strange waters, and, in spite of cramped accommodation, had given us opportunities for many hours of real pleasure and good fellowship.

## CHAPTER VI.

### THE RIVER VOYAGE OF THE *PHŒNIX* UP TO YENISEISK.

The Yenisei river—Its noble proportions—Scenery along the banks—The first tree—Our first mishap—The return of the tug—An exciting incident.

A HOUSE-BOAT.

On September 14 the ocean steamers *Biscaya* and *Thule* started on their return voyage to England, it having been arranged that the tug should pilot them down to the mouth of the river, and then rejoin us as quickly as possible. It almost seemed like parting with an old friend, as we got our last glimpse of the *Biscaya*; for, in spite

of her grimy decks and straitened quarters, we had all of us, somehow, come to look upon her as a sort of home; and when, after cheering ourselves hoarse, the two ships at length disappeared behind a distant headland, we realized that the connecting link with the Old Country was severed, so to speak, and the magnitude of the journey we had before us seemed to magnify itself. As a matter of fact, it is only now, on looking back over the six long weary weeks during which we were slowly making our way against the heavy stream, through hundreds and hundreds of miles of uninteresting scenery, and after quite a series of mishaps, that we can fully realize what the journey was like. For my own part, I should be sorry to undertake it again. However, to continue my narrative.

The two ships once out of sight, no time was lost, and preparations were immediately commenced for our speedy departure. The barges had to be properly stowed, a lot of spare timbers which had been brought down had to be cut up for the engines, and a host of minor details seen to before starting on our long journey. Two days were thus spent, and then at last, exactly a month after our arrival in the river, we made a start with our heavy load in tow. We made but slow progress, for the stream was strong. Still, we could not help feeling thankful at moving at all, after our long period of inactivity.

Although we were now nearly three hundred miles from the mouth of the river, there was no perceptible difference in its enormous width, which must nearly average ten miles for at least four hundred miles from the sea, while in many places it widens out into such enormous expanses of water that it can only be likened to a continuous series of huge lakes. As a matter of fact, between Golchika and Karaoul, at a distance of two hundred miles from the sea, there is one part where for nearly a hundred miles it is over sixty miles in width, and when there is a gale blowing, as was the case when we passed up it, the sea is quite as heavy as it is during a "sou'wester" in the English Channel, the flat character of the "tundras" (as the vast treeless plains in these regions are called) rendering the wind exceptionally bleak. Such noble proportions are thoroughly in keeping with the enormous length of this majestic river, which, with its important tributaries the Selenga and the Angara, is over five thousand miles, and takes its rise in Chinese territory, while, according to the French geographer Reclus, its water-system covers an enormous area of nearly 2,900,000 square versts (equal to about 1,950,000 English square miles). The largest rivers in Europe dwindle into absolute insignificance in comparison with it, for the Volga, Danube, Rhone, and Rhine, if added together, would barely make a Yenisei, while the poor little Thames would be but as a small muddy brook, even when compared with one of its least important tributaries—the Kureika, for instance. Yet on the whole of this vast highway, traversing as it does such a diversified tract of continent, there are only ten steamers, and these only kept going through the enterprise of such Siberian magnates as Siberiakoff, Gadaloff, Boudaresoff, and Kitmanoff. Siberia is still in its infancy, so the future of its magnificent resources cannot yet be gauged; still, should they eventually find a market in England through the medium of the Yenisei and Kara sea-route, it will be solely owing to British pluck and enterprise, as personified in Captain Wiggins, to whom is undoubtedly due the honour of being the first to land a British cargo in the heart of Siberia. Whether this bold and adventurous enterprise be destined ever to vie with that of the Hudson Bay traders, to which it can aptly be compared, is scarcely my province to discuss in a narrative which is purely descriptive; still, one cannot help contemplating it with pride that the old spirit which existed in our forefathers still remains, and that, while this exists, England will always retain her position as the pioneer of commercial enterprise all the world over.

For the next few days after leaving our anchorage, not only was the journey uninteresting as regards events, but also from a picturesque point of view. We were still beyond the northern limit of trees, and the banks of the river, though perhaps presenting some interest to the geological student, were certainly not strikingly picturesque, and offered no artistic attractions. This barren appearance, however, gradually changed, low bushes appeared on the hillsides and gradually increased in height, till at last, on September 18, we sighted the first actual tree we had seen since leaving Europe—a solitary and miserable specimen of the larch species; yet it was a very welcome sight, for it betokened our approaching return to more temperate latitudes and brighter scenes. But one must have been in the Arctic regions to understand how eager one is to get out of their dreary confines. In a very short time, trees became more and more numerous on either bank—in fact, it almost seemed as though we had crossed an invisible line beyond which they could not grow, so sudden was the change once past it. They were still a species of larch, though so small that some one remarked that they were not so "larch" (?) as in England. We also saw in the distance several white foxes along the banks; their being this colour is, as is well known, a sure sign of approaching winter.

We shortly reached the small church-village of Dudinskoi, the first station of any importance we had yet come to. We arrived too late to go on shore, much as we should have liked to; for it appeared, from all accounts, to be quite a flourishing little place, boasting of a population consisting of a couple of priests, a police officer, some exiles, and a number of natives, as well as a rich merchant who owns nearly all the place. However, we made up our minds to have a look round the first thing in the morning.

But "man proposes, God disposes." During the night our first mishap occurred. Without the slightest warning a strong gale sprang up, and the *Phœnix* had a very narrow escape of being wrecked. The river being certainly not less than six miles wide, there was quite a heavy sea on; our barges were pitched and tossed about like so many corks, and in a very short time became quite unmanageable, ending by being driven right up alongside in dangerous proximity to us. The confusion for a time was awful, and a blinding snowstorm coming on added still more to the excitement, as it was impossible to see more than a few yards on either side. Steam, indeed, was quickly got up, and it was immediately decided to get up the anchors and attempt to run before the gale up-stream. Before, however, we could get under way, one of the smaller lighters was swamped, and sank immediately. No one was on board of her at the time, fortunately. After proceeding some fifteen versts, we found a sheltered creek, and again anchored.

The gale abated as quickly as it rose, and the next day the weather was absolutely perfect. All that day we were busy replenishing our wood-bunkers, for although we had, to all appearances, an almost inexhaustible supply a couple of days before, it seemed to have positively melted away once the engines were started. As is the custom all over Siberia, nothing but wood is burnt, and this is easily understood when one comes to consider how vast is the forest region of Siberia, a region only comparable to the backwoods of North America.

At the various small stations, and also here and there along the banks of the river, are to be found huge piles of wood, placed by the villagers, ready cut, for the use of the steamers plying between Yeniseisk and the mouth of the river. This wood is for sale at an average price of one and a half roubles (a little more than 3s. 8d.) per cubic fathom —(N.B. the Russian fathom is seven feet, not six feet as in England)—not dear, considering how much time is saved by finding the wood all ready for use, as we afterwards discovered when on one or two occasions we ran short of fuel, and, there being no "station" near, we actually had to burn all our available spars and other spare timber, and eventually had to send men ashore to cut down trees—a long and tedious operation. The *Phœnix* burnt about fifteen fathoms a day, as I afterwards learnt; so my astonishment at the quick way the huge piles vanished down the bunker-holes is easily explained. I hear that some of the other river steamers burn as much as thirty fathoms in the twenty-four hours.

LOADING WOOD FOR THE "PHOENIX."

(To face p. 66.)

Just as we were finishing loading wood the tug hove in sight, much to our relief, as she was already overdue, and fear had been expressed for her safety. She was soon alongside, and we then learnt that she had safely accomplished her mission of piloting the two ships down to Golchika, but not, however, without a few mishaps, for she had had a serious fire in her bunkers, and on one occasion had been aground in a nasty position for no less than nine hours. However, "all's well that ends well," and our party was now complete again.

The next few days were uneventful. The weather was bitterly cold, and snow occasionally fell, so the surrounding landscape — if the dreary expanse of monotonous banks could be so called — looked, if anything, still more dreary. Then occurred the second incident in the long series of mishaps which followed us throughout the voyage.

We were busy loading wood one afternoon, when suddenly the captain rushed on deck, and, in an excited voice, called out that we had sprung a leak! It may easily be imagined the effect this announcement had on us—it came like a thunderbolt, so little were we expecting anything unusual. On further investigation it was found that the water was gaining rapidly, so without losing a moment all the men were instantly recalled to the ship and ordered to commence clearing the hold, in order, if possible, to discover the damage and, if not too late, make it good.

The excitement was great, for, although we were only about two miles from the shore, the situation was extremely grave, from what we could learn from those who had been down to see. Most of us, therefore, got our papers and valuables in readiness in case of emergency. In the mean time the pumps were going, and steam got ready, so that, in the event of its being necessary, the ship could be run ashore at a moment's notice. For some hours no visible headway was made against the enemy, till towards nine o'clock, after several hours of hard and persistent work in icy-cold water, the men were relieved, as it was discovered the water was abating. It afterwards transpired that, from some unexplained cause, a plate had been started, and the "list" given to the ship by the loading of the wood on one side only had caused the inrush of water. One of the engineers was fortunately soon able to patch it up and obviate any further danger. The prospect of having, perhaps, to abandon our comfortable quarters was not enticing while it lasted, and it certainly was with a great sense of relief that we got under way once more, and then sat down to an extra late dinner, with a bottle of champagne to commemorate our escape.

For the next twenty-four hours we fortunately were able to proceed without any special incident. The weather still continued very cold and wintry, and much snow fell. The few scattered trees on the banks now grew more closely together, till at length we reached a dense forest, which we never afterwards entirely lost sight of. Right away southward, with scarcely a break, I learnt, it stretches to the far-distant Chinese frontier, some five thousand miles, while to east it is bounded by the river Lena, which thus gives it an approximate breadth of two thousand miles—probably the largest tract of forest-land in the world, and, as I have previously remarked, only comparable to the backwoods of America. Very depressing was the effect of this continuous wall of trees, in all the various stages of growth and decay— in some parts the predominance of firs giving it almost the appearance of a huge plantation of telegraph-poles. The chief trees appeared to be pine, white birch, lime, and mountain ash.

## CHAPTER VII.

### THE RIVER VOYAGE—*continued*.

An awful fatality—Misfortune follows misfortune—M. Sotnikoff—Sellivanaka, the settlement of the Skopti—A visit from the village "elder."

DIFFICULT NAVIGATION.

OUR respite from misfortune was destined, unfortunately, to be but very brief, for on September 23 occurred an awful fatality by which we lost the commander of the *Phœnix*—Mr. George Lee, agent in Siberia of the Anglo-Siberian Syndicate. The circumstances of the tragic event in those far-away wilds were so impressive in their horror that they are as fresh in my memory as if it had happened only yesterday.

We had been moving slowly but surely, all day, against a strong head-wind; in the evening, after dinner, we were all seated in the cabin, smoking, and otherwise passing the time in our usual pleasant after-dinner fashion, when suddenly we heard a man who was taking soundings at the bows call out a quick change in the depth of water. Mr. Lee, who was reading a book, immediately jumped up, and, putting on his fur coat and cap, hastily went out, exclaiming as he did so that he "smelt something wrong." He had only been gone a few minutes, when we heard loud cries from the deck, the engine stopped, and almost immediately the captain rushed into the cabin in a frantic state. With some difficulty we gathered from his gestures that Mr. Lee had fallen overboard. In less time than it takes to write it we were all outside and on the upper deck. The excitement was indescribable. It was a pitch-dark night, and snowing hard; on all sides were men hurrying with lanterns, while the captain, through his speaking-trumpet, bawled out directions to the men in tug and barges behind us. For a few minutes, which seemed ages, we were peering into the intense darkness astern in the hope of seeing something which would guide us to the whereabouts of the unfortunate man, but in vain; when, all of a sudden, we heard shouts from the tug that they had picked him up. Our joy was great, but destined, unfortunately, to be of short duration. After some little delay, but really in wonderfully quick time considering, the tug was observed coming towards us, and soon was alongside. On its deck was a confused group of men, standing in awed silence, and looking strangely weird through the driving snow and under the flickering light of a lantern. In their midst, in a blanket which they were holding by the four corners, was something dripping wet, human in form. With little difficulty it was got on board the *Phœnix*, and then we saw it was the lifeless form of our ill-fated friend, who so few minutes before had been with us in the best of health and spirits, little dreaming his end was so near. It was a solemn sight, and brought before us with a power seldom realized that thrilling sentence, "In the midst of life we are in death." Although we persevered for no less than four hours with Dr. Sylvester's method, and tried every other known restorative, all was in vain—the unfortunate man never for one moment showed the least sign of life; so at last we were reluctantly forced to come to the conclusion that our efforts were futile.

We afterwards learnt how the accident had happened from the only man who had witnessed it. Mr. Lee, in his excitement to learn the depth of the water as shown by the sounding-pole, had stood on a log of timber covered with snow which was lying under the bulwarks, and, leaning over too far, his foot slipped on the treacherous surface, and he went overboard head first, so suddenly that he had not time to utter a cry. Considering how rapid the stream was, and the darkness of the night, the fact of his body being picked up at all was nothing short of miraculous, for we were going full speed at the time. Only a few days before, he had been telling us he could swim like a duck, and that evening during dinner had been relating some wonderful escapes from death he had had during his life. We had learnt that his heart was weak, so there can be very little doubt that the shock of the sudden immersion in the icy-cold water had had an instantaneously fatal effect, for his features showed no signs of any death-struggle, but were as calm as in sleep. A long consultation then took place, with the result that the London agent of the Syndicate took command of the ship, and she was again started ahead.

This awful event naturally cast a gloom over us all—although, as if in mockery of worldly griefs, the sun shone out brilliantly the next morning for the first time since we had left; in fact, it was like spring again. It was hard to realize that for the remainder of our voyage the *Phœnix*, so to speak, would be a floating hearse. No end of ghastly formalities had to be gone through, such as sealing up the dead man's effects, having a coffin made by one of the ship's carpenters, and a heap of other details, the custom-house officer now proving himself a really good fellow, and helping us as much as he could; in fact, I don't know what we should have done without him, speaking so little Russian as we all did. We learnt from him that we should have to stop at Turuchansk, the first important village we came to, and get permission from the police officer there to take the body on to Yeniseisk, and, as there was certain to be an inquest, we must make up our minds to some unavoidable delay. The only thing to be done, therefore, was to get on as quickly as possible, for we had no time to lose, with winter so close at hand.

But our misfortunes were not yet at an end. A day or so afterwards, owing to the strong current keeping us back, we ran short of wood when we were still some distance from the next station; so, in order not to let the fires out, it was decided (contrary to our usual custom, as we always anchored at dusk) to proceed all night. It was a nasty wet night, with a thick mist over everything, so our progress was very uncertain. All went well till about three o'clock, when suddenly, without the slightest warning, the water shallowed, and, with a nasty grinding sound which I shall long remember, the *Phœnix* ran aground. It was too dark and foggy at the time to make out where we were, but we evidently were stuck hard and fast, as was supposed, on a bank in the middle of the river. All efforts to back her were unsuccessful. The fog lifted shortly after, and it was then discovered that we had run clean ashore—so close, in fact, that one could almost have walked off the ship on to the grass. For several precious hours every possible device was tried in vain, and at one time things looked decidedly ugly, as we were on a rocky bottom. Our little tug, however, proved invaluable, for she at length succeeded in moving our bows, and then, to our great relief, we slid off into deep water, not without damage, unfortunately, for it was afterwards discovered that we had broken a blade of the propeller; still, we managed to get along somehow, in spite of it. It was high time, for we were at the very end of our supply of wood, and it was only by burning everything available, even to the hatches and some spare packing-cases we luckily had on board, that we could reach the next station, where we found wood in abundance.

We anchored opposite quite a "swagger" house, far and away the best we had hitherto seen in Siberia. It was two stories high, had carved window-frames, a bright-green roof, and other attempts at artistic decoration which one would hardly have expected to find so far away in Northern Asia. The owner of the place, we learnt, was a rich retired merchant named Sotnikoff, who had amassed a large fortune by mining and extensive trading operations. Vegetating in this dead-alive spot struck me as being a very unambitious ending to a long and successful life—however, *chacun à son goût*. We went ashore and paid Mr. Sotnikoff a visit, and were received with the usual hospitality of Russian people—I mean a regular sort of meal they put before one, generally consisting of delicious caviare and black bread, fish-pies, cakes, eggs, etc., washed down with copious draughts of vodka, and followed by the inevitable samovar. The house was furnished quite in a luxurious fashion, and the large room we were shown into boasted a really pretty suite of furniture, and had pictures on the walls. Mr. Sotnikoff, however, in spite of his great reputed wealth, was dressed in the ordinary costume of a Russian peasant, and with his long white beard presented quite a patriarchal appearance. He returned our visit later in the day, and strongly urged us not even to attempt to reach Yeniseisk with all our barges so late in the season, winter being so close at hand that the river might be frozen over at any moment, in which case we risked losing all our flotilla, if it caught us in any unprotected spot. Our best plan, he told us, would be to leave one of our least important barges in his charge till next spring, and proceed with the remainder without losing a moment, if possible. This advice so corroborated what we had already learnt that, as a result of a long and serious consultation, one of the barges was detached and left with him till the spring. We then again started, hoping that, with our diminished load, we should make better progress.

The next few days were uneventful; the banks,

with their fringe of dense forest, still continuing in dreary and endless monotony, while overhead flocks of migratory birds were continually passing us on their way south, sure and ominous sign of approaching winter. We could not help being surprised by the number of seagulls we still saw about; in fact, their name seemed almost a misnomer, so many hundreds of miles were we from the sea.

The curious huts of the Samoyede natives along the shores now gradually disappeared, and in their stead appeared other huts somewhat similar in form, only covered with strips of birch bark instead of skins, and inhabited by Ostiaks, a race of people not unlike the Samoyedes, but, from what I hear, certainly much more civilized—though that is not saying much, for they could not very easily be less so.

On September 30 we passed Selivanaka, a picturesque and flourishing little settlement, which is entirely inhabited by a portion of the secret sect called "Skopti," or "White Doves," who are perpetually banished from Russia on account of their peculiar doctrines. I had already read much about these curious people, and was hoping that we should stop here for wood, so that I should be able to go ashore and have a look round; but we were not in need of fuel, and our time was too precious to allow of any needless delays, so I had to content myself with as good a look at the settlement and its inhabitants as I could get through my binocular, for, although a boat containing three men rowed off to us, we did not stop. However, we had plenty of opportunity later on for a closer inspection of these men.

It happened this way: The boat returned to the shore, and Selivanaka was fast disappearing behind us, when we observed another boat rapidly catching us up, coming along close to the shore. In a very short time it was abreast of us, and we then saw it was drawn by three dogs, and contained the same men we had previously seen. They stopped when a little ahead of us, and, taking their dogs on board, rowed off to us and asked if we would allow them to tow behind us as far as Turuchansk, some few versts farther on. The desired permission being given to them, they shortly after came up on deck, and we therefore had plenty of time to examine more closely these specimens of one of the most curious sects in the world. I was lucky enough to get one of them, who turned out to be the "village elder," to let me make a careful sketch of him, as he had a face full of character; during which time I managed, through an interpreter, to obtain some interesting particulars of these "peculiar people." They are all eunuchs, marriage being forbidden among them. The Holy Virgin and the Christ they worship are appointed by their elders, and it is said they consider Peter III. as their god, imagining him to be

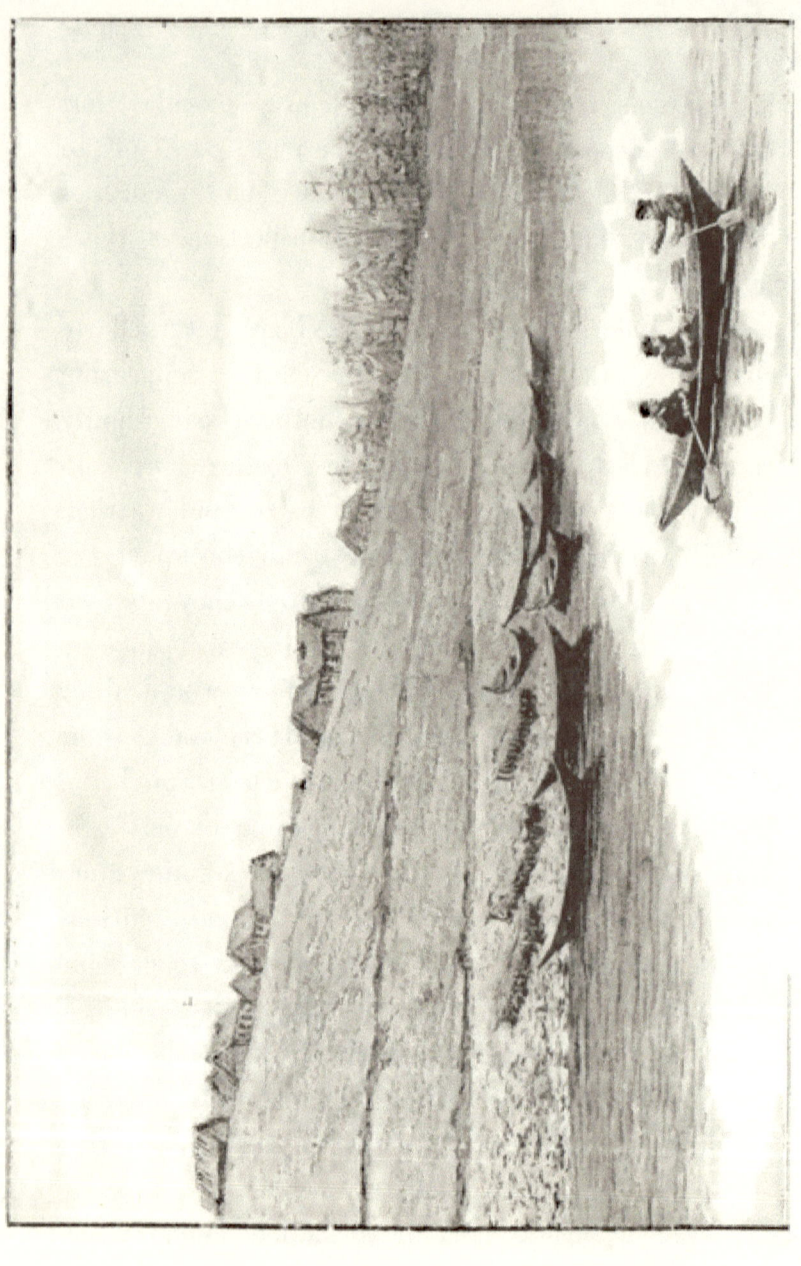

SULIVANAKA. [To face p. 78.

still living. They are also strict vegetarians and total abstainers, from which facts one gathers that, taking one consideration with another, a Skopti's life is not a happy one.

Afterwards I had a look at their boat, which was towing behind, and I could not help noticing the ready way in which their dogs made themselves comfortable during their masters' absence. The only harness they wear is a sort of band round the loins, which is connected with the boat by means of a long cord. Three is the number generally used, and wonderful are the distances which, I am told, they are able to accomplish—forty and even fifty versts at a stretch, and against the stream. No whip is ever used, their master's voice being quite sufficient to urge them on, for if one of them flags the others snap at him and make him keep up the pace.

THE PRINCIPAL THOROUGHFARE, TURUCHANSK.

## CHAPTER VIII.

### TURUCHANSK.

Visit to the monastery—Werchneimbackskoi—Our first visit from official Russia—The police officer of the district—The village priest.

DURING this time we were steadily advancing, and in the afternoon we came in sight of the beautiful monastery of Turuchansk, standing up above the trees like a big white lighthouse, its silvered dome glistening in the brilliant sunshine. It was our first real glimpse of Holy Russia, and a welcome sight after our long and wearisome journey. The river still retained its noble proportions, but was so full of sandbanks that we had to make a big *détour* before we could approach the shore. The beach, for it was nothing less, was covered with boats and quite a crowd of people, for our arrival was doubtless an event in this quiet place.

As it was uncertain how long we should be staying, we lost no time in getting ashore and making for the monastery. Its beautiful architecture offered a curious and striking contrast to the squalid wooden huts clustered round it, and in its quiet precincts we felt an indefinable sense of repose, which was very pleasant after the continual noise on board the *Phœnix*. We had no difficulty whatever in being shown over the interior of the building, which, I must confess, was somewhat disappointing, and did not equal the outside effect. As is usual in the Greek Church, sacred pictures constituted the chief feature, and, with their gaudy metal appendages, offered a great contrast to the bare whitewashed walls. As none of us understood Russian, all the interesting details given us by our guide (a monk, by the way, of most "unmonkish" appearance) were lost to us. Still, we were much interested in a very heavy sort of iron jacket and cross, which, we understood him to say, had been continually worn by some former ultra-religious inhabitant of the place. For what purpose he had thus afflicted himself we could not make out, but let us hope it did him a lot of good and brought him to an early grave, as was doubtless his wish when first donning it.

The few monks live in a wooden building just behind the church, and share their quarters with the police officer of the district—an arrangement, I hear, not at all to their taste ; still, they have to grin and bear it, as evidenced by the sentry-box which stood at the very door of the sacred edifice, and in which a Cossack is stationed when any Government money is in the district, for it is always kept for safety in the monastery itself. Our guide, the monk, had very comfortable quarters, and certainly far more luxurious than one would have expected for a man of his austere life. Here again Russian hospitality asserted itself. It is certainly a wonderful trait in the national character; I have never seen it equalled in any other country. Our genial host insisted on our breaking bread with him, and produced some delicious caviare and other eatables, which looked so appetizing we could not refuse.

On our return to the ship we learnt that the police officer of the district had gone on to the next village, some three hundred versts further up. As by this time the men had finished loading the wood, steam was got up, and soon we were once again moving onward, and, ere the moon had risen, peaceful Turuchansk, with its quaint monastery, was far behind us. In spite of all the adverse prophecies, the weather not only continued fine, but,

OUR FIRST VISIT FROM OFFICIAL RUSSIA.

[To face p. 83.

WERCHNEIMBACSKOI.  [*To face p.* 63.

during the next few days, became absolutely warm again. We made capital progress, as we had the wind in our favour, and reached the village of Werchneimbackskoi even sooner than we had expected.

Our arrival was hailed by a salute fired from a small cannon on the hillside, and the villagers crowded forth to have a look at us. It was a picturesque spot, and looked doubly so in the warm sunshine, the Oriental-looking little church, with its

INTERESTED OBSERVERS.

white walls and green cupolas, standing out in brilliant relief against the blue sky. In a short time the police officer arrived, accompanied by his clerk and a couple of Cossacks, and we thus received our first visit from official Russia. The Russians, physically, are undoubtedly a fine set of men; nearly all I have seen so far have been above the average height. This officer topped them all, for he must have stood at least six feet four inches, and, with his tall astrachan kepi and long fur coat, seemed a huge fellow, a very good-looking one to boot. Our passports had to be examined here, and a sort of inquest held on the body of poor Lee. As the proceedings had no interest for me, not understanding Russian, I went ashore and had a stroll through the village. It certainly was a great improvement on any of the others we had yet come to: the houses even had some pretence to architecture, and looked very pretty with their quaint wooden porticoes. Dogs, as usual, seemed more numerous than inhabitants; and, had it not been that I knew how peaceful they are, except among themselves, it would have required some nerve to pass through them, for the row they made was simply awful.

In the evening the police officer dined with us on board the *Phœnix*, and a very pleasant fellow he seemed. He told us that his jurisdiction extended over an enormous extent of country, which, on consulting the map, we found to be no less than *five times* the size of Great Britain, extending right away to the Arctic Ocean—an awful and desolate tract, which he was obliged to visit twice a year. During the winter, he said, the cold was so intense that at times he had experienced as much as 45 deg. of frost (Réaumur)! We could not help telling him that he looked remarkably well, in spite of all these hardships.

The next morning a messenger came to the ship expressly to ask if I would go ashore and take a

THE RUSSIAN POLICE OFFICER.

[*To face p. 84.*

sketch of the village priest and his family. This was rather a compliment, so I could hardly refuse,

THE VILLAGE PRIEST.

more especially as a few minutes later the worthy man himself arrived to show me the way. (Could it be possible, I thought, that they took in the

*Illustrated London News* in this far-away Siberian village, and had heard I was on board?) The priest was a person of remarkable appearance— tall, slim, and exceedingly good-looking, in an effeminate sort of way—with a long fair beard and flowing locks, quite a biblical-looking personage, so I immediately spotted him as a good subject for a sketch. We went up to his house, and I was presented to Madame, who was most commonplace-looking, and his children, who were still more so. Fortunately I had brought my camera with me, so to please him I took them all in a group, and shuddered to think how it would look when developed. I then asked the gentleman if I might make a separate study of him; and he not only said he would be very pleased to let me, but even offered to come on board to sit for me. So, during the morning, I made a careful pencil study of him. While doing it, to my astonishment the police officer, who had come to have a look at what I was doing, asked me if I would like to do him afterwards. This made it late in the evening before we got away. We, however, had an extra large amount of wood in the bunkers, so hoped to make up for lost time.

Nothing of importance occurred till a couple of days later, when there was a slight outbreak of fire on board, which, fortunately, we were soon able to extinguish, or it might have developed into a serious affair. As it was, it detained us some hours. It was caused by some dry wood on the upper deck igniting through being too close to the base of the funnel (the upper deck being a Siberian addition to the *Phœnix*). We were now nearing the famous Kamin Pass, which, with the rapids close to it, is the crux of the river navigation. It was all along considered doubtful whether the *Phœnix* would be able to get her four barges up at one time, or would have to make several journeys; no such load had ever been brought up the rapids before.

A VILLAGE BOAT.

## CHAPTER IX.

### THE KAMIN RAPIDS.

A whole chapter of accidents—First touch of winter—Arrival at Yeniseisk.

WE reached the entrance to the Kamin Pass on October 10, and all of us got up at six in the morning so as not to miss any of it. I was very disappointed, for, though the finest sight we had yet seen on the river, the scenery was not nearly so imposing as I had been led to expect. Still, I suppose it is very grand for Siberia, which does not abound in big effects. For about half a mile, high but unpicturesque rocks rose precipitously from the swirling waters, their summits covered with dense forests of rigid pine trees, which in themselves took away from the effect, so regularly did they grow. One of our

A RIVER PILOT.

party said it reminded him of the Hudson River. With the utmost difficulty the *Phœnix* managed to hold her own against the tremendous current, and, with the engines going at their utmost pressure, after eight hours' steaming got past the worst of the rapids, with all her barges in tow—an unprecedented feat in Yenisei navigation—and this notwithstanding her damaged propeller.

In the mean time the little tug was having a *mauvais quart d'heure*—for, with her heavy barge, the stream proved too much for her powers; it was very different work to towing on the Thames—and, as ill-luck would have it, eventually ended by her being driven ashore some distance away from us, and in such shallow water that we could not get near enough to render her any assistance with the *Phœnix*. For two whole days all our available men were working at her before they were successful in getting her off. It was dreary work hanging about the deserted ship during this time, for all the boats were being used, so we could not get ashore, although an adventurous member of our party tried to fix up a raft, but was not successful beyond giving us a couple of hours' hard work in hauling the confounded logs on board again after his fruitless attempt. However, at last we got under way again, and arrived at the village of Worogoro, where we had to stop for wood.

The village itself offered little of interest, but I had heard that a wealthy Tartar lived there, so was looking forward to seeing something quite startling and Asiatic in appearance, and had my sketch-book

THE RIVER VENUES AT WORGORO.

ready. Imagine my disappointment when there came on board what looked more like a middle-aged English butcher than anything else, even to wearing the usual sort of blue coat. There was absolutely nothing of the "Tartar" about him; he looked, on the contrary, a very mild and inoffensive sort of individual, very unlike what one used to conjure up in one's mind in the good old schoolboy days. Close to the village we saw the first cultivated ground we had seen since leaving Norway, in July.

The next morning an accident happened as they were getting up anchor, and caused tremendous excitement. By some means the anchor dragged, and the ship, swinging round with the swift stream, caused the chain to slip from the capstan, and it ran out with such tremendous velocity that the capstan was absolutely smashed to pieces. For a moment all the men around were panic-stricken, and although, to my mind, there was absolutely no danger, as we were quite close to the shore, I saw the captain and the custom-house officer devoutly crossing themselves and muttering prayers. Luckily, it all ended well, for we managed to recover the anchor and chain by means of the derrick, and the capstan was soon replaced by the carpenter, and we now began to congratulate ourselves that at last we should get fairly under way once more.

But we were destined to undergo many more vexatious mishaps before we reached our journey's end. The tug, which all along had been unable to keep up with us, and had proved itself our "old man of the sea," not having turned up when we anchored the previous night, and there being no signs of her, a boatful of wood in charge of three men was sent back in case she had run short of fuel. To our great annoyance, she did not turn up in the morning. Hour after hour passed by, and at last it was decided to leave the barges and run back to see what had happened. It was certainly most provoking, but the only thing to do. So back we went at a tremendous pace with the stream, and about ten miles off we came up with the laggard—anchored, as her fuel had run out. To our great astonishment we learnt that they had seen nothing of the boat with the wood we had sent them; it must, then, have passed them during the night, and they informed us their anchor light had gone out at one moment. So here was another delay, as we had now to go in search of this boat. Off we started, and another seven miles or so farther down we at last sighted it—much to our relief, for we were almost beginning to fear something had happened. The men, as ill-luck would have it, had evidently managed to pass the tug during the night at the exact moment when its lantern went out. The day was nearly gone by the time we got back to the barges again. Still, as there was a moon rising, it was decided to proceed without further delay.

The stream during the next few days was so swift that, with our broken propeller, we barely did two versts an hour; it was little better than standing still, and the vibration all over the ship was so great that it was impossible to read with comfort, still less to attempt to sketch or write. However, we were thankful to be making any headway at all, and to be able to pass a short time without any more mishaps. But our respite was not for long. We managed to run short of wood at some distance from the next "station," and, as we had on a previous similar occasion burnt up all our available spare timber, we had to stop and send the men ashore to cut down some trees. The water was so deep that, although the *Phœnix* was drawing eight feet, she was able to go so close in to the shore that we could put out a plank from her deck and walk off on to *terra firma*. Two of us took advantage of the opportunity to stretch our legs, and, taking our rifles, started on a ramble. The forest grew right down to the river's bank, and was almost impenetrable; dense underwood and huge fallen trees barred one's passage at every step, as though to warn one from endeavouring to penetrate too far into its gloomy recesses, while through the gaunt fir trees the rushing wind seemed to moan and sob as though at the approach of winter. It was a dreary, uncanny sort of place, and thoroughly realized my idea of the wilds of Siberia—so much so, in fact, that I felt glad to get out of its mysterious twilight into the broad daylight again.

Our custom-house officer and the first engineer the next morning took their guns and started off in search of game; they arranged to be back in a couple of hours, in readiness for our departure, but when we were ready to start they had not reappeared. Two hours more passed, and still no signs of them. We began to get anxious, and kept the steam-whistle going incessantly, in case they did not know the time. When at last they were quite four hours late, we could come to no other conclusion but that they had lost themselves, or that something had happened, so we immediately organized search-parties, and in a few minutes a dozen of us, fully armed, started off in different directions into the forest. It was a difficult task we had before us, and not unlike the proverbial "looking for a needle in a bundle of hay," as no one had the slightest idea which way the two men had taken. It was arranged that, as soon as they were found (for we seemed to have no doubt about it), the steam-whistle should be sounded four times as a signal to the other parties to return to the ship. Our satisfaction may easily be imagined when, half an hour or so afterwards, we heard the welcome sound which announced that what might have been yet another serious affair had come to a safe conclusion.

On getting back, we saw the two men in a state

of utter exhaustion; in fact, if one of the party who had found them had not had the forethought to take his flask of brandy with him, they would never have been able to get back without being carried, as they were dead-beat, having had nothing to eat that morning. They told us that they had come across a bear's trail, and in their excitement following it lost their way, and although they could hear the steam-whistle in the distance they could not localize the sound, and were actually going away rather than to it, as it appeared. They said they were on the point of giving in when they were found, for night was coming on, and they were famished with hunger and cold. We quite believed them, for they presented a pitiable appearance. They only had three damp matches and a few cartridges left, and had not even a compass to guide them. This bear-hunting experience will, therefore, probably teach them a lifelong lesson—not to venture into a dense and almost impassable forest without a compass and taking one's bearings on it beforehand. However, fortunately, as it happened, it was a case of "all's well that ends well," although another day had been lost.

We were now getting well within touch of our destination, and on arrival at the village of Nasy-movo, some eighty miles from Yeniseisk, sent a messenger on ahead with letters and telegrams with reference to Mr. Lee's death. He was a veritable messenger of death, and we felt what an awful shock it would be for his family. Still, it was better they should know of it before we arrived. This village, the last of importance we should stop at, was quite a big place, the principal street certainly being nearly a mile in length. There were several really good shops, in one of which, among a host of miscellaneous articles displayed, was a package of " Brook's Crochet Cotton." It was quite refreshing to see the English label.

That evening we had our first touch of real cold, the thermometer going down to 20° Fahr.— quite a respectable commencement, although none of our Russians seemed to think much of it. We now proceeded more rapidly, as the current was less swift, and we were looking forward to the speedy termination of the most tedious journey any of us had ever made. We began to count the hours which now separated us from civilization, for the little town which we were now approaching seemed a sort of El Dorado after our cramped shipboard quarters. No further incident occurred, and at eight o'clock in the evening of Saturday, October 25, we anchored off Yeniseisk, the goal which we had so long been striving to reach, and which we had reached, in spite of all adverse prophecies, thus accomplishing the feat of landing an important cargo of British goods in the very heart of Siberia.

STORING THE WINTER FORAGE: A VILLAGE SCENE ON THE YENISEI.

YENISEISK.

## CHAPTER X.

### THE CITY OF YENISEISK.

Custom-house officials—Novel sights in market-place and streets—My lodgings—Siberian idea of "board and lodging"—Society in Yeniseisk—A gentleman criminal exile.

VERY few Englishmen have any real knowledge of Siberia. To most of them its name raises a dismal vision of ice-bound wastes and wretched exiles passing their lives in hopeless and cheerless misery. Little do they know that, far away in the very heart of Asia, there exists civilization equal to what is to be found in any part of Europe. But this is actually the case, and when, sitting after dinner smoking a cigarette, in a luxuriously furnished and delightfully warm apartment, surrounded by rare tropical plants and with appointments not to be excelled in Paris, it was hard to realize how far one was from Europe, or that outside the cold was 28 deg. below zero (Réaumur), and that it was so short a distance from the wild uninhabited regions that had to be traversed before reaching this far-away Siberian city.

I shall never forget my impressions when, after the fourteen long dreary weeks passed in the Arctic Ocean and in river navigation, we at last anchored off Yeniseisk. It was towards eight o'clock, a cold wintry evening, though October was not yet passed. The moon was just rising, and in the still evening air the effect was almost that of a huge panorama: against the southern sky the many churches and the strange-looking wooden buildings of the Asiatic city stood out in sharply defined silhouettes, relieved here and there by the lights in the windows of the houses facing the river, while along the banks we could just discern, in the increasing twilight, dark masses of people hurrying down to greet us on hearing the sound of our steam-whistle, which was being vigorously blown to announce our arrival. The church bells began ringing as we let go our anchors, and immediately all the Russians who were crowded on the upper deck, from the captain downwards, uncovered their heads, and, bowing devoutly, crossed themselves again and again as they murmured a prayer of thanksgiving for their safe return.

It was a strange and weird sight, and made me involuntarily rub my eyes, to ascertain if I were really awake, and all this not a dream—the long and wearisome journey at length at an end—the goal attained. There was, however, little opportunity for soliloquizing, for within a very short space of time after the stoppage of our engines we were boarded and taken possession of by the inevitable custom-house officers and their assistants, and the voyage of the *Phœnix*, successfully accomplished, was a thing of the past. Much as we all naturally desired immediately to go on shore, we could not do so, for we were courteously though firmly informed that until our baggage had been examined none of us could leave the ship.

The next day was Sunday, and we were all awakened early by the sound of many church bells —not the familiar notes one knows so well in the old country, but a curious sort of jangle, without any attempt at harmony, in a low key, which reminded one of the noise produced by a child strumming with two fingers on the bass of a piano very much out of tune. Sleep after this was impossible, and we were all of us soon on deck, anxious to get a glimpse of Yeniseisk by daylight. The effect, though of course not so strange as when seen by moonlight, was undoubtedly imposing, and seen from the Yenisei the city certainly presents a grand appearance. No less than three fine churches stand in close proximity to each other facing the river, each one vying with the others in architectural pretensions, while all along the road facing the water are houses, or, rather, large villas, which remind one much of the South of France, except that they are of stucco instead of marble. Snow had fallen during the night, and, though the temperature was not cold, the aspect in the bright morning sunshine was decidedly wintry in effect. Shortly after breakfast the custom-house people (our old friend Bouldakoff included) started examining our baggage. From what I had always heard about Russian officials, I quite expected to have a *mauvais quart d'heure*, considering my large store of ammunition and my big cases of tinned provisions for my long land journey. To my astonishment, however, I was treated with a politeness and a courtesy which, in all my varied experience of this most irksome branch of Government officialism, has never been equalled. I could not help mentally contrasting it with what I have often experienced at Charing Cross, Newhaven, or Paris. In a very short time, my numerous bags, valises, and cases were disposed of, and I was free to land whenever I chose. Out of all my really large quantity of odds and ends, so to speak, I eventually only had to pay a slight duty on my photographic apparatus and films. After this, as you may imagine, we were all of us soon on shore, and exploring the place.

On closer inspection, Yeniseisk does not, like many foreign cities, lose in interest, for the streets are wide, and there are many fine buildings in them which would compare well with those of most Western towns. Novel and interesting sights were to be met with at every step. Strange-looking vehicles crowded the spacious market-place, surrounded by motley crowds of noisy peasants, who, however, were far too occupied with their bargaining to notice me by more than a passing glance, in spite of my costume, which, to say the least of it, must have been a novelty to most of them. I could not help picturing to myself the probable effect a Russian tourist would produce were he to turn up suddenly in an English provincial town on market-day and walk about among the crowd of rough country folk. He would possibly get more than a passing glance, and, doubtless, be glad when he had got out of the place. What struck me most at first sight in Yeniseisk was, to all outward appearance, the entire absence of shops, which, as a rule, give so much local

PEASANT WOMAN.

colouring and life to a place. Of course there are shops, but from the outside they are unrecognizable, as no goods are displayed in the windows, and only a name-board betokens their existence. This, I hear, is the custom throughout Northern Siberia, and it is easily understood, when one considers that in all the houses there are double, and in some cases even treble, windows, to keep out the intense cold during the winter, and that even in spite of these precautions the innermost windows are thickly coated with ice, notwithstanding the high temperature of the rooms!

I was much surprised to learn that there was no hotel in Yeniseisk—a fact, doubtless, to be accounted for by reason of the few travellers who visit this out-of-the-way place, those having occasion to do so probably staying with friends or taking lodgings. Perhaps, however, with the possible annual advent of English tourists by the Kara Sea route, some enterprising Yeniseisk citizen will find it a profitable venture to start one (on English lines, it is to be hoped). Fortunately, lodgings were readily to be got—and cheap into the bargain; so, with the aid of an interpreter, I was soon snugly quartered in two rooms, which for comfort and warmth left nothing to be desired, though there might perhaps have been a little more furniture, and also washing accommodation; but that, however, was a detail. I have stayed in many worse rooms when on sketching tours in France. "Board and lodging" I arranged for, but I afterwards discovered that, although they had agreed to provide "everything," I was expected to find such "extras" as bedding, sheets, blankets, towels, tea, sugar, milk, butter, eggs, and candles, if I desired such luxuries. When I expressed my surprise to the interpreter, I was informed that such is the Russian custom. I asked what "board and lodging" really meant, then; but he was unable to explain. As he was a Russian himself, he probably thought what strange ideas Englishmen have! However, in spite of this slight inconvenience, I managed to settle down comfortably in a very short time, and found the people I was lodging with very obliging, and ready to do their best to supply my wants when I tried to express them in the few words of Russian I had managed to pick up while on board the *Phœnix*. It was the commencement of the "season" when we arrived at Yeniseisk, and the town was full; for, with the advent of winter, the neighbouring gold-mines are deserted, and the rich owners return to their palatial town residences, so the place presents a much more animated appearance than it does during the summer, when the greater portion of the male inhabitants are absent, and the streets look comparatively empty.

The great industry of Yeniseisk is, of course, centred in its gold-fields, which were once among the most important of Siberia, but are now not so prolific as formerly. Everybody in the town has a direct or indirect interest in them, this being easily accounted for—the money made in them being all, as a rule, spent in Yeniseisk, so all the local trades profit by it. No less than eight thousand men are annually employed in the different workings—many coming from long distances to get employment—the pay, as a rule, being exceptionally good, and all their food found them. Some of the wealthiest of the mine-owners employ as many as six hundred men, and have a hospital and medical staff permanently attached to the works. The alluvial gold-mines of the Yeniseisk district have been worked since 1839. The quartz working has only recently been commenced, and it promises very great results. Better skill and appliances than are at present available are, however, needed, I learn.

During the winter months Yeniseisk is well provided with amusement. There is a capital club-house, which would pass muster anywhere, to which is attached a theatre and a ball-room, with a delightful "floor," and performances or dances take place two or three times a week. I shall long remember my first evening at Yeniseisk, when I was taken to see the club; there was a dance on, and in the large, brilliantly lighted rooms, with an excellent band playing a familiar waltz, it was hard to believe one's self nearly two thousand miles from a railroad, and in the very heart of Asia. Society in Yeniseisk, of course, consists principally of the wealthy mine-owners, or merchants, and their families, and the Government officials and theirs. These are sufficient pretty well to fill the club on big dance nights. Exiles, who naturally form an important contingent, are only allowed to enter subject to certain restrictions. For instance, the criminal ones are only permitted to come to the performances in the theatre, and are obliged to leave immediately after; while the political ones are permitted to remain after the performance, but on no account to dance. I learnt all this on inquiry, for to a casual observer nothing is noticeable of these arrangements, as the exiles fall in with them without demur, and everything is conducted in a manner which certainly reflects great credit on the management, and could not be excelled in any European club of the kind. Still, in spite of all this, I could not help feeling that Yeniseisk is a very democratic place. Everybody somehow seems to think himself as good as anybody else, and at a performance, during the *entr'acte*, when every one walks about, you become quite tired of the number of people who expect you to shake hands with them, from the rich mine-owner to the discharged convicted forger, in Siberia "for life."

One of these latter gentlemen, a well-dressed man (who, I afterwards learnt, had not only committed a big forgery, but also several minor felonies, for which he would probably have been "doing" fifteen years in England), introduced himself to me one day, and in very good French, but with no end of "swagger," asked me how I liked Yeniseisk, and on my replying that I liked it very much and thought it very pretty, he simply stared at me with amazement for a moment, and then said, "You have evidently not yet seen Moscow or St. Petersburg, or you would not think so. All I can say is, that it is a positive disgrace to send a gentleman like me to such a hole!" I had the greatest difficulty in preventing myself from telling him that he might consider himself lucky he had not committed the same offences in England, or he would probably be in a very different sort of "hole," as he called it.

A PRISON BEAUTY.

## CHAPTER XI.

### THE CITY OF YENISEISK—*continued*.

A visit to the prison—First impressions of the Siberian system.

I WAS naturally anxious to see something of the prison system here. On hearing of my desire, the governor of Yeniseisk, with whom I had got on very friendly terms, courteously offered not only to let me accompany him on one of his weekly inspections of the prison, but also to let me make some sketches of what I should see, if I so desired. I naturally jumped at the offer, and on the appointed day I was punctual to the appointment, and we drove together in his sledge. It was an intensely cold day ; in fact, the coldest I had yet experienced, there being no less than 28 deg. of frost (Réaumur), so one simply had to bury one's self in one's furs, and avoid talking as much as possible.

The building, which is on the outskirts of the town, offers nothing of interest from the outside, being an ordinary two-story brick building, looking much like most prisons anywhere. It is placed in close proximity to the barracks, so that in case of need military assistance is readily available. At the gates of the courtyard, where a sentinel was stationed, we were received by the *personnel* of the establishment—the director of the prison, a tall, thin, military-looking man in a shabby uniform, with a long sword by his side, and a huge astrachan *képi* on his head —and five undersized little jailers, who were armed with cutlasses and big revolvers, which looked much too large for them. I learnt afterwards that the director was a Polish exile, who had been sent to Siberia after the last insurrection in Poland, and, at the expiration of his sentence, had elected to remain in Siberia as the director of the criminal prison of Yeniseisk. We then entered the building. Once inside the heavy iron-bound doors, the temperature was delightfully warm as compared with outside, and, as is usual in Siberia, an even heat everywhere, on the stone staircases, in the corridors, and in the rooms. So far as warmth is concerned, the prisoners

certainly have nothing to complain of. After considerable unlocking of big padlocks and removing ponderous bars, we entered the portion of the prison occupied by men undergoing long sentences for felony and other offences. It was a big sort of vaulted hall, dimly lighted by a few heavily grated windows on one side. Under the windows the whole length of the room was a very wide sort of sloping shelf, which serves as a sleeping-place; and ranged against this shelf, shoulder to shoulder, stood a long line of prisoners in the usual prison garb of Siberia. On our entry, they all as with one voice called out, in a deep guttural bass tone, the word "*Sdrosteté!*" (Good day), to which the governor replied by a military salute. As we walked slowly up the line I had a good opportunity of a near inspection of the most awful-looking crowd of ruffians I have ever seen. Perhaps the ill-fitting garment they wore added to the effect; still, with very few exceptions, vice was written on their faces, and I was not astonished to learn that most of them were old criminals, and had been there many years. This hall led into another, and yet another, with the same long lines of unkempt ruffians. Somehow, on looking at them, I could not help thinking of the awful photographs one sees outside the Morgue in Paris. I remarked to the governor what a dreadful thing it must be for a young man for a first and perhaps trivial offence to be thrown among such a crowd of rascals, who have nothing to do all day but sleep and eat, and who are under no supervision whatever except that of an occasional visit from one of the insignificant jailers. He agreed with me that the system is a wrong one, but, said he, "Que voulez-vous? Il n'y a pas de place pour les caser tous seuls." My astonishment was that five such little warders could keep such a crowd in order; but doubtless the knowledge of the close proximity of the barracks has a wholesome effect.

In the corner of each hall, close up by the ceiling, was the indispensable sacred picture, or *ikon*, looking strangely incongruous in such foul surroundings. Still, even in this dismal place there was a touch of humour. As we passed slowly through, one miserable wretch complained to the governor that his coat did not fit, to which the governor very neatly replied that he could do nothing in the matter. If people wanted their clothes to fit they should not come there!

We then visited the murderers' department, which was in the upper story. There were no less than thirty men and women waiting their trial on this charge. Capital punishment does not exist in Russia, so the worst these prisoners can expect is hard labour at the mines for a certain number of years, after which they are free to live in Siberia, but not to return to Russia. In this portion of the prison the rooms were smaller, and only contained, at the most, a dozen men in each. All these prisoners, though as yet untried, were, without exception, in irons.

Several of the most desperate characters were in solitary confinement. In one of the "solitary" cells was a tall, good-looking man, who had murdered an old woman—a foul and brutal murder, I heard, and committed for the sake of a few roubles only. He complained bitterly about being shut up all alone, as, he said, he had done "nothing."

"How nothing?" said the governor; for the man

THE MURDERERS' DEPARTMENT, YENISEISK PRISON.

had been taken red-handed, and, in fact, had never denied his guilt.

"It was *only a woman* I killed!" was the whining reply, and then he looked astonished at the expression of disgust on our faces on hearing this little speech.

There is no doubt about it that the solitary-confinement system is the one with the most terror in it. I could not help trying to imagine the feelings of the caged ruffian as he saw the door shut, and heard the heavy bars drawn and the massive padlock replaced—very different, probably, to those of the rascals in the large hall below, who doubtless, as soon as we were out of hearing, recommenced their pandemonium.

The women's prison, which we afterwards visited, struck me as being a curious sight, and reminded me not a little of Dickens's description of the old "Fleet" or "Marshalsea" prisons. The inmates seemed free to do what they pleased—of course, with the exception of leaving the place—and the effect on entering was most extraordinary. The room was full of steam, for it was "washing day," I was informed, and overhead was quite a network of ropes with wet clothes on them, hung up to dry. Dirty, unkempt children crowded round us as we entered, while, through an open door leading to an adjoining department, appeared a lot of semi-clad females, who regarded us with a curiosity devoid of all modesty. There was here none of the respect which we were shown in the men's quarters, for these sullen-looking, half-naked women evidently looked upon our visit as an unwarrantable intrusion on their privacy.

As a result of my very interesting morning, I could not help coming to the conclusion that, at any rate as far as I could judge, the criminals of Siberia have little to complain of. They pass their forced seclusion in absolute idleness, if they so wish, for the work they do, if any, is voluntary—eating

CRIMINAL PRISONERS WAITING AT YENESEISK FOR CONVOY TO START FOR KRASNOIARSK.

(*To face p.* 113.

and sleeping, they while away the time as best they can, like so many caged beasts.

On another occasion I had an opportunity of seeing a batch of criminal prisoners start for Krasnoiarsk, where they were being sent for trial. They were all assembled in the hall of the Palais de Justice, and a strange crowd they looked, sitting along the wall on a bench, dressed in their drab kaftans, which serve them as overcoats. Round about lolled the guard which was to escort them half-way to Krasnoiarsk, half a dozen undersized soldiers (not "Cossacks," as they are often erroneously described), with rifles and fixed bayonets. All were well wrapped up for the journey, with huge woollen comforters round their necks, black gloves, and felt boots on. I had no difficulty in getting them to remain still while I made a sketch, for they seemed readily to understand what I wanted, even to the prisoners. As usual, when I had finished, no one evinced the slightest curiosity to see the result. A few minutes afterwards they started, under the command of a non-commissioned officer. And a curious procession it was, for none of the prisoners seemed to feel their position, and walked just as they pleased. I could not help thinking that the soldiers had the worst of it, burdened as they were with their heavy rifles, ammunition, and accoutrements, while the prisoners had absolutely nothing to carry. The soldiers from Yeniseisk only go half-way, when they meet a convoy

I

from Krasnoiarsk, and exchange prisoners. The journey takes about a week, as they only travel about fifty versts a day, and only during the daylight.

There is no prison for "political exiles" in Yeniseisk. Most of this class of *déportés* who are living in the town have already served their term of punishment elsewhere, and have elected to remain in Siberia, where they probably find the life not half so bad as it is painted; or, as is often the case, were banished "for life" from Russia, and condemned to pass the remainder of their days in Yeniseisk or some other town or village.

In the case of a well-connected and educated man being sent from, say, Moscow or St. Petersburg, or some other important city in Russia, for a long period to some remote Siberian village, the punishment must be a severe one. From the little I have seen of these villages on our way up the river, I can imagine no fate more dreadful than to be shut up alone in one of them, among a lot of unsympathetic and ignorant peasants, with no books to read, and entirely out of touch and hearing of the civilized world. Better almost to be buried alive! When, however, instead of to an out-of-the-way village, he is consigned to a biggish town like Yeniseisk or Krasnoiarsk, his fate is certainly not so hard. He is allowed to live how and where he pleases; if he has money of his own he is permitted to receive it; and if he is a sociable man he will soon find that he is not treated as an outcast, even by the officials, who, at any rate at Yeniseisk, are, I hear, the very embodiment of courtesy and politeness, though I believe it to be the same all over Siberia; and he will probably soon settle down to his new life, and, as is often the case when the sentence is not a "life" one, he will eventually decide to remain in a country which, though doubtless not all *couleur de rose*, is certainly not all black.

Still, there are many fine fellows whose fiery spirits not even exile to Siberia can tame, and who are only biding their time to return to Russia and start a fresh struggle for freedom—with possibly (or rather, probably) the same, or a worse, result to themselves.

There are a few of this sort here. One of them, M. X., an evidently well-educated man of about forty, was sent to Siberia for five years, two out of which he passed in a village, the rest in Yeniseisk. His time is up soon, when he will be allowed to return to Russia again, but not to live in a University town. His wife accompanied him into exile. I met them out one evening at a friend's house, and had a long and interesting talk with both of them in French, as I was anxious to learn something of his experiences. I could not help remarking to Madame that after what her husband had undergone he would, doubtless, on his return to Russia, not meddle with politics again. To my astonishment, she replied—

"*Nisnaia?*" (Who can tell?)

"What!" said I, "is not once sufficient to come to Siberia?"

But she shook her head, and answered, "It is very difficult to remain silent when one sees the state of things in Russia, and one knows how very different it is in other countries. If no one takes the initiative, it will never be changed."

We were on delicate ground, so I thought it best to change the subject, as one can never tell who may be listening. Moreover, politics are not in my line. However, I managed later on to have a further chat with M. X. on the subject, and he corroborated the words of his wife, in spite of my asking him if he had not had enough of it already in Siberia, for if he were again caught tripping he would doubtless not get off so easily, but, in all probability, be sent to the mines. "*Savorno!*" (It is all the same to me!) was his characteristic reply. The idea that they are wasting their lives on a cause which is not yet nearly ripe for solution, and which, for the moment, only time can help, never seems to occur to these men, who plod away cheerfully into Siberia with the firm conviction that they are making martyrs of themselves in the cause of liberty, whereas, in reality, they are only helping to colonize this vast continent.

STREET SCENE, YENISEISK.

## CHAPTER XII.

### YENISEISK—*continued*.

The hospital—Siberian houses—Their comfort—The streets of the city.

A FEW days after, I received an invitation to visit the hospital, and, as I heard it was a very interesting sight, I eagerly availed myself of it. The house doctor, an amiable old gentleman, who spoke German fluently, showed me over the place, and evidently took a great pride in it, although he informed me it was very old and was to be shortly replaced by a new building. The Yeniseisk sick-list was, unfortunately, very large at the time of my visit.

On entering the principal ward, every bed of which was occupied, I was much struck with the curious effect before me; it looked as if the place had been prematurely decorated for Christmas. Everywhere pine saplings were placed—between the beds and along the walls—reaching from the ground to the ceiling. On asking the reason, I was informed that it was to purify the air. It certainly wanted it, for the atmosphere was simply stifling. An English doctor would have stood aghast at the temperature. There was no attempt whatever at ventilation, and the triple windows were all hermetically sealed. Only a Russian could have lived in it, and all the patients seemed comfortable enough.

A WATER-CARRIER.

The fire brigade at Yeniseisk, as is usual in all Siberian towns—where the danger is so great in consequence of the many wooden houses—is remarkably well organized. In case of need, the numerous water-carriers of the town are bound to give their services and provide horses and water-carts; while in the tower over the fire-station is always a watchman, whose sole duty is to look out for the enemy, and to give warning of any outbreak by means of a big alarm-bell fixed on the upper platform.

GETTING WATER FROM THE FROZEN RIVER YENESEI.

[*To face p.* 118.

THE HIGH STREET, YENISEISK.

[*To face p. 118.*

What, I fancy, astonishes an Englishman most in Siberia for the first time, is the wonderful temperature he finds inside all the houses, from the richest to the poorest—a temperature so equable as to permit of the rarest tropical plants being cultivated with the greatest success. I may say, in fact, that many of the houses of the rich mine-owners present the appearance of conservatories, so crowded are they with exotics of all sorts, from climbing plants trained to grow round the doors to huge palms or plantains, and all in the most perfect condition. An Englishman's surprise is, therefore, comprehensible. He has heard of the frightful cold of the Siberian winter, so arrives in the country duly armed against it according to English ideas. To his astonishment he finds that, when the thermometer in

A SWELL.

the street registers 40 deg. of frost (Réaumur) the temperature of his room is still as genial as though it were spring, although there is no stove visible. His thick flannel shirts are naturally very much too warm; he only requires one thin blanket on his bed; and, when he goes out into the open air, his *dacha* is amply sufficient to keep out the cold. That most complete device for heating a house that was ever imagined, the Russian stove, robs, therefore, the Siberian winter of many of its terrors, and makes a visit to this interesting and little-known country pleasant even during the coldest period of the year.

The High Street of Yeniseisk is not unpicturesque; and the importance of many of the buildings is enough to upset all the previously conceived ideas of Siberian towns. It would astonish most Europeans if they could see the stately mansions owned by some of the millionaire mine-owners and rich exiles; these houses look as if they had been transplanted from the Champs Elysées or the Bois de Boulogne, and in the interior are to be found luxuries with which Paris, rather than Siberia, is generally associated. In my sketch I have, unfortunately, been unable to give any of these palatial residences, as I wanted to show the general effect of the town, with the schools, fire-towers, one of the many churches, and the inevitable telegraph-poles. The two Collegiate schools —one for boys, the other for girls—were founded by one of the merchant princes of the town—Mr. Kitmanoff. They are built in a style which would mark them as striking-looking buildings in any town in the world. They contain a fine laboratory of physical science, well supplied with apparatus, and a drawing-class room, provided with plaster casts and geometrical models; the walls of the rooms and corridors are hung with maps, drawings, and diagrams

THE TWO COLLEGIATE SCHOOLS, VENI-SISK.

[To face p. 120.

LIFE IN SIBERIA: AN AFTERNOON DRIVE, YENISEISK.

[*To face p.* 121.

useful for teaching, and the seats and desks are of the most approved design for schools. There are several European professors of competent attainments in this excellent educational institution. Yeniseisk, though only a place of ten or twelve thousand inhabitants, is quite a model abode of civilization.

It is worth while to see the ladies of fashionable society going out for an afternoon drive at Yeniseisk. When the temperature is not too low, say, 15 deg. below zero (Réaumur), one sees many smart sledges about. Four o'clock in the afternoon is the favourite time for driving, and one can then see horses as fine as those of any private carriages in London. The fair occupants of the sledges are, as a rule, too much wrapped up in furs to be seen to advantage, and, as the "grand chic" is to tear along at top speed, but a fleeting vision of beauty is all that is generally obtained, and before you have time almost to recognize who is in the sledge it is already far away.

The city of Yeniseisk at this moment is, of course, of great interest to Englishmen, on account of the scheme for sea traffic between England and the Yenisei —which, if it prove successful, will probably go a long way towards making the fortune of the smart little town—and, if the canal is ever finished which the Government is constructing to connect Yeniseisk with Tomsk, there will exist, by means of the Volga,

Obi, Yenisei, Irtish, Angara, and Amoor Rivers, one of the longest water highways of the world, and Chinese and Central Asian goods will be brought direct to the railroad at Tiumen, and thus to the gates of Europe, without transhipment.

READY TO START.

## CHAPTER XIII.

### FROM YENISEISK TO KRASNOIARSK.

My first experience of sledging—A delightful adventure—
Krasnoiarsk—The market-place—The High Street.

If asked which place I should prefer, Krasnoiarsk or London, to pass the winter in, I should, without hesitation, give the preference to this picturesque Siberian town, with its bright blue sky and exhilarating atmosphere, its gay and interesting society, and many festivities during the Christmas season. I do not think there was ever a country less known or more maligned than Siberia. I found this out more and more every day; but I formed that opinion from the time I landed, after my voyage through the Arctic Seas, and I have not had occasion to alter it, nor am I likely to do so.

In my last chapter I endeavoured to give you a description of Yeniseisk, the first Siberian town of any importance I had then reached, and where I managed to spend five of the pleasantest weeks imaginable among some of the most hospitable people I ever had the good fortune to meet. Far-away Yeniseisk will long remain graven on my memory, not only on account of its being the long-looked-for goal of the most eventful voyage I ever made in my life, but also as recalling many delightful hours and novel experiences.

The journey by sledge from Yeniseisk to Krasnoiarsk, a distance of 331 versts, if one travels day and night, takes forty-eight hours; this, of course, means hard going the whole time, but, as the various post-houses on the road offer but little inducement for the traveller to prolong his stay in them longer than is absolutely necessary, there is no temptation to loiter on the way. I had been strongly advised to buy my own sledge, and not trust to the ramshackle conveyances which could be hired at the different stations, so I determined to go by the advice of people who knew what Siberian travelling meant, and, with the assistance of a kind friend, was fortunate in picking up a sledge in excellent condition wonderfully cheap. All complete it cost me only fifty-two roubles, or about £6 15s.—such a bargain was it that, I was informed, I should doubtless be able to sell it again at the same price anywhere.

In fact, my lucky star seemed to be in the ascendant at that time, for just before leaving Yeniseisk I had a unique little adventure which made my first impressions of Siberian sledging too agreeable for description in plain Anglo-Saxon.

I had made my arrangements for starting, when a Siberian friend of mine called and asked me if I would escort a lady as far as Krasnoiarsk. The sledge held two, but I was alarmed at the idea, especially as I was informed that the lady was a widow. Like Mr. Weller, I avoid widows. It is one of my few guiding principles. I said, therefore, that my baggage was multitudinous and heavy. My friend had placed me under so many obligations that I could not refuse to reconsider the matter, so it was arranged that I should be presented to the widow on the next day to talk the matter over. I went to bed quite determined to have my sledge to myself. In the morning I called. The lady came into the room, and, instead of the wrinkled widow I had conjured up in my mind, behold a most charming and graceful creature of twenty-five, with a most vivacious manner and a smile which melted all the frost in my nature. (I mentally decided that if it cost me another sledge for the baggage the widow should be my companion.) So without the slightest hesitation I said, twirling my moustaches, that I should feel myself a thousand years younger if I might be permitted to escort her to Krasnoiarsk. I made this remark in English, so neither the widow nor my friend understood it; but I quickly assured them in my very best Parisian that on mature consideration I had discovered that there was room for two in the sledge, so the horses were ordered at the Government post-house, and at six o'clock that evening we started on our first stage, about twenty-five versts on the road. A party of friends accompanied us so far, and when we reached the post-house they produced chickens and champagne

"GOOD-BYE."

enough to have bribed the whole Press of Russia. Then good-bye, and away over the moonlit snow, galloping noiselessly through the night. I smoked a heavenly cigar; the widow puffed at a cigarette. And so we travelled, halting only at the post-houses to change the horses. My sledge was heavily laden with tinned meats and food to last me a long way. The post-houses supplied tea and minor necessities.

I was soon initiated by my charming companion into the mode of travelling by sledge here. I learnt that horses (the usual number is a *troika*, or three) were to be got at each post-house, the cost being three kopeks per horse per verst (rather under a penny for two-thirds of a mile), plus ten kopeks *progon*, or Government tax, per station. The *yemschik*, or driver, changes with each relay, and is included in the charges, but he naturally expects a small gratuity for himself. Although this is not obligatory, it is a usual custom to give sixpence or so, according to the length of the stage and how one was driven. The *padarojna*, or Government permit, authorizing the traveller to have the necessary horses, is a thing of the past, to all intents and purposes. Of course, there is nothing against the traveller wasting his money on one, if he so wishes, but he will find it a nuisance rather than otherwise. A good tip to your last driver goes a long way further towards helping one than all the Government padarojnas, in my humble opinion.

I have travelled right across Siberia without one, and had not the slightest difficulty in getting horses anywhere, and in no case was the delay longer than was necessary to get ready a cup of tea or bouillon-fleet to keep out the cold; but, of course, I was exceptionally fortunate in having had the advice of experienced friends before starting on my journey, and all went as merrily as a wedding-bell, although

I knew but the merest smattering of the Russian language. The distances between the different stations never exceeded twenty-five versts (about sixteen miles), and this generally took a little over two hours to do, so it may be remarked the pace was not slow. The post-station, I am informed, is usually the best house in the village (which is not always saying much), the owner being paid a certain sum yearly for the use of his largest room, which he always has to keep ready for travellers, and if necessary, for a small fee, to supply the inevitable samovar. Refreshments, also, he in most cases undertakes to provide; but, as a general rule, these only consist of black bread, milk, and frozen eggs, so the hungry traveller who is at all fastidious does well to provide himself beforehand with all his gastronomical necessaries. Of course, I am now speaking of travelling on the route from Yeniseisk to Krasnoiarsk, and not the "Great Post Road," which I shall have future occasion to describe. I found these houses, in most cases, clean and comfortably furnished, but always heated to such a degree as to render them almost unbearable; so stifling, as a rule, was the atmosphere that it was generally like walking into a badly ventilated Turkish bath. I never stayed a moment longer than was absolutely necessary, and was always glad to get back again into my comfortable sledge.

The road was in exceptionally good condition for

sledging; for the greater part of the way it was like travelling on a velvet-pile carpet. I never saw deeper snow anywhere, the horses at times being absolutely buried up to their withers in it, while the trees on either side of us were simply bent down with the weight of their fleecy pall. The scenery was at times very beautiful, having almost the appearance of an English park, and altogether very different to what I expected to find in the wilds of Siberia.

Taking it all in all, therefore, I found sledging a very pleasant way of travelling, and when snugly tucked up in my furs, as we dashed on through the darkness of the night, I was lulled gradually to sleep by the continuous jingle of the *duga* bells, the Strand, the Paper, and in fact London itself, seemed but as a dream of a far distant past. Of course this sort of sentimental reverie is only inspired when one is on a good road; if it is otherwise, well, one's impressions are not of quite so soothing a nature, more especially if they are caused by the corners of a box or the roof of the sledge!

I had reason to congratulate myself on having provided myself with quite a Siberian outfit in the way of furs, for I don't think I ever felt such cold in my life as I did on the road from Yeniseisk. If one's face was exposed to the wind for only a few seconds, one's eyes and nostrils were frozen together and one's moustache became coated with thick ice.

K

The horses, also, were so covered with white frost that their colour was absolutely unrecognizable. I found from my thermometer that the cold averaged each day no less than 35 deg. below zero (Réaumur)! It will give some idea of its intensity when I mention that whilst smoking in the open air, and having occasion to expectorate, my saliva would often fall to the ground as a solid lump of ice!

On reaching Krasnoiarsk, I was much surprised, and of course pleased, to find quite a decent hotel, where I was accommodated with a couple of really comfortable rooms well furnished, on fairly moderate terms. They would, I fancy, have been considered good anywhere; and when I add that they were fitted with electric bells, that there were sheets and bedding to the bed, and that I had a *real* "tub" every morning, you will understand that it seemed like getting back to civilization, with the ordinary "comforts" of everyday life once more. Krasnoiarsk is decidedly a picturesque town; and, if it be so in winter, it must be doubly pleasant in summer. Situated on one of the most beautiful portions of the river Yenisei, in the centre of an amphitheatre of high hills, every street has a sort of background of its own, so to speak, and the effect is very pleasing. It is, of course, a much more important place than Yeniseisk, being considerably larger, and is more advanced in every respect. I was struck with this on the night of my arrival, by the appearance and length of the lamp-lit streets we had to drive through before reaching the hotel.

The town was busy enough next morning, for it was market-day, and the traffic in the streets abutting on the market-place was so great that it required the services of several Cossacks, placed at different points for the purpose, to control it; and they had

IN THE MEAT MARKET, KRASNOIARSK.

their work cut out for them, for there is evidently no rule of the road here, to all outward appearance, and sledges of all sorts and sizes were dashing about in every direction in the most reckless fashion. The Bolskoi Oulitza, or High Street, presents a very animated appearance on a fine afternoon, and, if the weather be not too cold, one sees many pretty faces and smart equipages. Krasnoiarsk, owing to its sheltered position, is not so cold as Yeniseisk, the average here during the winter months being only 15 deg. below zero (Réaumur). Every afternoon there is quite a crowd of skaters in the fine public gardens, and the scene is a very picturesque one, for there are usually many officers on the ice, their striking uniforms harmonizing well with the furs of the fair sex.

Society in Krasnoiarsk is much gayer than in

A TYPICAL SIBERIAN INTERIOR, KRASNOIARSK.

Yeniseisk. I was fortunate in having letters of introduction to the Governor-General Telakoffski and other officials, also to the two richest mine-owners in the place, Messrs. Consnitsoff and Mativieff, so what with dinners and dances I never found the time hang heavily on my hands of an evening; in fact, it was rather too much the contrary, for so

SNOW SCAVENGER, KRASNOIARSK. [*To face p.* 133.

great is the hospitality of the Siberians that it was positively difficult to get an evening to one's self. Most of the people spoke French or German, and, as many visit Europe every year, they are, so to speak, well in touch with all subjects of social and artistic interest, and the general "tone" of the dinners, dances, and musical evenings was exactly like what one is accustomed to on the continent. Excellent musicians absolutely abound here.

I fancy it would have astonished most people in England, or, for the matter of it, anywhere, could they have been suddenly transported to the spacious ball-room of the club (*sobranje*) on Christmas Day, when the governor held his annual official reception. The magnificent suite of rooms was simply packed with everybody who was anybody here; all officers and Government officials in full uniform, the civilians in evening dress, whilst the many ladies who were also present, dressed in the latest of Parisian fashion, lent additional interest to a scene the like of which I certainly never even dreamt of seeing in the "dreary land of exile."

Of course Krasnoiarsk, like most places, has its "season," which lasts during the winter months only; during the heat of the summer the town has almost a deserted appearance, I heard, as all the rich people then go to their cool villas on the hills in order to escape from the scorching rays of the sun and the blinding dust, and the place is left to the *Oi polloi*.

## CHAPTER XIV.

### KRASNOIARSK—*continued*.

Privileged criminal exiles—Ordinary criminals—A marching convoy on the road—Convoy soldiers—The convoy—Proceedings on arrival at the Perasilny of Krasnoiarsk—The starostor of the gang—A stroll round the Perasilny—The married prisoners' quarters—A "privileged" prisoner in his cell—Scene outside the prison—Prison labour—I give it a trial—Details as to outside employment of prisoners.

THE CATHEDRAL, KRASNOIARSK.

HAVING given some slight idea of the bright side of life in Krasnoiarsk, a little about the reverse of the medal will doubtless be of interest.

In a vast country like Siberia, where a great part of the population—I mean of the lower middle class and working orders—is composed of criminal exiles, it may readily be imagined that there exists a peculiar state of social opinion, which is positively amusing at times. If a man conducts himself well, and is

liked, it matters not a straw that he be an exiled
"gentleman criminal" doing his time, for he is
received almost everywhere, and one need not be
ashamed to be seen associating with him, as even
the officials shake hands with him when they meet.
He himself makes no secret of his misdemeanour—
rather the contrary, as a rule—for most of them
seem to think that "coming to reside in Siberia"
absolutely whitens them again in the eyes of society.
As a matter of fact, they are encouraged in this
belief, for they are always spoken of as "unfortunates." Perhaps they are called so because they were
found out and sent here! On one occasion two men
I knew very well met in my rooms; both were
criminal exiles who had formerly occupied high
positions in St. Petersburg—one, a German, having
been "sent" for uttering forged bonds; the other,
a Russian, for embezzlement of Government money.
As they were not acquainted, I naturally introduced
them to each other. It was difficult to realize that
these two well-dressed and polished men, who spoke
several languages fluently, were each doing a ten
years' penal sentence. After a short preamble on
the usual everyday topics, the Russian asked the
German if he were an inhabitant of Krasnoiarsk.

"*Gott sei dank, nein,*" replied he; "I was only
sent for ten years, and my time is nearly up."

"Ah! then you're a *verschickte*? I thought you
were. So am I. What did you come for?"

"Oh, only for so and so. And you?"

"Oh, mine" (with a certain amount of pride) "was a big affair; I managed to get *over* forty thousand roubles out of the Government."

And so the conversation rattled pleasantly on, gradually drifting into (for me) more congenial subjects. There was not the least bit of shame about them—they talked of their offences, while smoking their cigarettes, as naturally as most men would relate an interesting episode in their lives, and I sat and listened—and wondered. The same unbiassed way of looking on the state of affairs exists among the lower orders; and soldiers, with gangs of criminals in prison garb and heavy clanking chains, push their way on foot through the crowd in the market-place, attracting no notice, the prisoners being, to all appearance, stolidly indifferent to their situation.

*Priviligierts*, or well-to-do criminals, that is to say, men of intelligence who have received a good education, either in a Government school or gymnase, and who have occupied good positions in their time, when they are only guilty of such petty offences as forgery or misappropriation, are never absolutely associated with the vulgar horde of ordinary, everyday criminals. On their way to Siberia, although they travel with the same gang, they do so apart, even in their own conveyance, if they have the means to pay for it. On arrival at the different *étapes*, the prisons in the villages, they are provided with a room to themselves, till the detachment is ready to start again, and on reaching their destination are turned loose, so to speak, and left to shift for themselves. I had no difficulty whatever in learning all this, for my various "criminal" acquaintances were not reticent; in fact, seemed glad to tell me all about it, as an interesting story.

All this naturally excited my curiosity and made me desire to witness personally, if possible, some of the proceedings, and, as good luck had it, I was soon enabled to do so. An officer with whom I had been very friendly was told off with his detachment to escort a large body of prisoners coming from Tomsk; he had to take them over from their previous escort some fifty versts back and convoy them to Krasnoiarsk; so he courteously let me know of the probable time of his arrival at a certain point on the road, so that I could drive out to meet him and make as many photos and sketches as I wished. It is needless to say I jumped at the invitation, and on the appointed day took an isvoschik and drove along the Tomsk road.

We had driven some considerable distance without seeing the slightest sign of life on the deserted highway, when suddenly on the crisp frosty air I distinguished a faint distant sound, so peculiar and weird that it immediately attracted my attention, as it was evidently approaching us. It was not unlike the noise which would be produced by hundreds of small birds singing all at once, yet I could see nothing of any sort anywhere on the vast plain, so I drew my driver's attention to it as well as I could with my limited vocabulary of Russian. To him it was neither novel nor interesting; he knew what it was at once. "The arrestanti are coming," he briefly told me; and shortly after, on ascending a rise in the road which had concealed them from our view, there came in sight a big body of men coming slowly along, and I then discovered that the strange noise which had so impressed me was produced by the clanking of the heavy chains they wore. But then, alas! all preconceived illusions vanished, for it was a loathsome and depressing sight, and rendered doubly so under the bright sunlight. There was absolutely nothing of the poetic about it that I had been led to expect from the descriptions I had read so often before coming to Siberia. It was simply a huge crowd of what looked like (and probably was) the very scum of the earth, for all races seemed to be represented amongst it, making as villanous and evil-looking a lot of men as one could possibly see. In front and on either side of the column were soldiers with rifles and fixed bayonets. By the way, many writers speak of these soldiers as Cossacks; as a matter of fact, Cossacks are now never under any circumstances used for this or any duty in connection with prisoners, nor have they for many years past. On the road,

A CONVOY OF PRISONERS ON THE MARCH.
(*Enlargement from an instantaneous Kodak photo.*)

[*To face p. 158.*]

as well as round the prisons, only special men are employed; these are known all over Russia and Siberia as "convoy soldiers," and form a big brigade, which is under the command of a special general and a large staff of officers. All the men must have served a certain time in the regular army before they are eligible for this branch of the service.

How any writer who has actually seen a gang of criminal exiles on the march can describe it in any way as a pathetic sight beats me, and my only astonishment is that convicts of other countries are not also spoken of in the same sentimental way, for they are probably far worse off than Siberian criminals, who, as a matter of fact, have a much better time of it, *considering their crimes*, than they would have anywhere else, barring, of course, the trifling discomfort of having to "foot it" the whole distance if they are able. If they are footsore or lame they are permitted to ride on one of the baggage conveyances. The more I learn about the prisoners' life, either on the road or in the ostrogs, the more astonished I am at the humane way in which they are treated, and how little is really known of it in the outer world. I am not referring to the system as a whole, which I feel convinced is not only a wrong but a demoralizing one, but to minor details, which show a kindly feeling on the part of the authorities which is somewhat unexpected. For instance, all Jews or Mohammedans receive ten kopeks

(3*d.*) per day, both on the road and when in prison, so that they can purchase their own food, and have it cooked according to their belief, the food and cooking being looked after by one of their own religion deputed by themselves. In a country where it is said that the Jews are so persistently persecuted by the authorities, this comes as rather an astounding revelation, in my opinion. I know nothing whatever about prison life in England, but I am anxious to know if we treat our convicts in the same way. Political prisoners never march (unless they wish to do so), but are conveyed on telegas or sledges according to the season, and always follow some distance behind the criminals, with whom they never are associated. Considering how slowly the column advances, for I am informed it is often no less than four or five months on the road, resting as it does every second day, this must be an awful journey indeed for those who are leaving friends, home, and in fact all behind them for ever. For these " unfortunates," when not criminal ones, all one's sympathy is due; but the canaille marching on ahead, and who are thus most *en évidence*, in most cases richly deserve more than their fate, and ought to thank their lucky stars they are Russian and not English convicts.

In the rear of the column followed about twenty open sledges, on which were women, children, foot-sore prisoners, and miscellaneous baggage. Even the drivers were soldiers, and with their rifles across

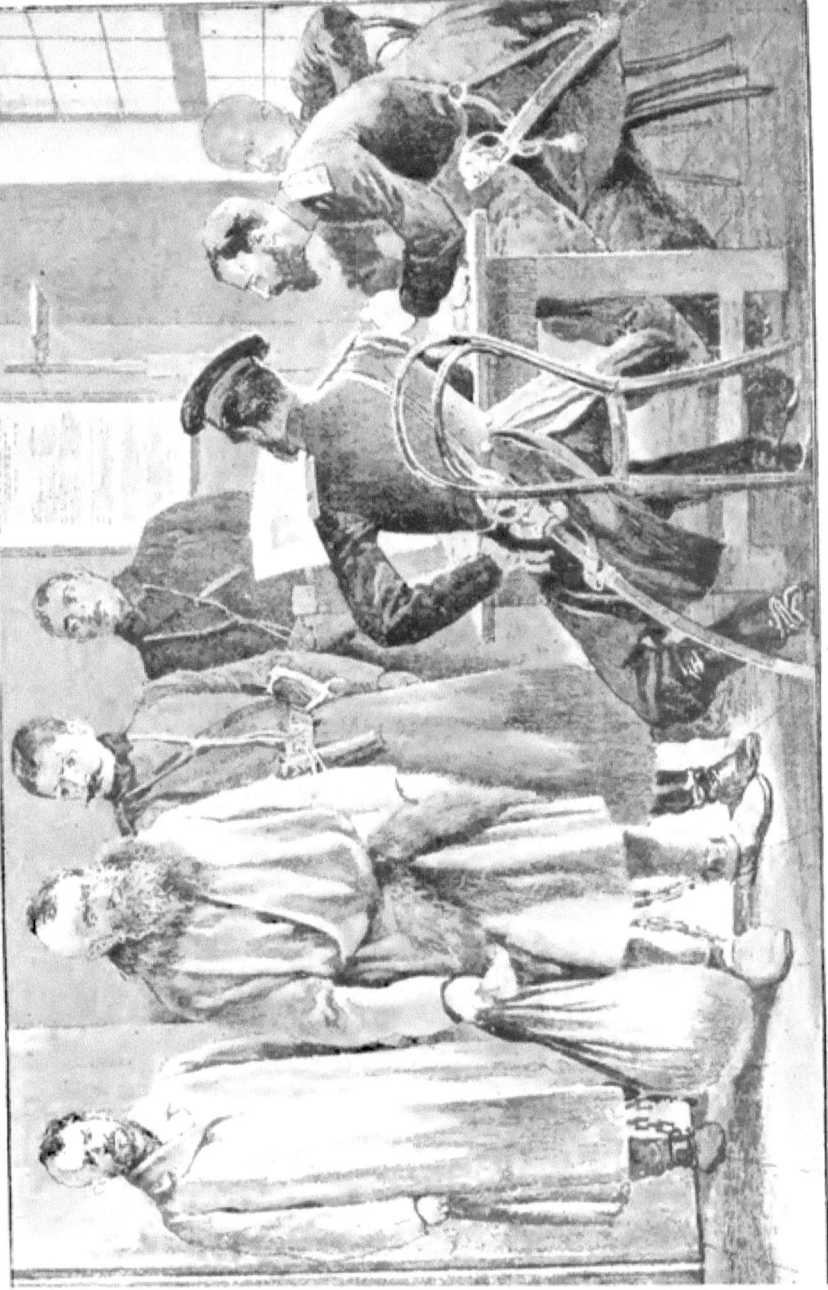

VERIFICATION OF PRISONERS ON ARRIVAL AT PERASILNY, KRASNOIARSK.

their knees presented a curious appearance. Last of all came my friend, the officer in charge of the detachment, in a luxurious covered-in sledge. There were no "politicals" with the party.

As I was desirous of seeing for myself all that takes place on the arrival of a gang of convicts at the *étape* or *perasilny* of a large town, I returned to Krasnoiarsk at the head of the detachment, and made sketches and photos to my heart's content of the unsavoury crowd of ruffians following closely behind me.

The perasilny of Krasnoiarsk is situated on the outskirts of the town, quite close to the *ostrog*, or regular prison, and, like most buildings of its kind I have hitherto seen, built entirely of wood, even to the high wall surrounding it. It is composed of several blocks of buildings in which prisoners are indiscriminately placed pending their removal to their ultimate destination. On arrival outside this building, the convicts were formed up two deep for inspection, and immediately after told off to unload the sledges and get their baggage; after which they were marched into the building preparatory to being "verified." In a large bare whitewashed room sat the officer who had brought the detachment and two prison officials, with a heap of papers before them. All the prisoners were in an adjoining room, at the door of which stood the *staroster*, or leader of the gang, waiting to call out the name as each man was required.

It may not be generally known that in Russia every gang of prisoners has its *staroster*, or captain, who is elected by themselves from amongst their number, and who on all occasions acts as their spokesman. It is difficult to ascertain on what

THE STAROSTER OF THE GANG.

particular merits he is elected—perhaps it is that he is known to be the biggest dare-devil villain amongst them, or that he is generally feared; at any rate, from all accounts, the staroster has always such unbounded influence and power amongst his fellows that if he were to decree the death of one of them there is no doubt whatever but that the sentence would be carried out. As a matter of fact, cases of the kind have been frequently known, the sort of liberty which Siberian prisoners enjoy amongst themselves rendering this an easy matter, and detection of the actual assassin absolutely impossible. A weak prisoner, therefore, who is in the bad books of his staroster must have a bad time of it, for he can be bullied and knocked about with impunity, and would never dare to report it. I have heard of an incident which happened quite recently, and which will give some idea of prison life here.

A prisoner had the foolhardiness (for one can call it nothing else) to inform the officials of the intended evasion of three of the most desperate characters in the prison. Whether he did it out of revenge or to suit his own ends is not known; at any rate, his treason (for such it would undoubtedly be considered amongst his fellows) got somehow to be known, and his death decreed by the staroster. In the mean time, however, he had been removed to another cell, so it was arranged that it should take place at the Government photographer's, when the gang went to be photo'd; but the officials heard of his danger, and he was removed to another room—only just in time, for he would have been lynched, to a certainty, otherwise. Although after this he was placed in another part of the building, the news had spread, and his life was made so awful for him that he was eventually placed in solitary confinement till he could be sent

GROUP OF PRISONERS (FROM A GOVERNMENT PHOTOGRAPH).

to another prison. Capital punishment not existing in Siberia (except in the rarest and most extreme of cases), criminals are absolutely reckless, as they know they cannot get worse than they have got, so there are many prisoners with a list of murders and other crimes against them which would probably make an English criminal open his eyes.

But *revenons à nos moutons* (or rather convicts). As the different men were required the staroster called out their names, and they then came to be "verified"—that is to say, compared with their photo, which is attached to the paper relating to each one. I omitted to mention that all convicts, before starting on the long march across Siberia, have their heads shaved on one side, to render them immediately recognizable as prisoners, and so as to prevent them from running away; and very hideous does this operation render them, as there is no concealing it. Still, in spite of it, numbers of them do escape, as I shall have occasion to tell you in a subsequent chapter. After the "verification" the prisoners were let loose into the courtyard of the perasilny, and left to shift for themselves and find accommodation where they could in the building. As I have already remarked, the perasilny is only a sort of depôt for prisoners; they never remain in it long, only till a detachment is starting for the prison or mine to which they have been consigned.

I was permitted to roam about all over the place with my sketch-book, quite alone, so made sketches amongst the unsavoury crowd of ruffians to my heart's content, and although they came closer to me

L

at times than I desired, still I was in no way molested. It was certainly a most extraordinary sight. Groups of evil, sullen-looking men were either roaming about the spacious courtyard, or else hanging about in groups, talking in an undertone to each other. Most of them were in chains, and their clanking noise harmonized well with the gloomy surroundings. It gave one the impression of being in a den of human wild beasts, and judging from their faces I should fancy most of them were but little better. They all seemed pretty well free to do what they pleased, and I noticed many were smoking cigarettes or pipes. The principal occupation, whilst I was there, seemed to be noting the new arrivals as they individually made their appearance inside the gate. In some cases the new-comers immediately found friends among the crowd, in which event he was introduced by them to the others, and the mutual greetings were most effusive, and doubtless sufficient to raise feelings of envy in the breasts of younger prisoners standing by, and who were unknown to criminal fame. I was told afterwards that new-comers, if they are absolutely unknown to any one in their cell, have to stand a sort of supper, or *bienvenue*—pay their "footing," as a matter of fact. Fancy this sort of thing in an English prison! I naturally asked how a prisoner would manage if he had no money. "He can always get enough for that," was the reply. How?

Whilst I was strolling about making notes and sketches, a warder came up and asked me if I would like to visit the building, and volunteered to show me over it. Naturally I accepted the offer, and was much interested, and I may say astonished, at all I saw. There were three blocks of wooden buildings, the windows of which were heavily grated; though why there were bars I could not make out, for all doors were unlocked, and the prisoners appeared to be free to go and come as they pleased. It was more like a large school-house than a prison. In the rooms, or rather dormitories, the same liberty prevailed, as there seemed to be no one to maintain discipline or order; in fact, there was such a row in all of them that the warder accompanying me had to call out several times at the top of his voice in order to get a little silence, as the noise was simply deafening. The sleeping accommodation in all the rooms consisted of the usual sloping wooden shelves fixed down the centre of the room.

What astonished me most in the whole place was the married prisoners' quarters; for in the large dormitory there were at least two hundred men, women, and children of all ages herded together indiscriminately. No words can fitly describe the scene. The evil faces, the babel of voices, the crying of children, the clanking of the men's chains, and, above all, the indescribable stench which seems inseparable from the Siberian prisons, all combined to make as hideous an impression as could well be imagined. All round, seated or standing, were little family parties, so to speak. Tea was going on at the moment I entered, and the women naturally were in their element; in fact, it was more like a picnic of the lower orders than a prison scene. The heat of the place, which appeared to be without ventilation, was as usual fearfully oppressive, and many of the men and women were in the very scantiest of attires, for decency did not

A "PRIVILIGIERT," OR PRIVILEGED PRISONER.

appear to affect them much, and the sight of so many poor little innocent children, in such foul surroundings, struck me as being particularly horrible.

We afterwards visited the room of a *priviligiert*, or swell prisoner, who was too good to associate with the ordinary horde of vulgar scoundrels, although possibly he may have caused as much misery in his time to his fellow-creatures as any of them. The "gentleman" in this case, I heard, "wrote too well." He was in ordinary civilian attire, and looked a well-dressed, gentlemanly fellow. His little son was with him in the room he occupied, which was really not an uncomfortable one, for there were two real beds in it, with sheets, bedding, etc., washing appliances, look-

PEASANT WOMEN SELLING PROVISIONS TO PRISONERS.

ing-glass, tea-things, plates, saucers, etc.—in fact, quite a little *ménage*. He was sitting on the bed when I entered, and my visit evidently did not seem to please him much, for he immediately turned his back on me and began muttering to himself. However, I went in all the same and had a good look round, and made a sketch of him in spite of his ungracious reception.

On coming out of the prison I was surprised to see quite a little crowd of peasant women with baskets of bread, etc., gathered round a hole in the outer wall, through which they were selling the provisions to such fortunate prisoners who happened to have a little money. It was a curious sight, and well worthy of a sketch, I thought—the grimy hands thrust out through the aperture, and in the background the mass of swarthy, evil countenances—a subject worthy of Doré.

As I was driving back to town with my friend, the conversation naturally turned on the scenes I had just witnessed, and I asked him if no work was ever done in the prisons. He then informed me that all work, except such as wood-cutting, getting water, etc., is optional; if the prisoners can find work and care to take it they are at liberty to do so, as there are specially reserved rooms for them to work in. Many, he told me, made money by making cigarettes, at which they were very clever, and naturally could turn them out cheaper than they could be bought at the shops. Being in want of some at the moment, I thought it would not be a bad idea to get some made by a prisoner, just out of curiosity. So the next day I purchased some tobacco and paper, and went to the *ostrog* (the regular prison, not the depôt) with a friend to interpret for me. It seemed a usual sort of proceeding, for the gaoler we spoke to about it said immediately, "*Morgenor*" (it can be done), and opening the large heavily ironed and barred door leading into the courtyard, called out at the top of his voice, "*Paperossnik*" (a cigarette-maker). There was a clanking of chains, and in a few minutes a miserable-looking wretch in prison clothes came forward. I had only brought a little tobacco, so it was not a big commission I had to give him. On asking what they would cost, he replied that he would make me a thousand for sixty kopeks (1s. 6d.), that these few he would make me as a sample, and I could give him what I chose for them. However, the result, though not exactly a failure, was not a success, as they were not particularly well made, and I had strong reason to believe that at least a third of the tobacco had been purloined, for I had got very many less cigarettes than I ought to have received. So much for convict labour in the prison itself. I shall have occasion, in a subsequent chapter, to speak about outdoor employment of the prisoners.

Of course, there are many political exiles living in Krasnoiarsk, but most of them are time-expired prisoners who cannot leave the district. At the time of my visit several were employed as clerks, and so forth, at the various Government offices; and, as far as I could see or hear (and I had many opportunities for so doing), were not treated with the severity one hears so much of in England. As a matter of fact, there is a great deal more complaint out of Siberia about the tyranny of officials than there is inside it, and the average notions about life there seems to me to be the outcome of entire ignorance. I must say, however, that the Russian officials take things too much *au sérieux*. They "drop upon" people for doing things which in England would be laughed at and forgotten in twenty-four hours. They don't believe in the safety-valve principle, but maybe one official thinks that if he doesn't take notice of a thing some other official will, and probably report the first official into the bargain. Everybody is watched, from a governor downwards. You don't see the working of the system, but it is there all the same. I will give an instance in proof of this. There was a fancy-dress ball at the club, and, as usual in Siberia, everybody wore a mask. One young fellow thought he would create a sensation—and he did. He appeared as a sort of walking advertisement. On his breast were written some of the advantages of life in Siberia. On his back were the disadvantages, so strongly worded that a police official tapped him on the shoulder and requested him to step into a private room. This he did, his mask was removed, and it was found that he was a young student at the Tomsk University. He was told to leave the place, notwithstanding the indignation of the other guests at the official's action. The official reported the matter; there was telegraphing backwards and forwards; the culprit was finally sent back to Tomsk, and I don't know what became of him. Probably he is at this moment in solitary exile in some out-of-the-way place. At any rate, as every one at the ball agreed in conversation about the affair, his life was practically ruined through a freak which, in any country not under Russian rule, would simply have been laughed at.

Local malefactors, whatever their offence, are first taken before the chief of police (*politeemeaster*), who, if the charge be only a petty one, disposes of it himself; if, however, it be of a grave nature it is sent for trial at the high court of justice of the district. I was informed that it goes very hardly indeed with a liberated criminal exile if he is ever caught committing a felony in Siberia, for he has then but a very slight chance of ever regaining his liberty. The police court itself offered little of interest, being merely a large room with a big table in it, at the head of which sat the chief and all his officers. The prisoners were brought in in charge of a soldier or a warder, and stood about anywhere, for there was no dock, and the proceedings, though novel, were not interesting.

I had heard a good deal about the "night refuges for the destitute," which exist in all Siberian towns, so was determined to visit one, although at first it seemed likely to prove a difficult matter, as my friends were not eager to go to such an uninviting den, even in the interests of art. However, at last I persuaded one to accompany me late one night. The refuge naturally was situated in the poorest part of the city, and we had some difficulty at first in finding it. It only consisted of two fairly large rooms, lighted by a swinging lamp. The effect was almost the same as in the prison, for there was the same fearful heat and stench, the same crowd of unkempt wretches, most of whom looked like old gaol-birds. The only difference was that these two rooms were simply packed to their utmost capacity, every available corner being occupied, even to the floor underneath the sloping shelf which served as the sleeping-place—so much so, in fact, that it was positively difficult to get in without treading on some one's face or body. As may be imagined, I hurried up with my sketch as much as possible, for I was anxious to get out into the open air again without delay. Beyond the sloping shelf no other "bedding" is supplied, the men having to provide any further luxuries themselves; but the heating arrangements were so complete that no coverings whatever were needed. Besides the actual lodging, the men are given a mug of tea and piece of bread for supper, and the same in the morning for breakfast. Those who are known to have a little money are charged five kopeks ($1\frac{1}{4}d.$) for the lodging. Before leaving, I was permitted to have a peep into the female dormitory, which was comparatively empty, for I only saw three miserable old hags in their "beauty sleep."

WATCHMAN ON DUTY IN FIRE TOWER, KRASNOIARSK.

[*To face p.* 155.

As in most Siberian towns where wood is principally used in the construction of the houses, the fire brigade forms a most important feature in the municipal arrangements. All over the city are to be seen large and in many cases handsome watch-towers, in which watchmen are always stationed, with a big bell close at hand to give the alarm when necessary; whilst below several manuals are in constant readiness with a supply of warm water during the winter, to avoid risk of its freezing.

The theatre is really quite an imposing building, and rendered more so by being situated in the centre of an immense open space. Performances take place in it three times a week during the winter, and, judging from the way they are patronized, histrionic art is evidently well appreciated here.

Taking it all in all, therefore, I found Krasnoiarsk a very interesting place, and well worth the six weeks' stay I made in it; in fact, I was quite sorry to leave it.

## CHAPTER XV.

### MY JOURNEY FROM KRASNOIARSK TO IRKUTSK.

My servant Matwieff—The Great Post Road—The post-houses—Tea caravans—Curious effect of road—Siberian lynch law—Runaway convicts—A curious incident—The post courier—An awkward accident—Arrival at Irkutsk.

MY SERVANT.

TRAVELLING in Siberia is evidently altered very much for the better during the last three years, for my experiences on the Great Post Road were very different indeed to those described by the author of a recent book of travel in these parts. Perhaps, however, the fact of my doing the journey during the winter may to a certain extent account for it; but whatever the cause, the impressions received are the same, and the eight days' journey, though certainly a somewhat tedious one, will remain in my memory as one amongst the many interesting episodes of my Siberian wanderings. After all I had read about the many difficulties and discomforts, not to say dangers, of this long journey, I must confess that it was not without certain misgivings that I at last decided to make a move and to start from my comfortable quarters in the Gostinnitza Gadaloff and push on further East, in accordance with the route I had planned out for myself. My numerous friends, on learning this, were so unanimous in their advice to me not to travel alone, in case of my being taken ill on the road or meeting with an accident, that I was at length persuaded, almost against my will, to listen to them and take a servant with me; and, as will be seen, it was very fortunate I did so.

Once it was known I was in want of a servant, I had no difficulty in finding men who were willing to go with me to Irkutsk, even on the off chance of my not requiring a servant when once there; in fact, it was an *embarras de richesses*, and I had my choice. The principal question was to find some one who was accustomed to travelling. Luckily, I suddenly heard of an ex-sergeant of gendarmes who was anxious to get to the capital, and who would be glad to give his services as servant to me in return for a "free passage." The mere fact of his having been in the Gendarmerie was in itself sufficient recommendation, as only men of exceptionally good character are admitted into this branch of the service; so without hesitation I decided on taking him, and he eventually turned out to be the best and most conscientious servant I have ever had; he also was the biggest, for he stood no less than 6 ft. 3 in., and was a typical fellow of his class. My journey to Irkutsk was therefore *une affaire arrangée*, for from the moment I arranged with Sergeant Matwieff all trouble on my part ceased, for he simply took charge of the arrangements as though he had travelled with me for years, and all I had to do was to decide when to start, and leave the rest to him, even to packing my things, ordering the horses, and the host of minor details inseparable from Siberian travel. It is almost unnecessary to add that he spoke no language but Russian, so our means of conversation were very limited, and most of the time I had to make him understand by means of pantomime.

At last my preparations were complete, and on the evening of Sunday, January 25, I started towards the next stage of my long journey, and shortly after Krasnoiarsk, with its many pleasant associations, was but a reminiscence of the past.

The road for some miles, after leaving the town, lay along the ice in the very centre of the river Yenisei. As it was a very bright moonlight night, the effect was novel and beautiful, the track was smooth and level, and the horses went along at their top speed. I was gradually lulled into a deep sleep, and woke to find the first stage of twenty-nine versts accomplished and the sledge in the post-yard of Botoiskaya. The little village was slumbering; not a light was to be seen in any of the windows; in the post-house was the only sign of life. Looking up the quaint street, which in the moonlight had a weird appearance, with its tumbledown cottages, I saw a most curious sight. The centre of the road had exactly the appearance of being laid with railway sleepers; as far as one could see, the long ridges in the snow followed each other so regularly, that I could not help asking what was the reason of so cutting up the road. To my astonishment I was told that these ridges were caused by the thousands of horses of the caravans which had passed along the road since the commencement of the winter. The horses instinctively know that they can get a better foothold by walking in each other's footsteps, and fall into the habit of doing so almost mechanically. I shortly after had the first of many opportunities of noting this for myself, for presently a large tea caravan came along, and I observed that it hardly ever happened that a horse stepped out of the grooves, so much so that the drivers strolling alongside seemed to have very little to do, as the animals appeared to know all that was expected of them.

This, my first sight of a caravan on the Great Post Road, was but the forerunner of what we met or passed both day and night almost without intermission the whole way to Irkutsk. While many were laden with European goods bound eastward, most of them were coming from China with tea. So great, in fact, was this traffic that I could not help wondering where all this immense quantity of tea can possibly go to, more especially when one comes to consider that what comes to Europe by the Great

Post Road is only a small proportion of the annual amount exported from China. The tea of China, packed in bales of hide, is brought across the Gobi desert by ox-waggons or by camels as far as Kiakhta, the Russian frontier town, where it is transferred to sledges or Siberian carts, according to the season, and the long journey to Tomsk is then commenced, a journey taking over two months. The same horses go the whole way; but they are allowed to take their own pace, and seldom do more than three miles an hour. At Tomsk the tea is stored till the spring, when it is taken by river steamer into Russia. Tea brought overland is said to retain more of its original flavour than that which, packed in lead, has made a sea voyage, but the difference is probably so slight that only an expert could detect it.

There are comparatively very few men in charge of these immensely valuable consignments, which often consist of as many as two hundred and fifty sledges—one man to about seven horses as a rule—and these at night take it in turns to keep watch; for on the Great Post Road a peculiar form of highway robbery exists: bales of tea are frequently cut loose and stolen in the dark hours by thieves, who lurk around to take advantage of a driver dozing on his sledge. The poor fellow then has to pay dearly for his "forty winks," as he has to make good the loss out of his wages—a very serious matter, considering the value of a large bale of tea. Last year, I am informed, these thefts became so frequent and the thieves so daring that at last the drivers combined to have their revenge, and when on one or two occasions they managed to catch a thief *flagrante delicto* they actually lynched him in quite a North-American Indian style. Bending a stout birch sapling to the ground by means of a rope, they fastened the back of the victim's head to it by the hair, and then cut the rope, releasing the tree, which immediately sprang back to its original position, and the unfortunate wretch was literally scalped. He was then left to his fate. It is probable that a few examples of this kind will have as deterrent an effect on intending thieves as on the victims themselves. But to return to my narrative.

We had no difficulty in getting horses, and, after a stoppage of twenty-five minutes, were rattling merrily along the frost-bound highway. It was a bitterly cold night, no less than 40 deg. below zero (Réaumur), but till now I had not felt it much, as the wind was at our backs. Unfortunately, a turn in the road brought it right against us, and then I felt such cold that in all my life I never experienced any like it. Although I was buried in furs, and the hood of the sledge down, there was no keeping it out. Moustache, nostrils, and eyelashes were frozen hard, and my dacha, where it came in contact with my face, was one solid mass of ice, caused by my breath, and to this my skin actually stuck.

M

The wonder to me was how the yemschiks stand it as they do; but I suppose they get case-hardened to it in time—frost-proof, in fact, for rolled up in their sheepskins they seem impervious to temperature, taking it all as a matter of course. As to the horses, although they were always so covered with frost as to have the appearance of being thickly coated with snow, they never seemed to mind it a bit, and would keep up the same pace the whole stage; standing afterwards in the post-yard as quiet as sheep while their icy coats were, so to speak, broken off with a primitive sort of curry-comb attached to the handle of the driver's whip. Twenty-five versts, or about two and a half hours of this sort of temperature was quite enough at a stretch, as I soon found, and the sight of the village boundary fence was always a welcome sight as betokening the end of another spell.

The novelty of sledge-travelling soon wears off, especially on a road like this, where there is so little to vary the eternal monotony of the dense forests or rolling plains on either side of one. The same dreary aspects seemed to repeat themselves over and over again almost at every turn of the road, whilst the various villages resembled each other so much that it was at times hard to believe we were not returning to the one we had just left. I do not propose wearying you with a detailed account of the forty-three stations between Krasnoiarsk and Irkutsk, for a description of one, which I have already given, suffices for all—so much so, in fact, that although I tried hard to see something more to sketch, I could discover nothing I had not already seen and sketched on our journey up the Yenisei or in Yeniseisk or Krasnoiarsk. Where, for instance, in France every little "pays" has its individual character, so to speak, here in Siberia from one end to the other of this enormous continent all is the same, and if you have studied one portion of it, you have studied all (of course, with the exception of the aborigines, who naturally differ according to their tribes). For my own part, I can assert that I saw absolutely no difference, either in the build of the houses, or the dress or customs of the inhabitants, all the way from Golchika, the tiny settlement on the tundras far away within the Arctic circle, and Kiakhta, a distance of nearly three thousand miles; and, from what I hear, it is the same from the Urals to the Pacific. It almost seems as though it had been ordained by Imperial Ukase that all over this vast empire the inhabitants should everywhere adopt the same costumes and build and furnish their houses always on the same pattern.

What strikes one most on the long stretches of road is the total absence of isolated cottages or farmhouses which so help to enliven a landscape in Europe. Once beyond the fence which encircles the limits of each village commune, all signs of habitation and even cultivation instantly cease, and no more are seen till the next commune is reached. The road then passes through a big wooden gate, with high posts on either side; just inside this is a small sentry-box, in which a watchman is always

ARRIVAL AT A POST STATION.

stationed during the summer months to see that the gate is kept closed, and so keep the cattle from straying outside the boundary. (In the winter the gate is always open.) In the distance one then sees the long dreary stretch of village street, with the green-roofed *ostrog*, or prison, and the public granary standing out in relief against the dilapidated wooden hovels. Everywhere, as a rule, there seems an entire absence of human life. The post-house is only distinguishable from the other houses by its having black and white lamp-posts on either side of the door, and the Russian coat-of-arms painted on a board over it.

Of course there were flourishing villages here and there, but so few. Kansk, Nijni Udinsk, Touloung, and the large village of Koutoulik, are really the only places worth mentioning in this long road. At Touloung the streets were actually lighted up at night. At these places, of course, the post-houses were better furnished and looked after, but they were but oases among the number of wretched and uncomfortable ones; although I must in justice admit that with only one or two exceptions they were all as clean as soap and water could make them; but then, soap and water does not restore dilapidations or rebuild ramshackle places, unfortunately, and many were very dilapidated indeed, and scarcely worthy being called "Government post-houses."

The same ideas of ventilation evidently prevail all over Siberia, for everywhere I found the windows hermetically sealed, and in most instances when the stove was in full blaze the atmosphere was simply stifling, as may be imagined after it has been confined in these stuffy rooms for the six long winter months, and being breathed over and over again by hundreds and hundreds of travellers. However, à la guerre comme à la guerre, and in the wilds of Siberia it would have been absurd to expect to find European notions of sanitation.

With but one exception I had no difficulty whatever in getting horses at each station; in fact, in most instances the fresh team was generally ready to start before I was, so I could not complain about being kept waiting. The one exception I refer to occurred at Kansk, where I arrived unfortunately too late at night to be able to look round this interesting and flourishing little town, as I should have had ample time to have done, for on reaching the post-house, the *staroster* (as the postmaster is called) courteously informed me that no horses could be had till three the next morning—six hours to wait. Luckily the waiting-room was as clean and comfortable as one could have wished it, so I decided to have supper at once and "turn in" on the sofa for a few hours. A tin of Irish stew, washed down (the Irish stew, not the tin) by a glass or two of vodka and a cup of black coffee, seemed a feast for a king after the hasty meals I had been having since leaving Krasnoiarsk, so when I did turn in an hour later it was to immediately fall into the deep sleep which naturally follows when one has "got outside" a square meal and one has a good digestion. Although I had particularly asked the station-master to call me as soon as the horses arrived, I suppose,

INTERIOR OF A POST HOUSE.

[*To face p.* 106.

like the Irish servant in Lever's story, "he did not like to knock too hard at the door for fear of waking me;" for I was only awakened at eight o'clock the next morning by the sun streaming into my eyes. Still, I was not exactly sorry for the few hours I had lost, as I had had a splendid rest, and after a good sluice in a bucket of ice-cold water felt "fit as ninepence" (though why ninepence should be fit I know not), and did ample justice to a good breakfast before starting.

Moreover, as it turned out, after leaving the town we passed through some of the finest forest scenery I have ever seen, and which it would have been a pity to have missed, for there was really so little that was interesting that I should have been sorry to have passed any that was, during the night. Either the big road, for some reason or other, was blocked, or else the driver thought he knew a near cut; anyway, we shortly after made a *détour* of several miles and went straight across the forest itself by a rough sort of track. It was a wild, desolate-looking place, the trees meeting overhead causing a dim twilight which considerably helped to heighten the effect—just the sort of place one would not have been astonished to meet a bear or a pack of wolves in; in fact, I was fondly hoping to see something and got my rifle ready. But in the still mysterious depths of the dense jungle no sign whatever of life was visible; over the thick carpet of snow, the sledge glided noiselessly, even the sound of horses' hoofs was muffled, and the deadly silence of the surroundings was only broken now and again by the subdued jingle of the duga bells. I could not help thinking how serious it would have been if an accident had occurred to the sledge or horses just about here; for the "near cut" was evidently not the usual road, as the whole length of it we were entirely alone.

It must have taken us at least three hours to do the next fifteen miles or so, for the track was so narrow in places, and so blocked by abutting trees, that at times it seemed doubtful whether the sledge would pass at all, so tight a squeeze was it. However, at last we got through and out into the broad daylight on the high-road again, when for a few seconds the light seemed absolutely dazzling after the semi-obscurity we had just left. Although we passed through many miles of dense forest after this, we did so on the regular road and in the full glare of the midday sun, so my impressions were very different to those received in the lonely track we had just come through.

The next day or two were uneventful, and as there was nothing new to see, the stoppages at the different post-houses usually came as a pleasant break to the the journey, and an excuse to get out of the sledge and call for the samovar. By the way, talking of samovars, it is really astonishing how quickly one takes to the Russian way of drinking weak tea without milk, boiling hot, out of a tumbler. There is no doubt about it that one can appreciate the full flavour of the tea better that way than as we drink it in England, although to drink out of a cup appears to me to be much more convenient than out of a tumbler; and I am surprised the Russians don't think so, for there is not the slightest doubt which is the more practical.

An interesting incident occurred shortly after leaving the village of Rasgonnaiaa. I had learnt at the station that a large gang of prisoners had passed a few days previously, so hurried on as much as possible in the hope of overtaking it, and at any rate seeing something which would break the monotony of the journey. The road, which hitherto had passed through forest-land, was now open on either side, and for miles ahead the rolling, snow-covered plains stretched, relieved, so to speak, only by the winding road and its endless vista of telegraph-poles. During the morning I had noticed that we were continually passing rough-looking men on foot, hurrying along, always in the same direction, as though on important business. Now, in any other country than Siberia such an occurrence would pass unnoticed, for "Shank's pony" is a cosmopolitan beast, and among certain classes generally the only means of locomotion. Here, however, in the wilds of Siberia, a foot-traveller is an extreme rarity outside a village. Hence my surprise. At last it occurred to me to ask Matwieff if he could tell me what these curious-looking men were, and what they were doing on the road so far from a village. Imagine my surprise when, without the slightest hesitation, he told me they were *bradiagga*, or runaway prisoners, from the *parti* on ahead. I could scarcely believe it, so he suggested our stopping the next one we met, and he would then convince me of the truth of his statement. To him there was evidently not so much novelty in the incident as to me, for as an ex-gendarme he could probably " spot " a prisoner at a glance.

I had not long to wait, for in a short time there appeared in the far distance another of these gentlemen hurrying towards us. I thought it would not be a bad idea to " take his photo," so ordered the yemschik to stop, and, getting out of the sledge, waited till the fellow got up abreast of us. Matwieff then called out to him to come over to where we were, for he was on the far side of the road, which (as is usual in Siberia) was of enormous width. The fellow, in his anxiety to get along as quickly as possible, had evidently not noticed that we were stopping, for when he heard us call out to him and he looked up and caught sight of us, a most curious look came over his face, which we could not help remarking. Whether it was the sight of my revolver (which I always wore outside my coat) or the gendarme cap Matwieff had on, I cannot tell, but he looked round wildly for a second over the snow-covered plain as though meditating a "bolt;" then realizing, perhaps, that he could not possibly get away, he seemed to make up his mind, and came slowly over towards us.

When he got close up we then saw that he was simply trembling in every limb with fright, whilst his mouth was quivering to such an extent that it was positively painful to see such a picture of abject fear. Although he was a great big hulking fellow, and had an ugly looking cudgel under his arm, he was as unnerved and cowed as a beaten dog, and evidently expected us to immediately handcuff him and take him back at the tail of the sledge to the *parti* he had escaped from. The delight of the poor wretch when he learnt that I only wanted to photograph him was almost curious to witness, and he offered no objection to my carrying out my fell purpose. Matwieff then, to prove to me that the man really was as he said, a *bradiagga*, coolly went up to him, and, lifting up his sheepskin coat, lo and behold, underneath were his prison clothes, whilst hidden by his high peasant boots were the ends of his chains still attached to the anklets, which he had not yet had time to remove. His head also, he showed me by removing his cap, had been half shaved in the usual convict manner. Whatever his crime, it was certainly no business of ours to re-arrest him, so I took the photo of him and then gave him a few kopeks for standing. Before letting him go, out of curiosity

I asked him where he was going to. To my astonishment he replied, "Moscow." The idea of his setting out, on foot, to accomplish over three thousand miles home, in the depth of winter, struck me as being an awful task to undertake.

At the next station, the staroster, on my mentioning the incident, informed me that in the village they were simply infested with runaway convicts after a convoy had passed, and that at night the barns and outhouses were always occupied; he had known as many as a dozen men sleeping in the bath-house of the station. (The baths in a Russian village are generally in wooden outbuildings.) The peasants, he further informed me, so far from interfering with the fuyards, or thinking even of giving them up, supply them on the quiet with bread and broken victuals, so that, at any rate, there is no fear of them dying of hunger within the village commune. As a matter of fact, the men themselves know that they can always reckon on something to eat in every place they have to pass through, and it has grown to be such a regular custom, this providing of food for them, that they take it as a matter of course.

The wind, which hitherto had somewhat lulled, now recommenced with renewed force. Fortunately, however, owing to the road going in a different direction, it was at our backs; for so hard did it blow, that the country presented the effect almost of steaming under it owing to the driving particles of snow,

THE IMPERIAL MAIL. [*To face p.* 173.

and one could only see a few yards ahead through the sort of white fog enveloping everything, and we should have doubtless had an unpleasant time if we had been going against it.

I was much struck with the scarcity of travellers we met, either on the road or in the stations, for only on two or three occasions did we meet any one or find the waiting-room occupied. At one place the Imperial Mail, bound for Irkutsk, came up while we were there—half a dozen of the shabbiest and most ramshackle of sledges, in charge of an equally seedy and shabby individual in a dirty old sheepskin coat, and with an enormous revolver in his belt. I could not help feeling somewhat disappointed, for from what I had previously read I had expected to see a dashing courier, resplendent in green and gold, and armed to the teeth, so had my sketch-book in readiness as soon as I heard that the mail had arrived. At another station I found the room occupied by a family, consisting of a lady and gentleman, and no less than four children and a maid. By some accident I discovered that the lady spoke German, so we had quite a long chat together. She informed me that they had come straight away from far Vladivostock, and were going to St. Petersburg, a journey which, from start to finish, would probably take them *ten weeks*, that is, if they stopped nowhere on the road. Her husband, who was a Government official, she told me, had been in bad health for some time past, and had been recommended to go to St. Petersburg to get the highest of medical advice. This is the longest journey I ever heard of "to see a doctor." I saw them start again shortly after, and although there were so many of them, they had such a huge sledge that they all seemed to pack into it quite comfortably.

You may imagine how refreshing, so to speak, it was, after the sort of wilderness we had come through, to find that the next station, Touloung, was quite a busy little town, its many and well-built streets actually lighted up, whilst several important-looking shops and large houses helped to give quite a lively appearance to the place. The post-house itself was also quite "up to" the town, and not only boasted of several large and well-furnished rooms, but also a big apartment, most handsomely decorated, in which, I was informed, the Governor of Irkutsk held receptions when he had occasion to visit the town. Touloung, though an old town, was certainly one of the prettiest and most flourishing I had passed through, and my only regret was that it was night when we got there, for I should like to have sketched some of the bits I saw, notably the beautiful house of the merchant, Mr. Shokounoff, which stands exactly opposite the post-station, for it struck me as being a splendid specimen of Russian architecture. After doing a little shopping, and a look round, and a "feed," once more I got under weigh.

The next few stations were wretchedly uncomfortable, or anyway they seemed so, perhaps out of contrast to the nice one we had just left; so there was little temptation to loiter in them longer than was absolutely necessary whilst waiting for the fresh horses. At Tiretskaya, where we had to cross the Oka, the road went along the centre of the river on the ice for several miles, and the high wooded banks on either side gave it a most peculiar and striking appearance, not unlike a railway cutting.

The next place of interest we came to was the large village of Koutoulik (or, rather, small town, for it contains over eleven hundred inhabitants). The post-house here was without exception the smartest on the whole road. The waiting-room, which was really well-furnished, was not only full of plants and flowers, but actually had pictures on the walls, not the usual cheap, religious ones, but good oleographs; whilst to add to the good impression caused by these attempts at luxury, I learnt that there was a "real dinner" ready if I cared to take of it. You may imagine I jumped at it after living on tinned food for nearly a week. The wife of the staroster had evidently been a professed cook in her time, judging from the result and the way I was served. After dinner I lit my pipe and had a stroll through the village, whilst Matwieff was looking after the horses. The streets presented so lively and animated an appearance that I spent more time than I had intended to, wandering about in search of subjects.

The inhabitants were evidently used to artists, for neither my sketch-book nor my camera attracted any particular attention.

During the night after leaving outoulik Koccurred the accident which I have already referred to. We had started from the station of Polovilnaya at about 1.30 a.m., and I was soon fast asleep. How long I had been asleep I know not, but I was suddenly woke up by an indescribable sort of sensation that the sledge had "changed front." I sprang up and, raising the hood, looked out, when, to my no slight dismay, I discovered that we were on a long and steep hill and that the horses had lost all control over the sledge which was "skidding" down sideways at a rate that increased every instant. Matwieff was immediately as wide awake as myself, and we both sat and looked out and waited breathlessly for the result, which was absolutely inevitable, for it would have been utter madness to have attempted to jump out, encumbered as we both were with our heavy furs and the stiff apron of the sledge. Although the driver urged the horses to their very top speed they could not get ahead of the heavy vehicle, which had obtained complete mastery over them and was simply dragging them along with it. Just before reaching the bottom of the hill was a slight rise in the road such as one sees on a switchback railway; here the driver was shot off his seat as out of a catapult, and a few yards further down the sledge turned completely over into a huge drift of snow by the side of the road. The luggage was so firmly wedged in that it barely moved, and both Matwieff and I were also so firmly boxed in that we found ourselves lying on our sides completely helpless. Fortunately a large caravan was coming along at the moment, and the men, seeing our predicament, immediately hurried up and soon righted the sledge again. The horses, I forgot to add, stopped at once as soon as they felt the resistance offered by the deep snow. This little misadventure was evidently a usual occurrence to them, and also to the driver, who turned up unhurt and smiling a few seconds after, and soon we were off again as fast as ever.

For the moment I thought we had got off scot free, for the sledge was uninjured, and neither Matwieff nor I felt any ill effects from the spill. A few stations further on, however, when going to get out of the sledge I felt a nasty pain in my right ankle, and found, on trying to walk, that my leg was so stiff I could not use it. Here was a pretty go! I was evidently in for a bad sprain, and I knew what that meant. Luckily Matwieff was an old soldier in every sense of the word, and rose to the occasion, for without the slightest hesitation he insisted on my not moving, and also on his putting me on a snow compress. In the mean time it was decided that we should hurry on to Irkutsk, which was now

N

only some forty versts off, without any unnecessary delay. In spite, however, of the cold compress, the pain in my foot, probably aggravated by the movement of the sledge, increased to such an extent that I was in positive agony when at last we came in sight of our destination, and the many golden cupolas and minarets of the capital of Eastern Siberia stood out clear and defined as a picture against the bright morning sky.

The scene was a beautiful one, and I could not help enjoying it in spite of the acute pain I was suffering. Our road lay right across the frozen river Angara, "the most beautiful river in the world," as it has been called. It was a Sunday morning, and crowds of gaily dressed peasants on foot and in sledges were making their way towards the city in the brilliant sunshine. The air resounded with the merry ring of sledge bells, whilst the many quaint costumes and curious conveyances gave an aspect of gaiety and life to a scene the like of which I had not yet witnessed in Siberia. My only regret was that owing to my being unable to move I could not get out of the sledge to make a sketch or take a photograph. However, I promised myself not to lose sight of the subject, and to return on the very first occasion when my foot would allow me. A few minutes afterwards the driver drew up outside a large triumphal arch standing at the entrance to the city and removed the duga bells before passing through, as nowhere in Siberia are these allowed except on the high-road.

My eight days' tedious journey was at last ended, and it was with a veritable feeling of relief that I found myself passing through the broad, well-built streets, with the prospect of soon being once again in a comfortable and well-appointed hotel.

IRKUTSK.

## CHAPTER XVI.

### IRKUTSK.

Unpleasant experiences at hotel—Hospitality of Mr. Charles Lee—First impressions of the city.

I WAS much disappointed to find, on reaching the principal hotel, the *Moskovskaia Podvorié*, that its glories, of which I had heard so much, were things of the past, and that as a hotel it no longer existed. True, the imposing three-storied building still remained, but under a new designation, for it is now the head-quarters of the Irkutsk military staff, and is known as the Etat Major of the city. A few *chambres meublées* in the upper stories are all that

THE MOSKOVSKAIA PODVORIÉ, IRKUTSK.  [To face p. 180.

remain of what was, two years ago, the best hotel in Siberia. I afterwards learnt that its failure was owing to its having been got up on far too grand a scale for the place, and that its promoters had lost a "pot of money" over it while it was open. Of course there were many other hotels, so I left the matter in the hands of the yemschik, for my foot was so painful that I felt absolutely indifferent as to where or how I was lodged, so long as I could get out of the sledge and lie down quietly somewhere. But it was evidently the height of the season in Irkutsk and the city crammed, for everywhere I was told they were "full." At last, however, after a lot of driving about, I found a place where they had one room just vacant. It was a really smart and imposing-looking hotel from outside, and quite a "find," as I imagined—till I got inside the building, when I found myself in one of the dirtiest places of its kind I had yet seen in Siberia. The contrast between the exterior and the interior was simply startling. Much, however, as I was disgusted with it, I was so sick of hunting about for lodgings that I determined to put up with it for a short time; at any rate, till my foot was better. With the help of Matwieff I therefore made myself as comfortable as I could on two chairs (for I did not like the look of the sofa), and composed myself for "forty winks" whilst waiting for the "something to eat" which I had ordered, for the accident to my foot had not interfered with my appetite. But I found it impossible to have a nap, on account of certain strange noises round the room. At first I could not make out what they were occasioned by, but I soon discovered after a slight inspection. The wall-paper, which was stretched over a wooden foundation, did not touch the wood everywhere, and the curious noise was produced by myriads of blackbeetles, cockroaches, and other vermin running up and down the wall and in and out of holes they had eaten in the paper. This cheerful discovery decided me at once to clear out of the place, and chance finding something better elsewhere.

Suddenly an idea occurred to me. I had a letter of introduction to a Mr. Charles Lee, an English engineer living in Irkutsk, a brother of the unfortunate man who lost his life on our way up the Yenisei, so I sent this letter to him, with a note telling him of my accident, and asking if he could recommend me some other hotel to go to. My good luck had not quite deserted me, for in a few minutes came back a message saying he would himself be round to see me directly, and shortly after he arrived. On seeing my helpless condition, this good Samaritan insisted on my immediately leaving the hotel and going to stay at his house, to be nursed till my foot was well; and, so as to ensure my not refusing, he gave orders for my luggage to be forthwith removed. In a very short time I was in a snug room, surrounded by every comfort; so, although the doctor said I should have to remain indoors and not move for a week, I felt that I should be in luck's way if my lines were always cast in such pleasant places. Under kind nursing my injured ankle got rapidly well, so much so that I was soon able to get about again, and with the assistance, though much against the wish, of my hospitable friend, find convenient lodgings in the city. So it was a further proof of "all's well that end's well."

Containing forty thousand inhabitants, the capital of Eastern Siberia covers an enormous extent of ground, being nearly two miles in each direction—the principal street, or Bolshoi Oulitza, itself over a mile in length. My first impressions on walking up this noble thoroughfare were very different indeed from what I had anticipated, for it was hard to realize how near one was to the Chinese frontier, and how far from a railway; the whole scene was one of absolutely European character, and reminded me not a little of many capitals I have visited. It was quite a relief, after the desolate look of the streets at Krasnoiarsk and Yeniseisk, owing to the apparent absence of shops, to see here the handsome buildings with large plate-glass windows, in which were displayed every description of European goods; and my surprise was the more natural, for, from what I had read, I was led to believe that nowhere in Siberia would I find the streets enlivened by the shop displays which give so much life and character to a place. But what astonished me most pleasantly in this far-away Siberian city was to see the fair sex dressed in the very latest of Parisian fashions, for I saw costumes in the Bolshoi Oulitza which would have looked smart even in Bond Street or the Rue de la Paix, and, as added to which I don't think I was ever in a place which for its size could boast of more pretty faces, the effect on a bright sunny afternoon may be imagined.

Irkutsk is not nearly so cold a place as Krasnoiarsk, for, according to Keane, the mean winter temperature is only minus 4 deg. Fahr., and the summer temperature equal to that of Melbourne, and considerably higher than that of Paris. Of course I was particularly fortunate in visiting Irkutsk in the very height of the "season," for, as is the case all over Siberia, and, I believe, Russia also, the time to see "life" is during the winter months, when the rich and fashionable classes are in town, and all sorts of festivities are going on.

As at Krasnoiarsk, I found "society" here absolutely European in its character, for most of the wealthiest people annually pass several months in the West, so are quite au courant with all that is going on in the world of pleasure, and manage to convey their impressions back to their Siberian palaces in the shape of luxuries and extravagances of every sort. Amongst the many hospitalities I was shown I had the pleasure of dining one evening at the house of

Mr. Soukatchoff, the Mayor of Irkutsk, one of the richest and most important men of the city. His magnificent house, with its large picture-gallery (in which are over two hundred and fifty examples of

AN IRKUTSK BEAUTY.

the best known of continental artists), its immense library, and its priceless collection of curiosities from every part of the world, made my visit to this gentleman a sort of " artistic treat "—a treat which was in no way spoilt by the very excellent dinner he gave us, and the interesting people I was introduced to, many of whom spoke French and German fluently.

ENTRANCE HALL OF MILLIONAIRE GOLD-MINE OWNER'S HOUSE, IRKUTSK.

and some of them English also. Here, as elsewhere in Siberia, on every occasion when I have dined out, either in Irkutsk, Krasnoiarsk, or Yeniseisk, the general "tone" and arrangements were delightful. I was also fortunate enough to be present at a big ball given by the millionaire, M. de Sievers, and I doubt very much if the most brilliant "crush" of a London season could present a more magnificent spectacle than did this ball—for the governor-general, with his party, and the head-quarters staff officers, were present in full uniform, blazing with orders and decorations, and the rooms were crowded with as smart a crowd of people as the most fastidious London dancing man could have desired. The "floor" and the music were both excellent. In the gallery of the ball-room was stationed the regimental band, while, by the fountain in the huge winter-garden, which was beautifully illuminated with quaint Chinese lanterns, the town string-band played all the evening. It was like being in dreamland to wander, with some pretty girl on one's arm, through the exotic shrubberies, and my thoughts were carried far away from cold Siberia, to the sunny south of France and to gay Monte Carlo. I should have been sorry to have missed seeing this dance, for it did more towards giving me an insight into Irkutsk society than all else.

Since the disastrous fire in Irkutsk in 1879, when almost the entire town was burnt to the ground, it has been forbidden to build any but stone or brick houses in the principal streets, so the result is broad thoroughfares, with lofty buildings of imposing architectural pretensions on either side, which would not disgrace any Western capital. For its size, I do not think there is any city in the world which can boast of more public institutions than Irkutsk. On first driving through the city this was the characteristic

STREET SCENE, IRKUTSK.

feature which struck me, for everywhere, almost in every street, was some important public edifice, many of the institutions being, I was informed, the result of private munificence. I had often read of these monuments as erected by Siberian millionaires more to satisfy their personal vanity and love of ostentation than out of any true charitable or public spirit —rather as a means of proving to the vulgar horde what wealth they really possess. Whether or no this is the case, of course it is impossible to say ; but, at any rate, the result is a conglomeration of public institutions which, considering the size of the place, could not be rivalled anywhere, I fancy. A brief list of them, in proof of my statement, may be of interest, as giving an idea of the importance of this distant Siberian city.

Of public schools there are no less than nineteen, all under the supervision of a Government Educational Committee.

Then there are six hospitals—namely, three town hospitals ; a foundling hospital, on the usual Russian system ; a military hospital, and a madhouse.

Of "homes" for children there are at least four ; three asylums for the aged and infirm ; a monastery for men and one for women ; a convict and a civil prison ; a geographical institute ; a large observatory (with an English telescope) ; and two clubs—one military, the other for merchants—making a total of over forty important public institutions for a population of less than forty thousand.

Of the handsome churches, of which there are no less than twenty-two, besides two cathedrals, many were also presented to this lucky city by its millionaire inhabitants, who, when they decide to spend their money, do so in no parsimonious manner, as is evidenced by the result. The monastery of St. Innocent, a short distance from the city, is as beautiful a specimen of Italian architecture as one could see anywhere, and cost its donors, several rich merchants, I don't know how many million roubles. It is not only in Irkutsk, however, that one finds such proofs of great private munificence, for I learn that the magnificent cathedral of Krasnoiarsk was presented to the city by a rich man who made his millions out of vodka!

Irkutsk, being the seat of the Government of Eastern Siberia (a district equal in size to the half of Europe), is naturally well stocked with officials of all sorts and grades, the governor-general and civil governor having each no less than three *remplaçants*. Considering what an important centre Irkutsk is, I was surprised to learn that it was only garrisoned by one battalion of 1000 soldiers and one *sotnia* (nominally 100, but actually 150) of Cossacks; so the energies of the military governor are not overtaxed. The Chinese frontier district comes within the government of the Trans-Baikal and Amour provinces.

The police arrangements struck me as being particularly good. In the daytime mounted men are continually patrolling the streets to prevent any congestion of the traffic—a very necessary measure, considering the reckless manner in which Siberians drive. At night there is a curious and truly Eastern custom still in vogue in this important

A COSSACK.  [To face p. 190.

AN IRKUTSK POLICEMAN.

city; watchmen parade the streets, continually agitating a peculiar sort of knocker which emits a sound not unlike that of the rattle our policemen used to be provided with. What is the reason of adhering to this primitive custom I have been unable to learn. Perhaps Siberian thieves are known to be nervous, and this arrangement frightens them, and deters them from contemplated misdeeds. Certainly the watchmen themselves would not have that effect on anything but a very old woman or a young child, for they were usually aged and decrepit fellows, who looked as though they ought to have been at home and in bed instead of out all night. Fortunately the Irkutsk streets are safe enough during the dark hours.

THE MUSEUM, IRKUTSK.

THE RECREATION GROUND, IRKUTSK PRISON.

## CHAPTER XVII.

### PRISON LIFE IN SIBERIA—*continued*.

The Irkutsk prison—Comparative liberty of prisoners—Incongruities of prison life—The "shops"—Prison artists.

THERE was always so much to see and do in Irkutsk, that the five weeks I spent there were fully occupied. The prison life of Siberia has always interested me highly, for I had read so much of it before coming to the country that I never missed an opportunity of seeing as much of it as possible. One of my first excursions, therefore, was to the gaol here. As at Yeniseisk and Krasnoiarsk, the officials were polite-

MARRIED PRISONERS WAITING TO BE SERVED WITH NEW CLOTHES ON ARRIVAL AT THE PRISON AT IRKUTSK.

[To face p. 183.

ness itself, and although the *ostrog* here is a really important one, containing as it does no less than twelve hundred prisoners (owing to the recent burning of the Alexandroffsky prison), I experienced not the slightest difficulty in being shown all there was to be seen. The authorities offered me every assistance in their power, and no secret whatever was made of it ; the governor-general of Irkutsk, to whom my mission as a special artist and correspondent was well known, even going so far as to send me a courteous message, saying that he would be pleased to let me see all I wished of the prison life, and hoped that I would only write the exact truth about it ! So I spent a long morning there, walking round with the director, the doctor, and other officials, and saw and sketched as much as I wished, and only had to ask to be told all I wanted to know.

What struck me most in the internal arrangements was the comparative liberty that existed inside the vast building ; for, with the exception of a few prisoners in solitary confinement, all seemed free to roam about in the corridors or the large quadrangle to their hearts' content ; and although a warder with a large bunch of keys accompanied us on our round, in no case did he find occasion to use them, for all the doors were unlocked. I was informed that it is only at night the prisoners are locked in. The system is certainly a curious one. Of course the men in the " solitary " cells were not allowed this sort of liberty.

o

The description I have given of the Yeniseisk prison will almost suffice for the Irkutsk one as well, with the exception that the various " halls," or " dormitories," there were infinitely better than those here, which—probably on account of their overcrowded state—were in a filthy condition, and little better than human pigsties. Every spot was occupied, and the stench was awful in consequence, for this is an old prison as compared with that at Yeniseisk. I was much astonished to see dogs, cats, and even pigeons and doves in some " halls," and on inquiry was informed that prisoners are allowed their " pets," and that each crowd had its special and distinctive favourites, fed out of the general "mess"! It was quite touching to see some hulking ruffian loafing about in the sunshine with a tiny kitten in his arms, or to hear the cooing of turtle-doves in some gloomy recess of a filthy cell. Although these incongruities of prison life struck me as being very extraordinary, they passed unnoticed by my companions, who were surprised when I drew their attention to them and observed how much more severe the English prison system is.

After going the round of the " halls" we next visited the workshops. As I told you in a previous chapter, work in a Siberian prison is purely optional ; a man can be as lazy as he likes, or else he can set to and earn a little money at his particular trade, if he has one, and such work is required. There are two kinds of work permitted by the Government—work in the prison itself in the various workshops provided for the different trades, and outdoor work away from the prison. In the Irkutsk prison almost every trade was not only represented but well employed also, for in many of the workshops I was informed the men were so busy with orders on hand that for the moment they could undertake no more. All the work being carried out was for townspeople. Of the money thus earned, a certain percentage goes to the Government, and the rest is divided equally among the men of the atelier.

We visited all the "shops," and it was quite refreshing to see the men hard at work, and working cheerfully together—as well they might, considering that it is to their mutual advantage to do so. They were working evidently under no restraint whatever, for I noticed no guards about. I was told that one could get almost anything made here—for in the "shops" were tailors, hatters, bootmakers, smiths, locksmiths, carpenters, cabinet-makers, cigarette-makers, jewellers, engravers, and even artists; for in the prison, at the time I visited it, were two men convicted of uttering false banknotes, and who, having artistic proclivities, passed their time in painting—the one, portraits from photographs; the other, *bons Dieux*, or the sacred pictures so dear to the Greek Church. I saw the portrait-painter at work in the same room as the cigarette-makers, and much out of place here did the easel and canvas look, almost as much so as the artist himself, in his prison garb, with a large palette and bunch of brushes and mahlstick in his hand. The fellow spoke German fluently, so we had a talk together, as he was not at all reticent, and did not seem to feel his position a little bit. He informed me that he always had as much work to do as he could possibly get through, so he never found the time hang heavily on his hands. This work—which, by the way, was very indifferent—I further learnt, was mostly for local photographers.

The other "artist," whom we subsequently visited, was quite a "swell," for he was in solitary confinement, and had been permitted to fit up his small cell quite as a studio. There were shelves on the walls full of half-completed pictures, a lot of the usual paraphernalia of art lay about, while in one corner hung a large framed oil-painting, a copy of a celebrated picture I knew well through the recently published photogravures of it in London—a beautiful composition, and looking strangely incongruous in so gruesome and dismal a place, for the only light entered by a small, heavily grated window high up near the ceiling. This gentleman, who seemed quite as busy as the portrait-painter, was, however, quite a different character, and as reticent and moody as the other was talkative, for when the director asked him if he did not speak French or German so that I could ask him a few questions, he curtly replied that he

THE PRISON ARTIST

# ГОСУДАРСТВЕННЫЙ
## КРЕДИТНЫЙ БИЛЕТЪ.

Государственный Коммиссія погашенія долговъ размѣниваетъ Государственные Кредитные билеты на звонкую монету:

**пять рублей серебряною или золотою монетою**

Управляющій
Директоръ Кассиръ

ГОДА 1857

№ 36563

ПЯТЬ РУБ. СЕРЕБ.

5 5

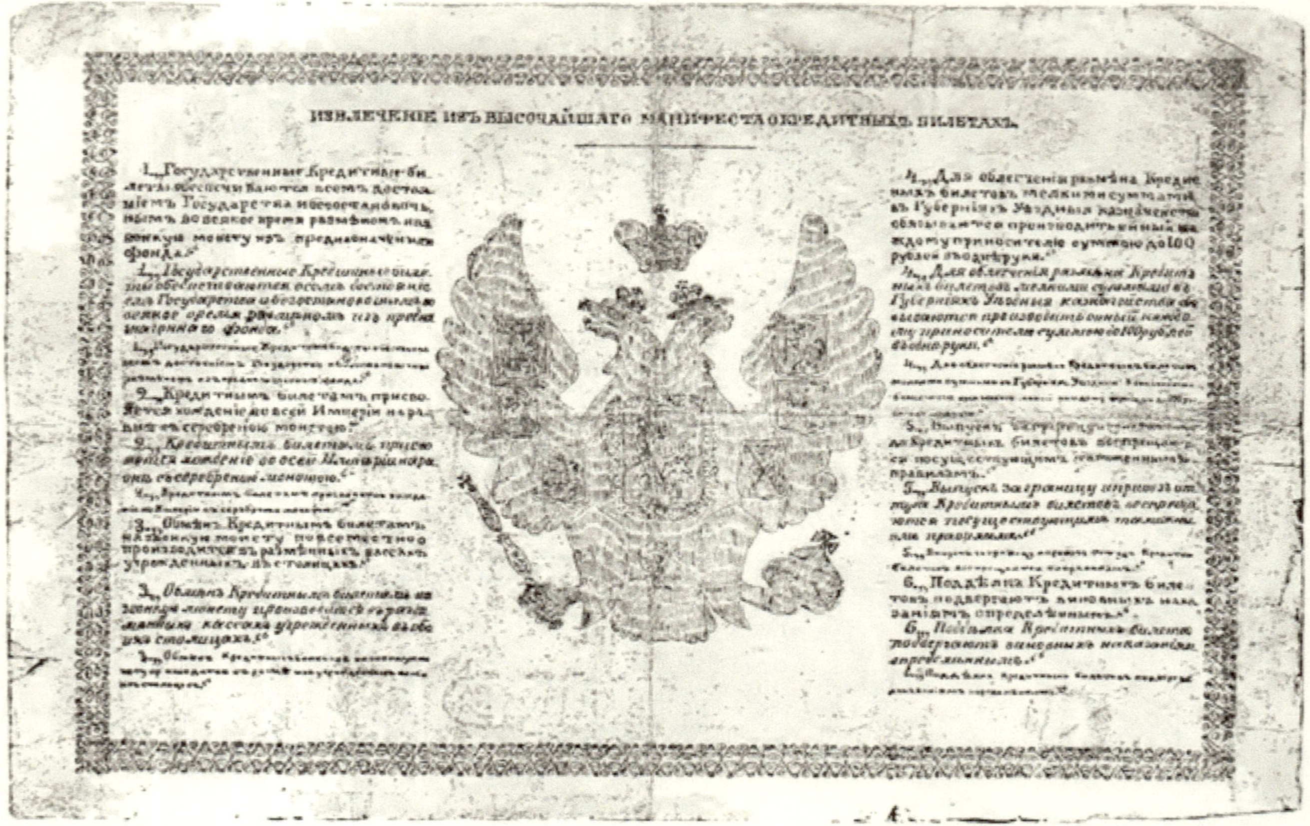
ИЗВЛЕЧЕНІЕ ИЗЪ ВЫСОЧАЙШАГО МАНИФЕСТА О КРЕДИТНЫХЪ БИЛЕТАХЪ.
2. Кредитнымъ билетамъ присвояется хожденіе во всей Имперіи наравнѣ съ серебреною монетою.
3. Обмѣнъ Кредитныхъ билетовъ на звонкую монету повсемѣстно производится въ размѣнныхъ кассахъ учрежденныхъ въ столицахъ.
6. Поддѣлка Кредитныхъ билетовъ подвергаетъ виновныхъ наказаніямъ опредѣленнымъ.

had forgotten whether he ever did or not, for he was now a "number," no longer a man. I afterwards learnt that both these men, though convicted, were not as yet sentenced, and that probably they would be sent for an indefinite number of years to hard labour in one of the Government mines, and that it was only pending their sentence that they were allowed to go on with their painting, though, my informant added, with a smile, they would probably be able to do a little even at the mines if they behaved themselves!

With so much labour of all sorts to be got almost for the asking, it may be imagined how *exploitée* the prison is by local tradesmen, who thus get their work done by these "unfortunates" at probably less than a third of what it would cost them if they employed town labour. I got a large double brass seal made, and engraved at both ends, for less than 2s. 6d., and then, when it was finished, the governor ordered the prisoner who had made it to engrave my initials on my stick into the bargain, which the fellow did without a word of grumbling. He looked very grateful, however, when I slipped a few extra kopeks into his hand afterwards.

The forged banknote which I give in facsimile was the work of a prison artist. All its elaborate pen-and-ink work represents when complete only the sum of five roubles (10s.). Yet for this small amount a long term of imprisonment was risked! (and got).

## CHAPTER XVIII.

### PRISON LIFE IN SIBERIA—*continued*.

Outdoor employment of prisoners—A chat with an employer of convict labour—The "convict's word"—An interview with a celebrated murderess—The criminal madhouse—Political prisoners in solitary confinement — I get permission to paint a picture in one of the cells—End of my visits to the prison.

OUTDOOR employment away from the prison is often granted to prisoners who have been remarked for special good conduct, and they are drafted off either to Government or private works, such as salt or iron workings. Those sent to private works are thus rewarded for exceptionally good behaviour whilst in prison; they get well paid whilst thus employed, and they work side by side with free men, receiving the same pay, and enjoying the same allowances, the only difference being that of course they cannot leave of their own accord. The pay struck me as being exceptionally good, for it averages twenty-five roubles (£3) per month for foremen, and ranging down to four roubles for ordinary labourers. Besides this pay each man receives eighty pounds of flour for himself, and if married forty for his wife, and the same amount for each child from the day of its birth till it is thirteen years of age. Eight roubles per year are also allowed for boots and gloves. Housing is provided by the owners of the works, but the convicts may if they choose live apart on the works at their own expense. At the Government works (not the hard-labour ones) it is very different, for although it is a distinct rise in the prisoner's position to be sent to them, the pay is very poor indeed, being only five kopeks (a little over one penny) per day, and the men are always under the supervision of convoy soldiers. There is no military guard over men working at private works.

I had an interesting interview with the owner of some salt works who largely employs convict labour. He told me that he would far rather employ convicts than ordinary labourers, as they were "more reliable." If a convict gave his "convict's word" to do or not to do a thing, as the case might be, he could rely on his never breaking it, for it would be contrary to the recognized code of prison honour. For instance, he told me, it would often happen, when the gang he had ordered arrived, the *staroster* of it would inform him that such and such prisoners were unreliable, as they had declared their intention of running away at the first opportunity. "But how about the others?" he would ask; "for it would be awkward to find one's self shorthanded at a critical moment." "Oh, the others," would reply the *staroster*, "have given me their 'convict's word' to remain and do their best, so you can rely on them." This system of thus utilizing convict labour is undoubtedly part of a huge scheme for gradually colonizing this vast continent, as round the works small villages gradually spring up.

After visiting the men's quarters we went to the portion reserved for the fair sex, which, beyond being very crowded, offered but little of novelty or interest. Just as we were turning to leave the building, however, the doctor said, "Let's go and see how the baroness is;" so we went back and down a corridor, at the end of which was a door by itself. Before going in I was informed that this was the cell of the famous poisoner, Sofie de Willup, Baroness de Sachs, whose trial, with that of her lover, a groom, some years ago in St. Petersburg, for murdering her second husband by slow poison, was *a cause célèbre*, for it then transpired that her first husband had also died in some mysterious manner. The case was proved to the hilt, I was told, and in England her fate, the gallows, would have been inevitable; but in Russia it was different, for she was a scion of a noble and wealthy house, and her relatives moving in the highest circles. Still, she could not entirely escape punishment of some sort, and she was eventually sent to Siberia for life, nominally to "hard labour at the mines," where a poor and unknown woman would undoubtedly have gone; but the governor of the province she was consigned to was a relative of hers, so she naturally never reached her destination, but remained in the Irkutsk prison as "an invalid." Her lover, being a nobody, was sent to work in chains for the remainder of his life in Saghalien, and is doubtless there still.

In response to a discreet knock by the governor, a female voice from within bade us enter. Imagine my astonishment, after having been told all the lady was, to find myself in a small but comfortably furnished room, with flowers and birds in cages in the window, and books and other "luxuries" lying about in profusion; whilst in a cupboard I noticed the usual extensive wardrobe of a stylish woman.

THE BARONESS.

On a carved bedstead in one corner of this unique prison "cell" lay the invalid, a healthy, not unprepossessing young woman of about thirty years of age; she was dressed in ordinary walking costume, and on hearing our knock had evidently hastily thrown herself on the bed and covered herself with a smart travelling rug, so as to carry out fully her invalid condition. The whole look of the place was certainly the most hollow mockery of justice I had ever seen, and I could not help involuntarily contrasting her surroundings with those of the poor wretches in other parts of the building, whose crimes were probably not half as bad as hers. The lady languidly gave us her hand to shake, and in reply to the doctor's question as to how "Madame la baronne" felt, said she felt a little better.

"By the way," said the governor, "you speak English, or French, or German, don't you, Baronne?"

"Oh yes," she replied, "all three."

So I was formally introduced, and had my first conversation with a real live murderess. It was rather embarrassing at the commencement, for I hardly knew what to say; but she helped me out of the difficulty by asking in very fair English how dear old London looked, and how long it was since I had left it, etc., and we ended by having quite a cosmopolitan chat together, first in English, then in French, and gradually drifting into German, as, so to speak, we wandered about Europe, talking of the different places we knew, whilst I meanwhile was making a rough sketch of the room and its occupant. She told me, to my surprise, that she hoped to be free in a couple of months, when, although she would not be allowed to leave Siberia, she could live on her means (which, I believe, were ample) in some designated village or town. "After six years of 'prison' life," she added, "any place will be an agreeable change for me."

On leaving the baroness the doctor suggested that the criminal madhouse might interest me, so we all adjourned to a neighbouring building standing within a high stockade. The unfortunate inmates were evidently well looked after, for the place was as warm as toast and as clean as possible. There were no dangerous madmen there when we visited it, so the padded rooms were empty. It gave one more the impression of a hospital than a madhouse. As we entered, a wretched-looking little individual rushed up to the director and loudly complained about his being still detained there because the governor-general of Irkutsk refused to pay him what he owed him. The director agreed with him that it was very unfair his being there under the circumstances, but assured him that the matter was receiving the attention it deserved, and doubtless in a few days he would be permitted to leave. This seemed to satisfy the poor fellow, and he withdrew, after thanking us all for having honoured him with our visit.

In another of the wards amongst the patients was an actor (absurdly like Willard). Immediately he caught sight of us he ran up to the doctor, and in excited tones informed him that he had not yet received the thirty thousand roubles, which were owing to him for his last performance. The doctor pacified him with the assurance that the money would shortly be forthcoming, but had not yet been received by the officials, and further, to humour him, asked how the performance for his "benefit" was progressing. In reply, the fellow gave us, in the centre of the room, what evidently was part of a scene he had once acted in, and went through some extraordinary performance, alternately weeping, tearing his hair, and grovelling on the floor, whilst uttering incoherent sentences, and then rushing about as though with a sword in his hand and singing operatic airs. It was a painful rather than an amusing sight, and one which I shall not easily forget—the poor half-witted chap in the centre of the large room declaiming to an imaginary audience, and all round, sitting or standing by their beds, were the other lunatics, watching his movements in rapt amazement.

We then went back to the prison, as I expressed a wish to see the prisoners in the solitary, or *sekrétene*, cells. This was the only part of the building which was really like a prison. And very gloomy and depressing was it; no less than three heavily barred

A "POLITICAL."
*(From a Government photo.)*          [*To face p. 295.*

iron doors had to be unlocked before we reached the corridor where these cells were situated. A warder is on duty here, I was told, night and day, for there were several political prisoners, and the rest were the most desperate characters. In each door was a little hole about the size of a sixpence, through which could be seen the interior of the cell. I had a peep into all; it was almost like looking at some caged wild beasts, the clanking of the heavy chains they wore on their hands and feet heightening the illusion. Some of the prisoners had, I was informed, been there for years, and only were allowed out for exercise for an hour a day, and were not permitted to mingle with the other prisoners. It was easy to distinguish which were the "politicals," for they were in ordinary civilian costume and had no chains on, as far as I could see. Most of them were quite young men, one being a mere lad, his curly hair and good-looking face not giving him the appearance of being so dangerous a political character as to necessitate such elaborate precautions being taken to prevent his escape. To my astonishment—for I had always read to the contrary—I noticed that all these political prisoners were not only allowed books to read, but in most cases were smoking also, and in every instance had their own mattresses and bedding; so their cells, at any rate, looked cleaner and more cheerful than those of the ordinary criminals, to whom filth seemed indifferent.

As we were crossing the quadrangle on our way out, a prisoner came up and offered to sell me a horsehair chain he had made. The fact of the governor and other officials being present did not seem to matter a bit, so as the work was curious I bought it of him, and as I had no small money about me, he took a rouble note and went and got change from some other prisoner!

This my first visit to the prison was followed by many others, and I made a heap of sketches; in fact, I fancy I got to be looked upon as quite an *habitué* of the gruesome place. I even obtained permission to make a painting of a prisoner in one of the solitary cells, and had a whole day's work at it under the supervision of a warder, a break in the poor wretch's awful existence which he will probably remember for many a long year, whilst probably wondering what the *Angliski Gospodin* could have seen worthy of being painted in so dreary a place.

On the morning of my last visit to the prison, when I went to fetch away my canvas and paint-box, I was rather surprised to notice as I drove up a tall, well-dressed woman walking up and down, accompanied by a gaoler, in the sunshine, outside the gates, in front of the group of warders and soldiers who were always lolling about smoking and chatting on the benches against the wall. On getting nearer, I found it was my murderess friend the baroness. We shook hands in the most unconstrained manner, and she told

VISITING DAY IN THE IRKUTSK PRISON.—"SWEETHEARTS AND WIVES.

[To face p. 236.

Irkoutsk,
February the 18th
in the year 1891

Honoured Sir!

You asked me to send you my photograph, and I make myself the honour, to send it you already to-day.

I have been much pleased to make, here in remote Sibiri, the acquaintance of so amiable an Englishman. It reminded me so lively, of former times, which seem to me, "long, long ago", when on my many journeys through Germany, France and England, most of my acquaintances and friends, were English people. I am sorry to say that I, in these last five years, not having had the opportunity, to speak English, find difficulty, to lead an English conversation, although the English language was the first I spoke; having an English governess, more than ten years, and I spoke it more fluently, than german. But in such way of life, were one scarcely was one thouroughly educated soul, it is not astonishing, if we forget most what we knew.

Permit me to say a few words, about relations which meet here the "exiled." The treatment here is humane and good, if we know how to behave our selves, if we are polite and submissive. The officers are almost all, educated men, and treat us so, how we show ourselves worthy. Who knows the way how to ask politely, never hears an unfriendly answer. Of course, who shows himself uncivil, rude and who thinks of prescribing and ordering, never to will be treated well. Who complains of rude treatment here, owes it to himself. All are eager to help the "exciled" to make his way, of course we must show ourselves worthy of it. All the same, the life in prison, and of exile, is a hard life, for us educated people, for not *that* is so hard, what we suffer phisicaly as what we suffer moraly. It is a life full of grief, humoliation, loneliness and resign. Most of all the shade of disgrace, that is cased on honour and name, is dificult to endure, and never can it be overcome. No one sees and knows, who of the exiled suffer by fault, or who by fate, and the only word of "exiled and sentenced" lie like a dark shade upon the heart.

Perhaps, honoured Sir, we meet again in life — and I should be glad to renew your acquaintance under more lyky circomstances.

Pray remember sometimes kindly one, whom a fatal destiny has made out of a favourite of fortune, a lonely, exiled and unhappy being.

I have the honour to sign respectfully

Sofie Wilupp
neé: Baronne de Sass

P.S. If you wish it, and you will give me your adress in England, I can sometime send you for your gazette a discription of my journy, from Russia, and of the mode of life I make acquaintance with here; and of life and people in Kourland, from where I am a native.

me in French that she was taking her usual "constitutional" after breakfast. We then had quite a long talk together, for she had news to give me. In a month she would be free again, and was going to live at a little place called Oussolić, near Irkutsk, where she intended building a house for herself. She then told me a lot more about her future plans—I almost felt inclined to ask if they included any more husbands! Whilst thus chatting, the warders in no way interfered with us; they did not seem to consider it in any way strange my speaking to a prisoner. Before leaving her she said she would be glad to write to me if I ever cared to hear from her, and would also send her photo if I liked. My murderess friend was evidently "smitten"! I gave her my address, and, to my surprise, a few days later received the letter, of which I give a facsimile, and also enclosing her photo, which I afterwards learnt she had had taken expressly for me. With this somewhat novel adventure ended my visits to the prison.

# CHAPTER XIX.

## IRKUTSK—*continued*.

A gold-caravan—Particulars as to the gold-mining industry of Siberia—The Foundling Hospital—The fire-brigade—Celebration of the Czar's birthday—Living in Irkutsk.

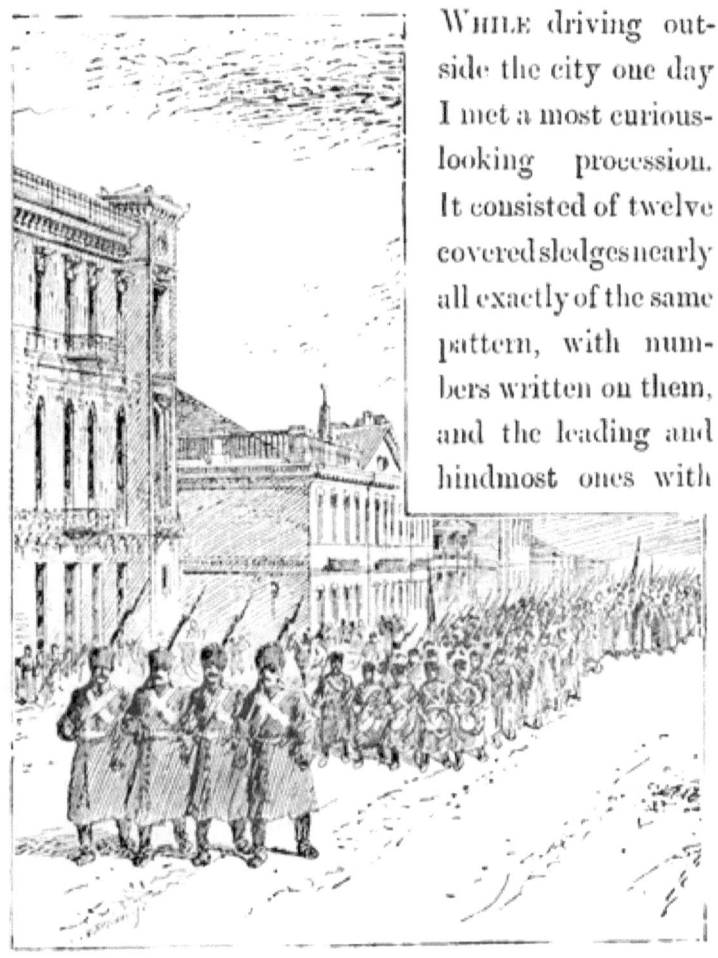

THE HIGH STREET, IRKUTSK.

WHILE driving outside the city one day I met a most curious-looking procession. It consisted of twelve covered sledges nearly all exactly of the same pattern, with numbers written on them, and the leading and hindmost ones with large lanterns fixed on the roof; in several of them I noticed were soldiers with rifles in readiness. The effect was so peculiar that on my return I made it my business to find out what it was all about. I was informed that what I had seen was a "gold-caravan" *en route* for Russia. My informant then, in reply to my questions, gave me a lot of interesting particulars about the gold-mining industry of Siberia which was quite new to me, and will doubtless be of interest to others. He told me that all gold found in Siberia has to be sold immediately to the Government, who buys it at the current price of St. Petersburg. A mine-owner is not permitted to sell to a private individual, nor even to have the smallest amount in his possession beyond a certain time. If he should desire to keep a small nugget, say, as a curiosity, he must *buy* it from the Government, who will then give him a special permit authorizing him its possession. All gold has to be delivered at the owner's expense at the Government smelting-houses, where it is made into ingots and then sent by caravan to St. Petersburg, the cost of smelting and carriage being also charged to the owner. The primary charges are, therefore, somewhat considerable. Gold is sold at per "pood," a pood being equivalent to thirty-six pounds English. At the then rate of exchange, a pood was worth 15,616 roubles (8 rs. 40 kopeks = £1, February, 1891); out of this must be deducted the cost of transport (usually per post)

P

to the smelting-house, which is considerable, and the further cost per caravan and rail to St. Petersburg, which amounts to forty roubles per pood. The Government keeps back for assaying, smelting, etc., 416 roubles per pood on all gold from the Lena mines, and 132 roubles in gold sent from the Amour district. I naturally asked the reason of the great difference in the charges against the two districts, and was told that in the Amour district, where only the width of the river separates the Russian from the Chinese empire, the temptation to sell the gold across the frontier would be very great were the Russian Government duties excessive; so it is for that reason they are so much reduced. The Lena mines are too far away for anything of the sort to be feared.

Through the courtesy of the officials I was enabled to spend a very interesting morning at the Government smelting-house, and witnessed several operations, to me very novel, from the unpacking of the gold as it is received from the mine-owners, its weighing, smelting, and eventual running off into ingots. Over £10,000 worth of gold was operated on, so I had a good opportunity of seeing the entire *modus operandi*. I noticed, by the way, that all the assaying instruments were English, and by a London maker. Afterwards I was shown, in the "safe," ingots to the amount of nearly half a million (£500,000), some of them so heavy that I could hardly lift them, all of which had the owner's mark on them, with date, weight, etc.

An enormous quantity of gold annually leaves Siberia for St. Petersburg. Last year, I am informed, the weight amounted to 1295 poods, or 46,620 lbs. Each caravan, such as the one I had seen, by which it is sent as far as the railway at Tiumen, consists of twelve sledges or tarantasses, according to the season, and is accompanied by two officers and six soldiers, which is certainly not a big guard, considering the immense value of their charge, for each conveyance contains 25 poods (or 900 lbs. of solid gold), so the entire caravan carries no less than 10,800 lbs. of the precious metal.

To my surprise, I learnt that no Siberian goldsmith is allowed to buy or work in gold, the penalty for breaking this law being very severe. In spite, however, of these regulations, I hear that a lot of illicit gold-buying and even goldsmith's work exists; for, as is always the case when such stringent precautions are taken, there are weak points in the law, which serve as loopholes to the many people whose consciences do not prick them, with the result that a deal of Siberian gold crosses the frontier into China, where it finds a ready market.

Amongst the many imposing buildings in the city there was one which struck me as being particularly fine. On inquiry I was informed that it was the Foundling Hospital (*Vospititelni Dom*).

I had read so much about these unique Russian institutions, that my curiosity was aroused. Without any difficulty whatever I obtained permission to visit it, and I was very much interested in all I was shown, for I had never seen anything of the kind before. It was, of course, a *replica* on a smaller scale of the colossal institutions of the kind in St. Petersburg and Moscow and other Russian cities, which are so ably described in "Murray." As their *raison d'être* may not be generally known, a few extracts from the work just named may be of interest.

In speaking of these hospitals at St. Petersburg and Moscow he says—

" The fate of illegitimate children and the responsibilities of their parents have been, and in all probability will remain, one of the most difficult subjects for legislation in most countries. But though some laws regarding it are necessary, there can be no question that natural affection, nay, even common humanity, should inculcate upon those who can possibly raise the means the duty of bringing them up at their own expense. The facilities afforded by this hospital militate, we think, against this principle. . . .

" We cannot help thinking that a visit to this remarkable establishment—the St. Petersburg one—cannot fail to excite very serious reflections in the mind of the English traveller. If the institution is to be viewed in the light of a charity, it is charity upon a very questionable principle; but be this as it may, this vast breeding-cage will give visitors a very clear idea of the power and immense resources of the State. . . . Though this is called a foundling hospital, it is in reality a general receptacle for all children, who are received up to a certain age without exception, it being entirely left to the option of the parents to state their names and conditions, and to contribute or not to the future support of the child. . . . If a boy be left by his parents without any accompanying deposit, he is brought up for the army, and, unless he displays very unusual mental powers, is destined for life to serve as a common soldier; if, on the contrary, a certain sum is left with him, he will become an officer. Thus the boys brought up in this institution become in all cases the property of the State, and furnish a constant supply of recruits for the various gradations of military service. . . . The majority of the girls, beyond a common and useful education in their own language, are employed solely in manual labour, the produce of which goes partly to the funds of the institution and is partly put by for them, to form their marriage portion."

I do not think I was ever in a cleaner-looking place than the Irkutsk Foundling Hospital. The floors actually rivalled the walls in whiteness, and the neat costume worn by the wet-nurses enhanced an effect which was as pretty as it was unique. Each nurse, I was informed, has charge of two infants, and I noticed in several instances the woman walking about with the two babies at the same time, one on each arm. Considering how many children there were in the place, the rooms were remarkably quiet, for I had quite expected to hear the usual deafening "nursery row" going on—a row which, though doubtless very amusing to mothers and nurses, never had much attraction for me. There was nothing particularly striking about the interior of the building, which consisted of several very large and lofty rooms; in the centre of each of these, which probably contained about six cots, was a sort of high table or desk with a ledge round it, and on which the babies were dressed, or, rather, tightly packed up in swaddling clothes—a curious process which gave them the appearance of miniature mummies all exactly of the same pattern, for the rolling always seemed done on a sort of systematic principle. I was much astonished to learn that many of the wet-nurses were the mothers of the children they were nursing, for they are often so appointed if they wish it, when there is no reason to the contrary. The infants are usually kept in the hospital for about six weeks, and are then sent out to nurse amongst the peasants round about, for which a small monthly sum is paid by the institution; and then when they reach a certain age,

"About six years old, they are taken from their foster parents (what a parting this must be to thousands every year!), the girls to St. Petersburg for their education, and the boys to a branch establishment at Gatshina" (Murray).

Of course the Irkutsk foundlings are brought up and remain in Siberia.

Amongst the many other charitable institutions here, I also visited one of the children's homes (*dedski prioutt*), where orphans of both sexes are received up to a certain age, and educated and brought up free. Also the "Home" for the aged and infirm who, through no fault of their own, find themselves stranded at the end of their lives—a "Home" unique in its way, being neither a workhouse nor an almshouse as we understand it in England. What most impressed me in these institutions was the marvellous cleanliness and order which existed everywhere.

The fire-brigade is quite a big affair here, as well it may be after the terrible experiences of the inhabitants in 1879, and, as is the case in all Siberian cities, large watch-towers are placed in all the most prominent positions, from which watchmen can discern any outbreak, and then give the alarm by means of a big bell; whilst in the stations below

IN THE COURTYARD OF A FIRE STATION, IRKUTSK.

the men, horses, manuals, and water-carts are in constant readiness, and can turn out in wonderfully short time—in fact, so smart are they, that had I not seen a proof of it on one occasion, I could hardly have believed it possible to harness the horses and get away so quickly. There is a steam fire-engine at Irkutsk, and I was gratified to note that it was by an English firm, Shand and Mason. Very proud the men seem of it, too, for it shone all over like a looking-glass, and is evidently kept in tip-top condition. In this distant Siberian city its familiar form seemed like a connecting-link with far-away London.

I was much struck with the number of overhead wires one sees in Irkutsk, and on inquiry learnt they were mostly telephone wires, and that all the Government offices and most of the big business houses are connected by this means. The wires are worked by a private company, and the charges are not excessive considering, the cost per year, including hire and fixing of machine, etc., being only twenty-five roubles (£3). Irkutsk is also in direct communication with a St. Petersburg Central News Agency, and every item of news of importance is received here by telegram as soon as it is known at the Russian office. In this way I learnt of the last Whitechapel murder on the very evening of the day it had occurred, for everybody at the club was talking of it, such an impression did it make even right away here in the centre of Asia. Talking of clubs, there are two really well-arranged ones here, one a military, the other a merchants', though neither of them can come up to the one at Krasnoiarsk in my opinion.

The museum, which I visited one morning, well repaid me for the couple of hours I spent there, for the five rooms contain, besides many valuable specimens of Siberian and Mongolian curiosities and mammoth bones, a complete stuffed collection of

Siberian animals and birds. The rooms are also used for the periodical meetings of the St. Petersburg Imperial Geographical Society, of which Irkutsk is the Eastern Siberian section.

As far as outdoor amusement is concerned, the principal place during the winter months is the skating-rink, in the principal street, which is the favourite resort of the *jeunesse dorée* here, and from four till six of an afternoon the ice is generally crowded with pretty girls and smart-looking officers and civilians, most of them excellent skaters. A band, which plays twice a week, and fireworks and illuminations on certain evenings, add also considerably to its attractions. Beyond the clubs there is very little in the way of public amusements, for the only theatre was burnt down two years ago and has not yet been rebuilt, although it is proposed to do so shortly on a magnificent scale. Meanwhile, amateur dramatic performances occasionally take place in a large hall transformed for the nonce into a short of theatre. I was present at one of these "performances," and although I understood but very little of what was said, I could not help coming to the conclusion that Irkutsk is not bubbling over with amateur histrionic talent, for the show was very tame and uninteresting.

It is said that in Russia at least one-half of the year is given up to religious or other holidays, and I can quite believe it, for scarcely a week passed

without a *prasnik* of some sort occurring during it;
so much so that my astonishment is that any business
can be carried on successfully with such continuous

THE GOVERNOR-GENERAL'S HOUSE, IRKUTSK.

interruptions; for on these holidays all the shops are
closed, and nothing whatever goes on all day except
church-bell ringing and subsequent parading of the
streets by the towns-people in their well-used holiday

attire. The most important of all these *fêtes* occurred whilst I was in Irkutsk, March 10 (February 26, Old Style), being the anniversary of the Czar's birthday. The city was gaily decorated for the occasion, and as it was quite a warm spring-like day the streets were thronged with people, and presented a most animated appearance. After the customary thanksgiving service in the different churches, a royal salute was fired, and a parade of the garrison took place in front of the cathedral, in the presence of the governor-general and his staff. The troops, who were without their rifles, performed several evolutions with a smartness which quite surprised me, for, although undoubtedly a serviceable-looking lot of men, they had never given me the impression of having any smartness in them. After marching past, first in quarter column and then double column of companies, they were formed up in line, the wheeling being remarkably steady, and the proceedings ended with a cheer for his most holy Majesty the Czar of all the Russias. One sees so little of the military in Siberia, except when they are off duty, that it is seldom one has an opportunity of judging what "stuff" they are made of.

Living in Irkutsk is not cheap—rather the reverse, I thought, after my Krasnoiarsk and Yeniseisk experiences—for, in spite of rent, food, and labour being as cheap as anywhere else in Siberia, the charges at all the hotels were as high as they would have been anywhere in Europe. One could understand it if everything had to be brought from a great distance; but considering that Irkutsk is the centre of a huge producing district, it ought to be one of the cheapest places to live in rather than the contrary. Still, it is a city well worth seeing, and had I not visited it I should certainly have missed the real "life" of Siberia.

STREET SCENE, IRKUTSK.

A BIT ON THE ROAD TO LAKE BAIKAL.

## CHAPTER XX.

### FROM IRKUTSK TO THE MONGOL CHINESE FRONTIER.

*My journey to Kiakhta, the city of the tea princes—Across Lake Baikal on the ice—Interesting experiences.*

THE weather was beginning to get so warm and the snow so rapidly disappearing that I made up my mind to continue my route to the frontier without delay, as I was anxious to cross Lake Baikal on the ice whilst there was still the opportunity. True, I had been informed that there was really no necessity to hurry, that it could often be crossed thus even as late as May; but such opportunities were doubtless exceptional, and this year the season showed every sign of being an early one, so I felt there was no time to be lost if I wished to see this vast inland sea in its winter garb, and I had heard so much about the wondrous beauties of this enormous expanse of ice and the novel experiences of the journey across, that I decided not to remain any longer in Irkutsk, but to push on to Kiakhta, the frontier city, and finish up my work there. Moreover, I had very positive confirmation of my views, for shortly after the news reached us that the ice on the Angara river had commenced to break up, and that for many miles the river was already clear.

I now learnt that I could not go the whole way from Irkutsk to Kiakhta by sledge, as the snow always ends some miles before the frontier is reached, and the remainder of the journey has to be made in a conveyance on wheels. I was advised, therefore, to do the snow-covered part of the road on a cheap, open sledge, which I could sell for a few roubles at the last post-house. So my big sledge, in which I had travelled so many thousand versts, had to be disposed of, and I was fortunate enough to find an enterprising dealer who took it off my hands at a fair price, probably on the off-chance of making a good thing out of it next winter. My next concern was to buy the cheap open sledge for the journey; this I had no difficulty in procuring, and for eight roubles (less than £1) I got a big, awkward-looking vehicle, not unlike a huge clothes-basket covered with sacking—a great contrast to the luxurious *paroska* I had hitherto been travelling in. Still, it was in itself a welcome sign that, for me, the long Siberian winter was nearly past, and that I was soon to be *en route* for the sunny South.

My preparations did not take long, for the journey to Kiakhta only occupies two days, and on the evening of March 11 I left the gay capital of Eastern Siberia for the Mongol frontier. I had been advised to start at night, so as to reach the lake—which is only sixty versts off—early in the morning, and accomplish the crossing by daylight. I had not thought it necessary to hamper myself with a servant for so short a journey, so was travelling quite alone.

For many miles after leaving the city the road lay along the ice in the very centre of the river Angara, and as it was quite a warm evening and the track very smooth, the motion was so pleasant that the idea of perchance the road ending abruptly never entered my head, and it was quite with a feeling of regret that I saw the horses at last turned towards the bank and we were on land once more. But only by the wildest stretch of the imagination could it have been considered a sledge-track, my driver having actually to search for bits of snow here and there, and make for them as well as he could across the intervening mud; in fact, it seemed absurd attempting it in a sledge. However, we managed somehow to reach the first station, and found the yard full of *tarantasses* (the summer posting carriages, which I shall have occasion to describe further on), which had just arrived with travellers bound for Irkutsk; my sledge looking strangely out of place among the tall, unwieldy vehicles. The postmaster shook his head, and said he very much doubted whether he ought to let me proceed, except on wheels; eventually he only let me have horses on condition that I did not start till just before daybreak, so as to reach the bad part when it was light. I shall long remember that "bad part," for I don't think I was ever on such a road before in my life, even in a wheeled carriage, and certainly hope never to be on such a one again in a sledge. Many times I got out and tramped along in the mud out of sheer compassion for the horses, who were "pulling their hearts out" to get the unwieldy sledge through the awful quagmire, for it was nothing else.

It was a lovely morning, with every promise of another spring-like day, when we once more sighted the river Angara. But to my astonishment, this was no silent expanse of ice as when I had seen it on the previous night, for before me was a broad, swiftly running river, its clear limpid waters sparkling like crystal in the bright rays of the rising sun, while on its surface no trace of ice could I discern.

It was a beautiful and impressive scene, though positively startling withal, to see a moving river once more after the dreary ice-bound wastes one had got accustomed to look at during the past four months, and I could scarcely realize that this was the same river along which I had travelled on the ice so few miles back. The Angara here must have been at least as wide as the Thames at London Bridge, the opposite banks, which were clothed with dense pine forests, rising precipitously from the very edge of the

THE RIVER ANGARA NEAR LAKE BAIKAL.

water. On account of the pureness of the atmosphere everything appeared so much nearer than it really was, that at first I could hardly believe that what I took to be curious little bushes on the opposite side were in reality big full-grown trees. I could not help thinking that if the scene is so weirdly beautiful even during the winter months, what must it be when

Q

all these grand hills are clothed with the gorgeous verdure of an Asiatic summer? Then indeed must the effect be almost of surpassing beauty, and one which must fully justify its title of "the most beautiful river in the world." Considering the importance of the Angara, its resources are undoubtedly as yet in their infancy, for this mighty river is the only outlet of the waters of Lake Baikal, being, curiously enough, the only river which flows *out of it*, and is, as may be seen by a glance at the map, the big connecting link of the whole of the huge watershed of Central Asia—a watershed so vast and extended that in comparison with it that of the Mississippi and Missouri pales into insignificance.

Unfortunately, however, there is an impediment to the entire utilization of this great waterway which up to the present has defied the combined ideas of some of the greatest practical engineers of the world, for not far from where the Angara leaves Lake Baikal it forms a big rapid over two miles in length, and before gaining its subsequent level actually falls over a ledge of rock which bars its entire width. It is this huge "step" which must be removed before the river can be entirely used for navigation. Engineers for years past have been studying the possibility of removing this obstacle, but as yet nothing has been attempted. Meanwhile, however, that Siberian magnate, M. Siberiakoff, has undertaken the task of making the river navigable the whole way for steamers running from Irkutsk to Lake Baikal, and he proposes carrying out his scheme on a chain-hauling principle on the plans of the Swedish system. Whether or not this will be successful on a Siberian river remains, of course, to be seen.

The navigation of the river Selenga, Lake Baikal, and the river Angara is at present only carried on by nine steamers, only three of which ply between Irkutsk and the rapids. All these vessels, except one, are owned by Russians. The one exception is owned and worked by an Englishman resident in Irkutsk, Mr. Charles Lee, a gentleman to whom I have already referred. The Russian steamers offer but little of interest, having been purchased in Russia, and only put together in Siberia. Not so, however, the English one, which was not only built and launched at Irkutsk, but every portion of her construction, from her engines to her outer plates and rivets, was made in Irkutsk under the supervision of Mr. Lee, who is a practical engineer of great ability. This, as being, I believe, the first attempt at actual shipbuilding (not merely putting together) in Siberia, is of great interest, and more especially so when one learns that the credit of the enterprise is due to an Englishman; not the least interesting part of it being that this was Mr. Lee's first experience in shipbuilding, and that the whole of the work was done by convict labour; also that the ship, when finished, was launched sideways, in itself a somewhat novel feat.

We now followed the banks of the river the whole way; it widened more, and when we at length sighted the lake, it must have been considerably over a mile in width. Here, right in the centre of the seething rapids, is the celebrated "Chaman" stone, a huge rock which from time immemorial has withstood the tremendous rush of the waters round it. It is the subject of many legends amongst the peasantry, one being that on the day it is at length carried away, the waters of Lake Baikal will escape and inundate the surrounding country. Without attaching any faith to such legends, there are many people in Irkutsk who would regard with unfeigned dread any tampering with the Angara rapids, and who believe that the rocks which cause them alone hold the waters of mighty Lake Baikal in check, and that the day they ceased to exist an awful disaster would happen.

I was prepared now for any surprises, after the transformation that had so startled me in the early morning; so when a bend in the road brought us in full view of this vast inland sea, I was not astonished to see that it was still held in the icy grasp of the Siberian winter. The ice commenced again at the very mouth of the Angara, a most extraordinary phenomenon, for it was as though it had been cut away by man to allow of the escape of the imprisoned waters. From one side of the stream to the other the line of ice was as straight as if it had been ruled. The part of the lake we had now reached is the narrowest end; the distance across it here from shore to shore being about thirty miles, though the great height of the mountains on the opposite side makes it look much narrower. Our road now lay along the shore, a sort of rocky beach, reminding me very much of bits of Devonshire I know well. Under the lofty cliffs ice and snow

LISTVINITZ, ON LAKE BAIKAL.

became more plentiful, so my driver no longer had to search for a likely sledging track, and for the next few miles, till we reached the post station, we went along splendidly. The road in one place left the shore for a short distance, and went right across a sort of little harbour crowded with shipping; in fact, we actually had to dodge in and out of the vessels, and duck our heads to avoid the ropes and spars.

My driver evidently knew the place well, for we went right through the sort of fleet at full gallop, and a few minutes later reached the quaint little village of Liestvinitz, the point at which the journey across the lake is commenced. And after I had had a good sluice in a bucket of cold water, I was soon comfortably settled at breakfast in one of the cleanest post-houses I had yet seen. A real square meal, followed by a good cigar, put me in the right sort of trim to fully appreciate the novel experiences in store for me, and when I gave the order to start, I was lounging back in my sledge literally basking in the genial sunshine, prepared to enjoy myself to the very utmost. Try and imagine what it would be like starting from the Lord Warden Hotel at Dover on a warm, spring-like morning, with the intention of *driving* over to Calais or Boulogne, and you will have some idea of this part of my journey.

The opposite shore for which I was " bound " was quite invisible ; and the ice, owing to its smoothness and the unusual absence of snow on its surface, almost presented the appearance of a very calm sea under the bright blue morning sky.

Lake Baikal, or, as it is called by Russians, "the Holy Sea of Siberia," is one of the largest fresh-water lakes in the world. Its elevation is 1500 feet above the level of the sea. This magnificent sheet of water covers an area of 12,444 square miles, equal to sixty times that of the Lake of Geneva, and is 420 miles in length, and forty in breadth in the widest part. The principal characteristics of this big inland sea are its great depth, the severe and sudden storms which rage upon it, and the curious fact that seals are annually caught in it to a great extent. That this immense lake owes its origin to volcanic agencies has, I think, never been doubted; its enormous depth alone carries out this supposition, for in parts, where

A LAKE BAIKAL STEAMER.

lines of 5000 feet and 6000 feet have been used, no bottom has been found, while in most places its average depth is 5404 feet. I hear that it is said in Irkutsk that it is only on Baikal that "a man learns first to pray from his heart," for so unexpectedly do its awful hurricanes arise, that no one can tell, however promising may be the outlook when starting, under what conditions the opposite shore will be reached. Of course I had no opportunity of judging for myself, but I heard anything but good accounts of the three steamers employed for the journey, which usually takes about six hours under favourable circumstances. Other remarkable features of Lake Baikal are the marvellous transparency of its water and the rapidity with which it freezes when winter sets in. The appearance of the ice on the lake depends entirely on the weather at the time the water congealed. If the surface was then much agitated, the ice everywhere will present a broken appearance like waves, plainly showing how sudden and irresistible was the icy grasp of the Siberian winter. I am informed that along the coast the curious phenomenon has often been noticed of *frozen waves*, the curl of the water and even the foam being plainly distinguishable in the solid mass. I was fortunate in finding the ice perfectly smooth; it had evidently been a dead calm at the time the frost set in.

The road the whole way is indicated by means of a double row of pine saplings stuck at intervals in the ice—a curious effect being thus produced, not unlike an endless miniature boulevard stretching away till it is lost in the distance. I could not help noticing the way the horses are shod for the work: huge spikes are fastened to their shoes, which, as they gallop along, splinter the ice in all directions, but give them a firm foothold on its treacherous surface. In a very short time after leaving picturesque

Liestvenitz we were well out in the open, and tearing along at the horses' top speed, the motion being simply delightful. For about a mile from the shore the ice had a thin layer of snow over it, but we gradually left this sort of dazzling white carpet, and at length reached the clear ice, when I saw around

CROSSING LAKE BAIKAL.

me the most wonderful and bewitching sight I ever beheld. Owing to the marvellous transparency of the water, the ice presented everywhere the appearance of polished crystal, and, although undoubtedly of great thickness, was so colourless that it was like passing over space. It gave me at first quite an uncanny feeling to look over the side of the sledge down into the black abyss beneath; this feeling, however, gradually changed to one of fascination, till at last I found it positively difficult to withdraw my gaze from the awful depths, with nothing but this sheet of crystal between me and eternity. I believe that most travellers, on crossing the lake on the ice for the first time, experience the same weird and fascinating influence. About half-way across I stopped to make a sketch and take some photographs. It was no easy matter, as I found on getting out of the sledge, for the ice was so slippery that in spite of my having felt snow-boots on I could hardly stand. The death-like silence of the surroundings reminded me not a little of my experiences in the ice of the Kara Sea. This wonderful stillness was occasionally broken, however, by curious sounds, as though big guns were being fired at some little distance. They were caused by the cracking of the ice here and there. I was told that in some parts of the lake were huge fissures, through which the water could be seen. It is for this reason that it is always advisable to do the journey by daylight.

We reached Moufshkaya, on the opposite coast, exactly four and a half hours after leaving Liestvenitz, the horses having done the whole distance of over thirty miles with only two stoppages of a few minutes each. It was evidently an easy bit of work for them, as they seemed as fresh when we drew up in the post-yard as when they started in the morning.

THE KUPETSKI TRACK.

## CHAPTER XXI.

### FROM IRKUTSK TO THE MONGOL CHINESE FRONTIER—
*continued.*

The road from Lake Baikal to Krakhta — The " Kupetski track "—Incidents on the way—I change my sledge for a tarantass—Exciting adventures—Arrival at Troitzkosavsk, the business surburb of Kiakhta.

FROM Moufshkaya to Kiakhta I had the choice of two roads—one, the regular Government post-road, which passes through Verchni Udinsk, and then branches off to the frontier; the other, a private track made by the merchant princes of Kiakhta, which goes straight there without touching at any town, thus saving at least two days' journey. This road, I had been informed,

could be used without any special permission, so, after
my recent experiences of Siberian posting, I did not
hesitate which of the two to go by, especially as I had
been told that the " Kupetski track," or merchants'
route, was by far the more picturesque, while Verchni
Udinsk and the few scattered villages on the post-
road offered but the usual monotony of Siberian travel,
which I knew only too well. I was well repaid for
my choice; for not only did the road pass through
some magnificent mountain and forest scenery, but the
post-houses, with only two exceptions, were better
than I had usually found on the Government roads.

For many miles after leaving the lake the road
passed through a narrow gorge with high mountains
and dense pine forest on either side. Night was
coming on, and in the deepening gloom around me,
whence issued the sound of a rushing torrent, the
effect was very weird. Here the snow lay thick, so
there was no doubt about the practicability of
sledging, and we got along very well; but we did
not reach the next post-house till it was quite dark.
After but a very short delay, just to get fresh horses,
I started again. The night was so black that had it
not been for the snow on the road it would have been
a most difficult matter to find it at all; as it was,
we shortly after had a slight accident. In one part
of the road, where it was exceptionally narrow, one
of the horses somehow got out of the track and fell
into a deep hole full of snow. The other two

sagacious animals fortunately had the instinct to stop, or we might have had an awkward time had they started kicking. The yemschik was evidently used to these little *contretemps*, for the incident did not seem to put him out very much, and we soon got the half-buried brute on *terra firma* again. It occurred to me that all such incidents might not end equally well, so I decided to wait in the next post-house till daybreak, as the road seemed to get darker and darker, and more and more uneven. On reaching the station, however, one look was sufficient; it was so infested with cockroaches and other vermin that rather than spend the night in it I determined to push on at all hazards. So uninhabitable, in fact, was the place that I positively could not remain in it even while the horses were being got ready.

After leaving this station the road appeared to get more sandy and with less snow on it; so, in order to make it easier for his horses, the yemschik followed a narrow track leading right through the forest. I soon fell asleep, and was in the midst of a delightful dream when I was awakened by the man calling to me to get up. At first I thought we had reached the next station, but on looking round I saw we were in a sort of clearing in the very depths of the forest. It was snowing so thickly at the time that one could scarcely make out anything a few yards distant. On either side of the sledge were two trees so close to it that I immediately suspected what was wrong, so without hesitation I jumped out, and the yemschik explained to me that he had lost his way, and had somehow got the sledge wedged between these two trees. Here was a predicament! For the next hour we were trying all we knew to get the clumsy vehicle

A POST-HOUSE ON THE KUPETSKI TRACK.

free, and it was only after endless futile efforts that we literally had to cut it out—with no little difficulty, for the wood seemed as hard as iron. By the time we got under way again, and after searching for the track, day was beginning to break, and it was broad daylight when we reached the station. It had taken over five hours to do the last fifteen miles. The postmaster here, who spoke German fluently, informed me that it was out of the question attempting to proceed any further in a sledge, and that I should have now to continue my journey in a *tarantass*, or post-cart. As he agreed to purchase my sledge for exactly what I had given for it, I could not object, though I felt that the remainder of the route to Kiakhta would not be enjoyable, as I should, at every station, have to repack my baggage in a fresh conveyance. However, there was no help for it. A Tarantass is a most curious and distinctively Russian vehicle. In shape it is not unlike a very unwieldy barouche, with a large fixed hood at the back. As in a sledge, the luggage is packed inside so as to form a seat, and, though not an elegant-looking conveyance, it is well adapted to the rough roads of the country. I was once more travelling on wheels, for the first time since I had left England.

The country now began to assume a much more barren and steppe-like appearance, and there was hardly a trace of snow anywhere. The trees also seemed to have disappeared, and for miles ahead there was a bare undulating plain. I could not help noticing that everything was now beginning to look more Chinese, or, rather, Mongolian. Even the tea caravans we passed were composed of quaint-looking carts, undoubtedly of Chinese origin, whilst the drivers, with their swarthy sunburnt faces, looked strangely out of keeping with the cold landscape.

In the afternoon we reached a small river, over which, as usual, the road passed on the ice. My yemschik, quite a young lad, was, however, in no hurry to cross when we saw a cart which was coming towards us suddenly half disappear through the ice,

A TEA CART.

which was evidently very rotten. The water, fortunately, was only four feet deep at the utmost, so beyond the difficulty of getting his horse and cart out again he ran no risk. After watching the fellow (who was standing up to his waist in the icy-cold water) in his vain efforts to move the lumbersome vehicle, I decided that we could not stay where we were all day, and that we had to get across somehow, so I persuaded my youthful Jehu to try a narrower spot a little further down, in the hopes of the ice being stronger there. Well, we went at it full tilt, hoping to get across with a rush; and so we did till within about twenty yards of the opposite bank, when, with a sickening crash, the ice gave way, and we were in the water. The horses immediately began kicking and plunging to such an extent that I expected every moment the heavy tarantass would turn over and all my baggage be lost. For a few minutes my driver absolutely lost his head; but, finding that the horses in their mad endeavours to get out had so loosened the ice as to clear the way, he cooled down, and we managed to reach the bank without any further mishap than getting slightly wet. As we drove full gallop along the road to make up for lost time, I looked back and saw the peasant with his horse and cart still in the water, and taking it very quietly. A basin of hot Bouillon Fleet at the next station soon set me right, and I felt no ill effects from the cold water.

I was now rapidly nearing my destination, when on reaching the last station but one, as evening was coming on, the postmaster said something which I did not quite understand, that he did not like to let me go on, about its being soon dark and the road a bad one, also something which I did not catch. However, I had made up my mind to reach Kiakhta that night if it could be done, so I peremptorily ordered the fresh tarantass and horses at once, and after but a short delay I was soon on the move again. The road now lay right across the turf, and, owing to the nature of the soil, was scarcely visible in the rapidly failing light; in fact, in many places I wondered how the driver found his way at all, for I could see no sign of any track.

It was quite dark when we came to what looked like an immense white plain. This, the yemschik told me, was the river Selenga. This majestic river, which flows into Lake Baikal, was here as wide as the Thames at Gravesend, and in the darkness the opposite bank was scarcely visible. Our road lay right across its ice-bound surface. At the edge of the ice my driver drew up, and, getting down, said he would go and look round before venturing on it, as a man who had that afternoon came in from the next station reported that the ice was beginning to break up. I immediately remembered the incident which had happened only a few miles back, and visions rose up before me of what would be the result in the event of such an accident occurring on this mighty river, so I felt just the least little bit uncomfortable when, after being absent some twenty minutes, he came back and said he thought it would be all right, so on we went. It may have been my fancy, but the heavy lumbering vehicle seemed to weigh more than ever now, as it rattled over the ice

DAY-DREAMS: A SKETCH IN THE TRANS-BAIKAL.
*(The curious hanging arrangement is a cradle.)*

of the river. We had reached, I suppose, about the middle, when suddenly the horses drew up of their own accord, snorting with fear. A large dark mass was in front of them. Nothing could induce them to go on, so the driver got down to see what it was, and almost immediately returned and, getting up, hastily drove in another direction, informing me, in an awed whisper, that it was water. I then made out that the dark mass was a huge gap in the ice. The instinct of the horses had undoubtedly saved us!

After a considerable *détour* we reached what appeared to be the opposite bank, only to find that it was an island, and that there was another broad piece of ice still to be crossed. The driver had now the greatest difficulty in getting the terror-stricken animals to go on at all. It was only after a lot of coaxing, and eventually leading them himself, that they could be persuaded to venture on the treacherous surface. This time, however, we got across without further incident, and it was with a genuine feeling of relief that I felt the tarantass once more rolling over the grass.

After a short search the track was again found, and an hour later I reached the last post-house before Kiakhta, after a most exciting "stage." There is, of course, no other means of crossing Siberian rivers during the winter but on the ice. Towards the end of the winter, just before the *débâcle* begins, it is always advisable, where possible, to cross the big rivers by daylight, on account of the many fissures in the ice. I remember nothing of the next twenty versts, for I went off into a deep sleep, probably occasioned by the recent excitement, and never moved till I was woke up by the yemschik calling out to me that we had reached our destination, and wanting to know where he should drive me.

I sat up and looked round me; no easy matter, for it was snowing so thickly that I could scarcely see anything, and the dreary-looking deserted street looked still more wretched as, in the piercing wind, the blinding flakes were whirled about in clouds. It was as uninviting and wintry a scene as could be well imagined, and for a moment I wished myself back in my comfortable quarters at Irkutsk.

So this was the frontier city of Kiakhta, the delightful place where, as I had read, it never snows, and where, pinning my faith on this outrageous statement, I had been fondly imagining I should find a genial temperature; but the Siberian winter evidently holds good to its reputation to the furthermost confines of the vast country. However, it was no time for this fanciful musing, for we were in the middle of the night, and the road also, and I knew not where to turn for a lodging. The only hotel of Kiakhta was not strongly recommended (which means a great deal in Siberia), so I had made up my mind to seek accommodation elsewhere; but the

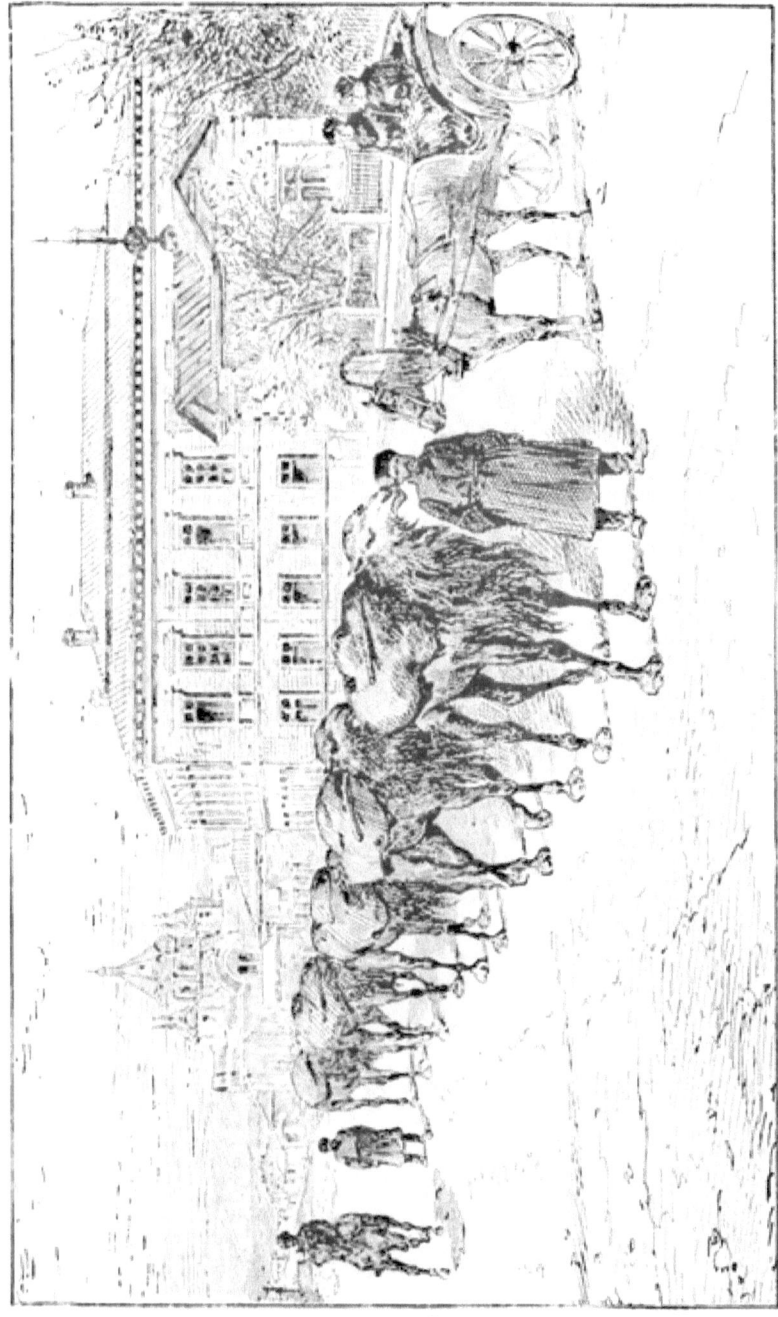

THE HIGH STREET, TROITZKOSAVSK.

[To face p. 215.

whole town was asleep. The yemschik then said he knew of some people who had a room to let, if we could manage to wake them up. So we went to the house, and, happily, were successful. The room, on inspection, proved not only comfortable and clean, but wonderfully cheap in the bargain. So I decided to remain there during my stay in the town. And how thankful I was when I at length "turned in" for a good night's rest after my somewhat eventful and fatiguing journey!

My lodgings were in the High Street of Troitzkosavsk, the business suburb of Kiakhta, for in the frontier city itself there are not above fifty houses, nearly all of which belong to the great merchants. The frontier commissioner also lives there. I suppose it was the recollection of all the gaieties at Irkutsk, for I found Kiakhta and Troitzkosavsk terribly dull after the capital—so much so, in fact, that had I not made up my mind to complete my work I should have pushed on towards Ourga without delay, more especially as the weather continued bitterly cold and it snowed almost every day. There was only one redeeming feature in this dead-alive little frontier city, and that was the novel sights one occasionally sees in the streets. After the unvaried monotony of costume in other Siberian towns, it was refreshing here to see wild-looking Mongolians dashing up the quiet street on their wiry little ponies; or an occasional camel-caravan, with tea, arriving from the desert. It was a sign that a warmer and more picturesque country was close at hand, and made me long the more to get out of cold Siberia. But the novel and interesting sights at Kiakhta were but poor specimens of what I hoped to see further on; so I decided not to begin sketching them till I saw the genuine article in Mongolia itself.

By the way, a somewhat interesting incident occurred whilst I was here. I had made friends with a local photographer, a man of some considerable talent, and would frequently while away an hour in his company. One day that I was visiting his studio for the first time, I was much struck with a " background " painted on a large canvas lying against the wall. It was so exceptionally good that I could not refrain from making a remark upon it, when I was informed, to my astonishment, that it was the work of his assistant, who was standing by. One does not expect to meet artists of talent in local photographers' employ in these far-away places, and I could not help saying so. I was still further impressed when the young fellow, in reply to my question as to whether he had any other work to show, produced a portfolio of sketches which indicated a talent rarely met with. Becoming enthusiastic, I told him he must be mad to be wasting his time at photography in this out-of-the-way town when St. Petersburg would be acclaiming

MY FIRST GLIMPSE OF MONGOLIA. [*To face p.* 246.

him as a born artist. After a deal of beating about the bush, and evident reluctance on his part, I learnt the true facts of the case, that he and his employer (both eminent artists, as I was afterwards informed), were political exiles, suffering a long term of banishment. Many of the sketches shown to me (one of which I give in facsimile) related to prisoners' life, and were evidently done during the long march across Siberia. I could not help being strongly impressed with

A BOURRIATE LADY.

the idea that a system which would allow a prisoner to beguile the tedium of the march by following his artistic proclivities cannot, however faulty its theory may be, in practice be so cruelly *disciplinaire* as many would have us believe.

Meanwhile, my work progressed rapidly, and after a little over a fortnight's stay, I saw my way clear to arrange for my further journey to the sacred city of Ourga, and then across the Gobi desert to China; but of all this I will tell you in my next chapter.

SKETCH BY A POLITICAL PRISONER MADE WHILST ON THE MARCH
ACROSS SIBERIA.
(The original is in sepia and white.)

[To face p. 248.

ON THE ROAD TO OURGA.

## CHAPTER XXII.

### ACROSS MONGOLIA.

The Russo-Chinese frontier—Maimachin—The Mongols of to-day—Curious customs—Hair-dressing extraordinary—A pestilent farmyard—Exciting incidents—A forced encampment—An awful night's experiences—The Manhati Pass—Magnificent scenery—I pull off a successful "bluff"—"Angliski Boxe" in the wilds of Mongolia—Arrival at Ourga.

THERE are two means of getting from Kiakhta, the Siberian frontier town, to the Mongolian capital, Ourga—either by camel caravan or in an ordinary

Russian tarantass, drawn by horses. I chose the latter conveyance. The distance, a little over two hundred miles, takes four days, as the same horses have to do the entire journey, there being no means of getting fresh relays on the road.

It was a lovely, springlike morning when, in a fairly comfortable vehicle with three strong horses, I crossed the frontier, my saddle-horse being fastened loosely alongside the tarantass, to be ready at a moment's notice in case of need when fording rivers or for sporting purposes.

What actually marks the "frontier" it would be difficult to say. Beyond a narrow, dirty strip of what I believe is called "neutral ground," but which is evidently used principally as a sort of Russo-Chinese dust-bin, there is nothing to denote the borders of the two vast empires, and the road passes right across into Mongolia without a break. Many years ago, I learnt, some sort of barrier existed, but it has long since been done away with. The Russians, who, as a rule, are so fond of sticking up their national coat of arms and placing their black-and-white sentry-boxes wherever practicable, doubtless consider this remote corner unworthy of such ostentation, for there is here a striking absence of these (in Siberia) familiar objects. Mentioning this noteworthy absence of any national insignia here, reminds me of a remarkable instance of clairvoyance on the part of a traveller who crossed this frontier *within the last five years*, and who described, in his subsequent " Impressions de Voyage," in a most graphic manner, having passed, on that auspicious occasion, "a guard-house and high wooden gates," which were burnt down *nineteen years* previously! Once, however, on the other side of the neutral ground, one finds one's self in quite another world, so to speak, for here is the wonderfully quaint little Chinese town of Maimachin, which presents as great a contrast to the neighbouring Siberian town, Kiakhta, as could be imagined.

From the outside, little can be seen of Maimachin, as it is surrounded by a high wooden palisade; but once entered through the picturesque archway, Siberia is, as it were, left so completely that it takes a few minutes to get used to the wonderful transformation, for at one step, so to speak, one finds one's self in the Far East, with all its brilliant colouring and strange costumes. There are probably no two nations in the world which present a greater dissimilarity in point of artistic taste than the Russian and the Chinese; so, going direct from one to the other, the contrast is positively startling. Maimachin is a poor specimen of a Chinese town, but is almost like a museum compared with the monotonous aspect of Siberian cities. This town, with about two thousand inhabitants, is of some importance as the final stage for the camel caravans with tea before they reach Siberia and the consignment is handed over to the Russian merchants. It therefore always presents a busy and animated appearance. A most striking peculiarity here is the entire absence of women; for, according to Chinese law, no female of that nation is permitted to dwell beyond the Great Wall. The Chinese who seek their fortunes in Mongolia readily, however, console themselves with Mongolian ladies, in the absence of their own countrywomen.

After passing through Maimachin, the road—a broad, well-defined track—lay for many miles across level grassy plains, bounded in the extreme distance by a low range of hills, and was flat and uninteresting in the extreme. A few wretched *yourts*, or huts, with some camels and cattle browsing here and there, were the only signs of life in the vast solitude.

Before proceeding further into Mongolia, a short description of the Mongols and their habitations may be of interest. A yourt is a sort of cone-shaped hut, covered with a kind of coarse felt made out of sheep's wool. Its walls are held up on the inside, to a height of about five feet, by a circular arrangement of wooden lattice-work; this also supports the roof, not unlike a huge umbrella, the ribs fitting tightly into the lower part; the centre of this is something like a big wheel, from which the ribs radiate, being left open to allow the smoke from the fireplace to escape. This fireplace in the centre of the apartment is usually a rough sort of iron basket on feet. One portion of the interior is invariably furnished with a kind of altar, on which are placed various religious emblems; for the Mongols are a sincerely devout people, and their devotions form an important item in their daily routine. The residence of a noble or rich Mongol is usually composed of several yourts for the different members

A MONGOL YOURT.

of the family, and is often gorgeously furnished, one or two I have visited having valuable carpets and curios in them which simply made my mouth water. In such dwellings of rich Mongols one yourt is specially set apart for the reception of visitors; but these abodes of wealth are very few and far between, possibly because there are not many rich Mongols.

By " rich," I mean being the possessor of many horses or camels and head of cattle and much *yamba*, as Chinese bar silver is called, for gold is not valued at all by the Mongols. The average yourts were indescribably filthy, not only serving as shelter for

A MONGOL.

families of several persons of both sexes herded indiscriminately together, but in many cases for sheep or goats with their young. As, added to which, the smoke from the fire as a rule only partially escapes, the atmosphere under such conditions may be imagined. Living, therefore, in such human pigsties, it is not to be wondered that the ordinary Mongol presents an extremely unsavoury appearance, so that it is often difficult to tell whether nature gave him a black or a white skin; for they are not a water-loving race, cleanliness evidently not being one of the appurtenances of godliness from Mongol-Buddhist point of view.

The curious fashion of the women fixing their hair in a sort of circle round their faces by means of massive silver ornaments has often a very incongruous effect, as I have seen old hags, dressed in a mass of rags which a professional London rag-picker would pass in disgust, with quite a little fortune on their heads, in many cases even among the poorer classes to the value of £30 or £40! All the family savings go first towards providing a wife with the orthodox jewellery, as a girl is not spoken of as a "woman" till her hair is dressed properly—never mind the rest of her wardrobe. Among the very poorest classes I have occasionally seen strips of wood used when silver could not be afforded, but this is very exceptional. Of course, in their dress, as in their dwellings, there are social class differences, and the rich or noble Mongols wear clothes of the finest silks of the most gorgeous hues, their wives and daughters being decorated with costly silver jewellery of exquisite workmanship. Among women of the higher classes are to be found actual beauties, and the curious method of arranging

the hair is really very becoming when it encircles
a pretty face with sparkling eyes and pearly teeth.
I remember on one occasion seeing a princess riding
through Ourga who was so startlingly beautiful that
the apparition simply took my breath away; it was
like a vision from the "Arabian Nights," and for
several days after I felt quite "smitten" with the
lovely unknown one, and my appetite suffered considerably in consequence!

Although as a distinct nation the Mongols are
slowly disappearing, owing to gradual fusion with
the Chinese, still there are many amongst the
descendants of the old princes who yet cling to
the idea that the glorious times of Genghis Khan
will again return, and that some day another such
leader will appear and restore to this once so mighty
race its old prestige. In fact, there is one sect
amongst the people who believes that Genghis Khan
is not dead at all, but has only disappeared for a
time, and will on some not very distant date again
return to earth; and in the national songs the name
of this hero and his great deeds are continually
appearing. *En attendant* this millennium, however,
the Mongols have lost all trace of the formidable
warriors they were in the past, and have lapsed into
such quiet and inoffensive beings that it is hard to
realize they are descendants of the mighty horde
which once conquered Russia, and threw all Europe
into a state of panic. Of their old national cha-

racteristics but one really remains—their wonderful horsemanship; for I believe that the Mongols as a nation enjoy the undisputed reputation of being the finest horsemen in the world, and this in spite of their, to European ideas, somewhat ungainly seat in consequence of the use of a short stirrup. One can imagine what magnificent cavalry these men must have made under their old leaders. However, *revenons à nos moutons*.

As we gradually neared the confines of this "steppe," trees appeared on either side, till we were in a sort of open forest when we reached the foot of the hills. Out on the plains, in the brilliant sunshine, there had not been the slightest trace on the ground of the recent heavy falls of snow; but among the trees and on the higher ground it still lay thickly, and gave a very cold and wintry appearance to the scene. The extreme mildness of the temperature was, however, rapidly doing its work, and under the genial rays of the sun the remaining vestiges of winter fast disappearing. The road, in consequence, was in an awful state, in many places the water and mud being so deep as to render it almost impassable. Our three game little horses, however, struggled bravely on, and, without any further excitement than the waving of the driver's puny whip, managed to get us along.

With the exception of a couple of hours' rest in the middle of the day, we pushed on steadily till

s

nightfall, when we reached the station where the halt for the night was to be made—a couple of yourts close together forming a sort of Mongol farm, where my driver from experience knew he was certain to be able to get hay and water for the horses. I do not think I was ever in a more gloomy or depressing spot. It was a sort of narrow valley between two high hills, with scarcely a trace of vegetation. Heavy clouds, gradually coming up, now quite obscured the sky, and the deadly stillness of the air betokened some approaching change in the weather during the night. All around were curious looking objects lying on the ground. In the twilight I could not at first distinguish what they were, but on a nearer inspection I discovered that these were dead oxen. I counted fourteen lying within a few yards of the huts; and, judging from the odour, I imagine they must have been dead some considerable time. On inquiring of my driver the reason of so wholesale a slaughter, he told me that they had not been killed, but had died from starvation, owing to the severe winter. The wretched inhabitants of the two yourts, in the apathy caused by their misfortunes, had not the energy to remove the decomposing carcases out of sight. I could not help feeling thankful that we had encamped far enough away to be clear of the perfume of this pestilent farmyard.

The night I passed comfortably enough wrapped up in my *dochа* in the tarantass, whilst my driver, used to the peculiarities of Mongol life, sought his couch inside one of the yourts. Towards morning it came on to blow and rain, and in a short time such a tornado burst over us, that I expected every minute the ramshackle vehicle would be blown bodily over; fortunately, however, it was heavy enough to withstand the gale, which abated almost as suddenly as it had arisen, and when towards five o'clock we made a start, it was a beautifully clear morning, with every promise of a fine day. The country presented now, if anything, a more desolate appearance than any we had hitherto passed through —it was a "desert" in every respect. All around were low sandy hills, without even a bush to break their monotonous appearance; not even a blade of grass was to be seen on the wide expanse of stone and sand. The aspect was uninteresting in the extreme, so I got my driver to "hurry up a bit," so as to get out of the dreary surroundings as quickly as possible. We had to do the next eight hours with scarcely any stoppage, as there was no sign of any human habitation anywhere in this solitude, and no human beings meant no water or hay for the horses, so we were obliged to push on at any cost. About one o'clock we at length sighted a few wretched yourts, and in a few minutes drew up at the station, after the longest stage we had yet made. The horses did not seem very fatigued, however; as long as they got plenty to eat and drink, the distances between the stations affected them but little—the hard work they were used to. Four hours we had to pass in this dreary uninteresting place. I managed somehow to while away the time with my pipe and sketch-book, and very glad was

OUR MIDDAY HALT.

I when we at last started preparations for continuing the journey.

The day, which had commenced so brightly, had not fulfilled its early promise; the sky had gradually become obscured, and, as on the previous afternoon, the wind also showed signs of renewed activity; so when the yemschik told me that we had forty versts (twenty-eight miles) to do before we reached the next station, and that on the way a nasty bit of river had to be crossed, I was still more anxious to push on, so as to reach our encampment before dark if possible. For several miles the road now lay along a level plain, intersected here and there by small brooks, swelled into rushing torrents owing to the recent rains, and which in many cases were only with great difficulty crossed, as the banks were generally very steep. Owing to the many delays and the frequent big *détours* we had to make, night was upon us when we at last reached the river the yemschik had told me of in the afternoon. By this time the wind, which fortunately was at our backs, had changed to a piercing cold gale from the north, and snow was beginning to fall heavily. There was every prospect of an extremely dirty night, and one which I should not have cared to be out in anywhere under any circumstances, still less in a rickety tarantass on the desolate steppes of Mongolia. In the darkness I could hear the rushing sound of the swollen river as it raced by, and I could just manage to discern its turbid stream by the large masses of ice floating by like ghosts in the gloom.

It was anything but an encouraging spectacle, and had there been the slightest sign of anything to afford a kind of shelter, I should have persuaded the driver to wait until daybreak before crossing; but all around was bleak, open plain, over which the merciless wind blew with ever increasing force, and the driving snow felt like so many needles, so there was absolutely nothing for it but to chance getting across the river, as the man said the station was only some ten versts off. The horses, however, evidently took a different view of the matter, and it was some time before they could be got to advance even to the water's edge, and still longer before they would venture into it. It was an awkward moment, for they started plunging and kicking to such an extent, that I expected every moment to find myself in the water with the tarantass on the top of me. We had nearly got over, and without any incident, for the water was barely four feet deep, when my saddle horse was seized with ungovernable fear, and managed to break loose somehow, and bolted back as fast as he could. A few minutes after and we were safe on the opposite bank.

In the mean time the snow was coming down so thickly that everything was already completely covered with it, so much so that it was impossible to distinguish the track leading from the river. In vain did the yemschik get down and search about on his hands and knees for some clue to guide him as to its whereabouts. His efforts were futile, for there was absolutely nothing to go by; and although after a few minutes' search he got up and drove off full speed, I felt convinced by his manner that he was on a wild-goose chase. And so it proved, for in a very short time he pulled up again and once more got down to have another search. But it was useless, as I could see by the bewildered way in which he was looking about, and every minute made the chances of hitting on the track still more remote, for all this time it was snowing so thickly that it was almost impossible to see a yard ahead. The cold was also intense.

On the man getting back on to his seat, as I thought with the intention of driving on further, I asked him what he intended doing, as I felt sure it was useless risk going on blindly, and perchance getting turned over into some gully or losing ourselves quite hopelessly. At first he did not reply, and when he did it was only to mumble out something about hearing dogs barking close by, so there must be a yourt near. I listened, but heard absolutely nothing but the roaring and screeching of the wind; when, on looking at the fellow again, I saw to my horror that *he was going to sleep*—the long exposure to the cold was beginning to take effect. Sleep under such conditions I was well aware meant *death*, so I immediately sprang up and commenced shaking him as hard as I could, and after a while succeeded in waking him. I then told him that I had decided not to risk going on any further, but to remain where we were till morning, and that we should have to unharness the horses and make them as comfortable as we could with some oats.

which we providentially happened to have left. Suiting my action to my words, I got out and lent him a hand as well as I could, although it was more to show him that I intended to stand no nonsense than to really help; for Siberian harness is a complicated arrangement of tied ropes and straps, which wants some knowing before meddling with it in the dark. My determination had the desired effect, for in a very few minutes we had the horses stalled on either side of the shafts, which we managed to prop up, and by placing a piece of loose sacking over them, made a very good impromptu manger, out of which the three hardy brutes were soon eating their oats as tranquilly as though in a stable, paying not the slightest heed to the snow or wind, so used are they to be out in all weathers.

All being secure, I then ordered the man to get into the tarantass and roll himself up in his sheepskin, and after a stiff glass of vodka apiece, to keep out as much cold as possible, I attempted to go to sleep. I say attempted, for very little sleep did I get, and I hope never again in my life to spend such a wretched night as I did that 8th of April. The cold seemed to come in at every corner and crevice of the hood which sheltered us, and it was almost impossible to get even the chill off one, whilst the whistling of the wind around and the uneasy movements of the horses combined to keep me from anything but just dozing off till the welcome dawn appeared; and with it the weather cleared up and the storm abated. Then what a magnificent spectacle presented itself to my eyes on looking out of the tarantass! in spite of being cramped in every joint with the cold, I could not help being impressed with the grandeur of the effect. We were right at the very foot of the mountains, which, covered with snow, towered high up above us, like dim white monoliths against the deep blue sky, their summits, which caught the rays of the rising sun, glowing like solid gold.

The yemschik, who had got up some little time before me, had been meanwhile reconnoitring for the lost track, and eventually found it only a short distance away, but quite in another direction to the one we had been proceeding in; so it was fortunate we had not gone on, as he himself owned. The horses, though naturally not looking over-bright, appeared none the worse for their exposure to the storm, so, before proceeding to the station, the man suggested his galloping back on one of them a short distance, to look if he could see anything of our runaway. This I agreed to; so off he went, and, as luck had it, returned in less than an hour with the delinquent in tow. He had found it on the bank of the river, close by where it had bolted. We were not long in reaching the station after this, and, in spite of its grimy interior, I managed to make myself really comfortable in front of its cheerful fire till it was time to start again.

We had now reached the *crux* of the journey to Ourga, the pass through the Manhati Mountains. I gathered, from what the Mongol of the yourt was telling my yemschik, that the road further on was in a very dangerous condition, and that therefore he would go with us part of the way, to lend a hand in case of accident. We therefore made a start, under the pilotage of our good-natured host, and he and I rode on a little distance ahead to ascertain the condition of the track after the storm. The sharp, exhilarating morning air and the bright sunshine considerably helped to liven me up again, and even my wiry little horse, with a good feed inside him, was as game as possible, and evidently not a bit the worse for his night's outing. It had undoubtedly been a very severe frost during, or immediately after, the storm, for the steep track was simply coated with ice; so we had to proceed very cautiously indeed, and pick our way along as well as we could between the rocks, the heavy tarantass following us up very slowly. In many places the road followed the very edge of a precipice, where any accident would probably have been followed by disastrous consequences. It took us two hours to reach the top of the defile, and then, after a few minutes to rest the horses, during which time I had opportunity to fully enjoy as fine a panorama of forest and mountain as I have ever seen, we started on the downward journey, which, if anything, offered still more difficulties than the part just accomplished; for this side of the mountain facing the south, had evidently been but the previous day a sort of series of torrents caused by the melting snow, and the severe frost during the night had been sufficient to coat them thickly with ice, but naturally not strong enough to bear the weight of a man, still less a horse, so my poor yemschik was more than half the time floundering about up to his knees in icy cold water, as he had to lead the horses the whole way, so treacherous was the ground, and timid the animals in consequence. In spite, however, of the almost impassable state of the defile, we managed fortunately to get through without the slightest incident worth mentioning, and exactly four hours after starting reached the plains once more, where the whole aspect of the surroundings changed suddenly as it were.

In front of me, stretching away into the far distance on either side, till where it was bounded by a faint blue wall of mountains, was a vast prairie, and on its surface not a trace of snow was to be seen. In the long grass cattle were grazing peacefully, or standing knee-deep in a rippling stream, which sparkled like a silver ribbon thrown across the green sward. Some little distance off, a group of Mongols, dressed in yellow and red *khadats*, were galloping merrily along, the sound of their voices and laughter reaching me quite plainly on the still atmosphere; while a gorgeously coloured tent near by gave a still further note of colour to this delightful picture. In the warm sunshine the effect was almost one of having reached a "promised land," so great a contrast did it offer to the cold wintry appearance on the mountains close by.

The rest of the journey was all clear sailing; for, with the exception of the last part of the road, which was again very mountainous, the track was very level, and we made good progress, encamping for the usual halts at the yourts of friendly Mongols, known to my driver. By the way, an incident occurred on one of these occasions, which may be of interest. At a yourt where we had halted for our midday rest, a large tea caravan, consisting of several hundred carts, was also encamped; all the oxen were out on the plains, and the drivers, a crowd of some twenty swarthy Bourriats and Mongols, were loafing about, smoking and whiling away the time as best they could. My arrival was, of course, quite an event, and, although my man asked them not to do so, they crowded round me in a very offensive manner as soon as I left the tarantass. One may imagine what would be the effect if a Mongol were suddenly to arrive in the midst of a crowd of English roughs. My position was somewhat similar, except that there was no friendly policeman near. I felt instinctively that I was going to have a very unpleasant time of it unless I managed to score off them somehow; nor was I mistaken, for in a few minutes a sort of Mongol-Bourriat chaff commenced at my expense, although, of course, I understood but very little of what was said. Well, this went on for a little while, during which I was positively hemmed in by the crowd, who would persist in feeling my clothes and otherwise making me very uncomfortable. My usually small stock of patience was getting exhausted, and I felt my "back getting up." At last I could stand it no longer. The leader of the gang, who had been doing his best to distinguish himself in his attempts at "chaff," having asked me several questions in Russian which I did not understand, I told him curtly that I did not understand him, as I spoke but very little Russian.

"Ah," said the fellow, imitating my accent, "you don't speak Russian, don't you?" and there was a general roar of laughter at his imitative powers, at the same time one of the crowd was violently pushed, or rather thrown, against me from behind.

This was sufficient. My blood was up, so, swinging round my elbows to clear myself some room, I deliberately turned up my cuffs and, going up to the leader, shook my fist close under his nose, at the same time telling him as well as I could that although *I* could not speak Russian *that* could any language, as I would soon show him if he wanted to try. My determination had a magical effect, for he retreated a few paces, and, smiling in a sheepish sort of way, replied that he did not understand the

*Angliski Bore*, and added something in an undertone to the men near him, at which they all gradually moved off and left me master of the situation. I was not interfered with again after that. I had pulled off a successful " bluff " !

On nearing Ourga snow once more began to show itself thickly on the ground, and the temperature gradually lowered till it was so chilly even in the sunshine that I had to keep my furs on. We were now in sight of the last spur of mountains which separated us from the plain in which Ourga is situated, and had a very steep bit of track to do for the next hour or so. At last we reached the top, where was a huge cairn, consisting of bones, stones, and all sorts of rags and odds and ends, offerings to Buddha by pious Mongols on reaching the end of their journey, or the top of the mountain. As it was now all downhill work till we reached our destination, I lit my pipe and composed myself comfortably for the remaining hour before me. But my comfort was destined to be but of short duration, for the track down the mountain-side, in fact the whole way, was simply awful, and the shaking and bumping I got during that hour makes me feel sore even now to think of. The heavy springless tarantass having to go over rocks and gullies which would have smashed up any ordinary conveyance in a few minutes, I got the man to drive slowly in the hope of lessening the shocks as much as possible, for I was doubtful whether my inside could hold out long under such treatment; but slow or fast seemed to make but little difference, so at last in despair I ordered the man to get over the ground as rapidly as possible, in the hopes of getting to my destination with, at any rate, some of my most vital arrangements unimpaired. At length a welcome turn in the road showed me that my sufferings were nearly ended, for on the plain below I saw a huge conglomeration of dirty yourts and wooden palisades, with here and there a somewhat higher building to break the dull level monotony. This dreary place, looking doubly wretched in the wintry surroundings, was the capital of Mongolia, the sacred city of Ourga, of which I had heard so much and travelled so far to see. It was a disappointing sight, to say the least of it, and, with the recollection of my long and comfortless journey still fresh in my memory, the first thought that crossed my mind was, *le jeu ne vaut pas la chandelle.*

## CHAPTER XXIII.

### THE SACRED CITY OF OURGA.

The Russian consul, M. Feodroff—Hospitality of the Consulate—The "lions" of Ourga—The colossal statue of the "Maidha"—The "Bogdor of Kurene"—An impromptu interview—Prayer-wheels—Praying boards—Religious fervour of the Mongols.

A STREET MUSICIAN, OURGA.

DISAPPOINTING though the first view of the sacred city undoubtedly is, when seen from the mountains, it certainly improves on a nearer inspection. As I drove through the broad principal thoroughfare, which was thronged with as noisy and picturesque a crowd as could well be imagined, I could not help coming to the conclusion that, however uninteresting its buildings were, among its inhabitants, at any rate, I should find ample scope

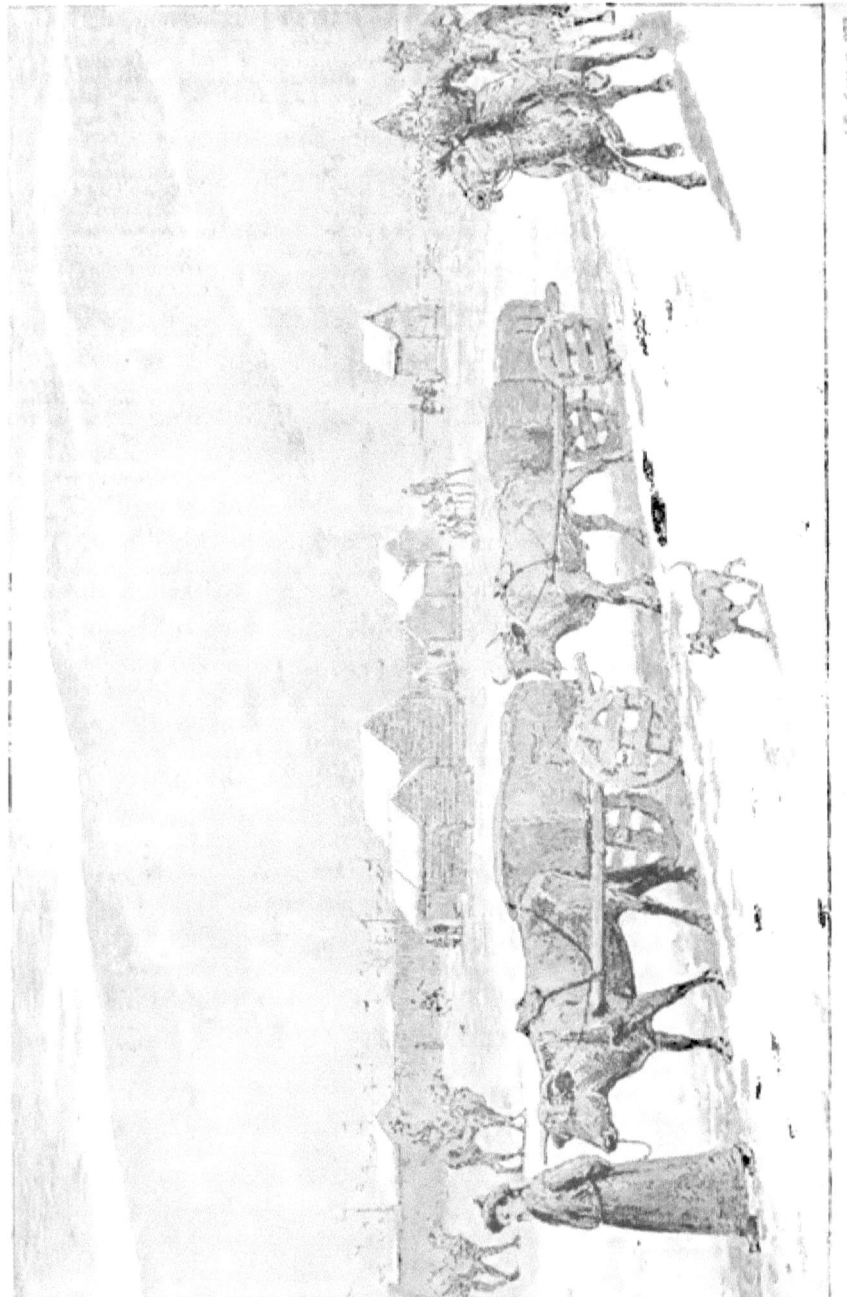

THE PRINCIPAL THOROUGHFARE, OURGA. [To face p. 273.

for my brush and pencil during my stay. On reaching the house of the merchant on whom I had a letter of credit, and where I had anticipated being able to find a lodging, I learned, to my disappointment, that there was no room to spare for the moment, but that the Russian consul had sent word (as evidently my arrival had been expected) that I was to stay at the Consulate; so, without losing time, I ordered my man to drive there at once, as it was getting dark and the horses had evidently had enough work for the day. It took half an hour to reach the large block of buildings, with the gilt dome, which represents the kingdom of the Czar at Ourga.

For reasons best known to the authorities, the Consulate is situated at least two miles from the city, and stands quite alone, out in the desert, some distance from any habitation. Most of the few travellers, I believe, who have visited this out-of-the-way corner of the world have been received and entertained under its hospitable roof during the few days their stay has usually lasted, for accommodation in Ourga itself is very difficult to find, owing to the few Europeans living there. Putting up at a Mongol yourt being, of course, out of the question, and as I had come with the express intention of studying this city and its inhabitants, so little known, I presently decided that I should have but little opportunity of so doing if I fixed my quarters so far

T

from the centre of interest; so I made up my mind to put up with anything in the shape of accommodation in Ourga itself. I received a very kind and truly Russian welcome from the Consul, M. Feodroff. The fact of my being a total stranger, unprovided even with a letter of introduction to him, appeared to make no difference. He had heard I was coming, so took it for granted that I, like other travellers, would stay at the Consulate. On my informing him of my desire to find, if possible, a lodging in the city itself, he good naturedly offered to do his best to help me, but added that he doubted my being able to get anything comfortable, as there were only seven European houses, and these so small that their accommodation was naturally very limited. In the mean time he begged me to make myself at home at his place.

The Consulate, I found, was quite a little colony in itself, consisting of the men employed by the consul and their families, each having their own quarters. One wing of the building was used as a post-office; for, although on Chinese territory, the postal service across Mongolia and through China to Peking and Tientsin is conducted entirely by Russians. Besides the actual *personnel* of the establishment, there was also a guard of five Cossacks under the command of a non-commissioned officer. In spite, however, of the attractions of the comfortable quarters I was in, I reminded my hospitable host the very next day of his promise to help me find a room in the city, so shortly after we drove into Ourga together, with a mounted Cossack galloping on ahead, as is always the case whenever the consul leaves his house. After a lot of persuasion one of the merchants agreed to take me in as a boarder at his house, and to give me half a room occupied by one of his *employés*. The next day, therefore, saw me installed in what were to be my "diggings" during my stay in the sacred city, and as they were in the very centre of the busiest part of the place, I had not to go far in search of my subjects, for I could almost get them by looking out of the window. The charge for the accommodation, considering how rough it was, struck me as very dear for Ourga; but I was informed that living in Mongolia is (for Europeans) not cheap, as almost everything has to be brought from Siberia.

Ourga, or, as it is called by the Mongolians, "Bogdor Kurene"—which means the settlement of the Bogdor—though it contains nearly fifteen thousand inhabitants, cannot even by the wildest stretch of the imagination be called a city with any architectural pretensions to beauty. With the exception of the Chinese portions of it—only a small part—its streets consist of mere rows of high wooden palisades, which enclose the space in the centre of which is erected the inevitable yourt; for so nomadic is the Mongol by nature that, even when settled here in the capital, his old instincts compel him to continue dwelling in his original tent. The effect, therefore, of these long monotonous rows of rough logs, relieved at regular intervals by tall wooden doors, all exactly of the same pattern, is indescribably dreary; and, were it not for the two or three large open spaces where a bazaar is daily held, there would be but little to see, for Ourga has but few "lions." There is really only one building of any pretension in the place, and that is the large wooden Buddhist temple which enshrines the huge gilt-bronze figure dedicated to the apostle "Maidha."

Either the Mongols don't know or won't tell—most probably the former, but, at any rate, I was unable to find out anything about this mysterious figure, or how or when the immense mass of metal was brought to the desert city. It is certainly not less than forty feet in height, and is in the familiar seated position in which Buddha is always represented. In fact, I should have taken it for that divinity had not my informant, a Mongol, insisted on its representing "Maidha," who, I afterwards learned, is one of the Mongol Buddhist apostles, and one much prayed to in Mongolia. The body and extremities of this immense figure are draped in yellow silk, and are almost lost in the surrounding obscurity; but the face itself, which is surmounted by a majestic crown, is lighted up by a hidden window in front of it; so it stands out in foreshortened relief against the darkness of the dome, which gives it a certain weird appearance that is somewhat increased by the eyes being painted a natural colour.

Still, Ourga is most interesting, representing as it does one of the standpoints of the Mongol Buddhist faith, and the capital of a fast disappearing nation; for here is the abode of that most holy of holy personages, the "Bogdor of Kurene," and long and weary are the pilgrimages frequently made by devout Mongols for a glimpse of this mysterious man, who occupies in their faith almost the same position as the pope does, or rather did in former times, to the Catholics. It is for this reason that Ourga is spoken of as a sacred city, and ranks immediately after the mystic capital of Thibet, Lhassa, where is the abode of the prophet of Buddha, the living God, the mighty Dalai Lama, and which is yet a forbidden place to unbelievers.

A PILGRIM FROM THIBET.

The Bogdor of Kurene is a sort of branch establishment, in Ourga, of the head office at Lhassa; for all

Bogdor are supplied exactly of the same youthful age, when required, by the Dalai Lama himself. It is difficult to learn what are the special aptitudes necessary for this high position, for the average Mongol is very reticent on matters concerning his faith; but, at any rate, whatever they may be, the Bogdor seems to have a very good time of it here, for he has little or nothing to do but to live on the fat of the land and to say prayers all day. What more can a man want? He has no voice in municipal and State matters, which are conducted entirely by a Manchurian general, representing China, and by a Mongolian prince. There is, however, just one little drawback to being so august a personage. If the Bogdor conducts himself as his numerous Lamas consider he ought to do, all goes well; but unfortunately youth will have, or tries to have, its fling, and even a Bogdor is, after all, only an ordinary mortal; so when, as has been usually the case up to now, the youth, arrived at years of discretion, wished to meddle in affairs which did not concern him, or to indulge in pleasures not consonant with his austere position, he suddenly died; he was snuffed out, so to speak, how or when was never known, nor were any questions asked; and in course of time another Bogdor arrived from Lhassa to take his place, and perchance also to meet the same fate. Very few of these holy youths have lived much beyond the age of twenty. The first of the line, two hundred years ago, however, was an exception, for he died a natural death, at the advanced age of seventy; he evidently knew how to take care of himself. The present representative, who is twenty-two years old, is likely, I hear, to prove another exception; for it is said that he is of a very different stamp to his predecessors, and is, for a Mongol, a most enlightened man, taking a great interest in all modern subjects and inventions. He has even had his photo taken (for strictly private circulation only), and has a piano in his palace, which was presented to him by a former Russian consul here.

Although to obtain an audience of the great man is, for a European, an absolute impossibility, still he can often be seen; for he rides out constantly, and on several occasions I have seen him, accompanied by his suite. In fact, the first of these occasions formed rather an amusing incident, and may be interesting. Seated on horseback, I was one afternoon busy making a sketch near his palace, when suddenly I heard shouting, and, looking round, saw that the people near were trying to draw my attention to a sort of cavalcade, preceded by two horsemen bearing a huge white silk standard, approaching me, and which I had not until then noticed. To start a fresh sketch was the impulse of the moment, for it was a gallant sight, which almost recalled the Middle Ages. The costumes were really gorgeous. In the centre of the main group was a pale-faced youth dressed in bright yellow silk, the crown of his fur-trimmed hat covered with gold, which glittered like a halo on his head. Although I had some idea that he must be some very exalted personage, in spite of the frantic shouting of the people around, I went on quietly with my sketch, just for the fun of seeing the adventure out. In a few seconds they were close to me, when, to my astonishment, they all galloped up to where I was, and I was surrounded by a curious and inquisitive crowd, who had probably never seen a sketch-book before. The pale-faced youth, who looked something like an Englishman got up for a fancy-dress ball, appeared to be the most interested in my proceedings, and put several questions to me in Mongol, which, of course, were unintelligible to me, so I replied in Russian, saying I was an Englishman and did not understand Mongolian. Evidently this was considered a capital joke, although I had not intended to be humorous; for they all laughed heartily for a few moments, and then some one said something to the pale-faced youth, and they continued their ride. Immediately they were gone the people came up, and, pointing to the horsemen, said, "Bogdor! Bogdor!" in a reverential sort of way, making signs that the youth with the gold roof to his hat was that august person himself. So I suppose I can claim the honour of being the first European who has had an "interview" with this inaccessible personage.

The Bogdor of Kurene is supported on the same principle as are some of the London hospitals—that is, by "voluntary contributions only;" yet so fervent are the Mongols in all matters connected with their religion, that the amount of donations of all sorts which annually reach him is sufficient to support him and his numerous suite of Lamas in a grand and fitting style. All is grist which comes to the Bogdor's mill; so everything, however small, is acceptable, and the poorest Mongol can offer his humble tribute.

By the way, I was much struck by the number of Lamas I met everywhere in Mongolia: almost every other man seemed one. On inquiring, however, I found

A LAMA.

that, although there are so many, most of them are only so in name, but a comparatively small proportion are really priests. It is customary, out of every family where there are several sons, to make at least one of them a Lama. From his earliest childhood his head is shaved, this being the great distinguishing outward mark between the Lamas and ordinary individuals; and though, perhaps, he may not in after life serve as a priest, still he can never marry. The title of Lama, therefore, in most cases, is but a very empty one, and carries nothing with it except the obligation to wear always yellow and red, and to dispense with the pigtail and many other comforts of life.

Still, I could not help feeling that the Mongols are, in their way, a very religious people, and, as I have remarked before, their devotions form an important item in their daily routine; though, perhaps, to an unbeliever in the Mongol Buddhist faith, these devotions may seem to take a form which is somewhat astonishing. Still, it cannot be denied they are carried out with great sincerity. Among the principal features of Ourga are the "prayer-wheels," which are placed for public use in most of the big open spaces. These wheels, or rather hollow wooden cylinders, are placed under cover of rough wooden sheds, and present at first sight a very curious appearance. Most of them are covered with Thibetan inscriptions, and all are completely filled with prayers written on pieces of paper. In order to pray, all that is necessary—beyond, of course, a sincere faith in what you are doing—is to walk round and round inside the shed, and turn the cylinder with you; the more turns the better. Many of the old people, while operating the large wheel with one hand, at the same time diligently turn a small portable one with the other; a rosary suspended from the wrist is also considered an almost indispensable adjunct. Many of the wheels were very large, so that several people

A PRAYER-WHEEL, OUEGA.

could pray together; but most of them were small, and evidently were only used for private communion, the sheds in many instances being decorated with odds and ends of silk and bits of rags, intended as offerings to Buddha.

Apart from the wheels are the "prayer-boards," also placed for public use in various parts of the city, and on which are continually to be seen prostrate figures lying on their faces, and thus literally humbling themselves to the very dust. From a little

PRAYER-BOARDS, OURGA.

distance, these boards presented a very ludicrous appearance, which so reminded me of the familiar spring-board in a swimming-bath that I never passed them without an inward grin—if you can imagine what that is—for any outward sign of mirth at the strange proceedings would probably have got me into trouble. The whole action of the people using them was exactly like that of a person preparing to make a run along the board and take a "header" rather than a prelude to a devotional exercise.

I don't think I was ever in a more strangely religious place than Ourga. Everywhere, at the most unexpected places, at all times, one often saw people throwing themselves suddenly face downwards, full length on the ground, saying their prayers, just as the fit took them, I suppose, these curious proceedings attracting no attention. Many a time I have been riding quietly along, when all of a sudden my horse would be made to swerve violently by some hideous old man or woman, who was seized with an irresistible impulse to say a prayer just in front of its feet. And their devotions do not end here, for every yourt, however humble, not only contains a family wheel, but is decorated outside with innumerable "prayer-flags," or rather bits of rag, tied on to strings suspended from poles all round the palisades. Till I was informed what they were, I took them for bird-scares, for they could not, even by the wildest stretch of the imagination, be taken for flags. If the Mongols were only a quarter as industrious in ordinary everyday pursuits as they are in their religion, the Chinese would not, as they do, monopolize all the trade of the country, while its inhabitants sit about on their hams twirling their prayer-wheels or manipulating their rosaries, quite content if they only earn enough to keep them from day to day.

The sight of a nation's decadence is always a saddening spectacle; but that of the once so powerful Mongol race being gradually but surely extinguished, by the people they once conquered, is a still further and overwhelming instance of Darwin's theory of the survival of the fittest. Although, beyond the annual rearing of a few ponies, camels, and cattle by some of the richer families, there is no actual industry, and the bulk of the populace live from hand to mouth, there are but few signs of actual want. Of course there are poor, wretchedly poor, people in Ourga, who live, or, rather, manage to exist, in the most awful hovels. But still, during the whole month I spent in the sacred city, I was never once pestered by a beggar; indeed, I never saw one. Ourga, in this respect, offered an agreeable contrast to most of the Siberian towns I was in, where one could never leave one's hotel or lodgings without finding quite a little crowd of them lying in wait. Whether this is a relic of the old national pride, I cannot, of course, tell, but I give it as a curious and remarkable fact.

The absence of beggars was, however, but the one redeeming feature of this dirty and disappointing city—or, rather, I don't think that this could be called a redeeming feature, for it was more than counterbalanced by the immense quantity of dogs

"THE OLD OLD STORY ALL THE WORLD OVER."

[*To face p. 286.*

with which the place is infested—huge fierce brutes, more like wild beasts than domestic animals. They are not unlike certain breeds of Scotch collies, only considerably larger. Till I went to Ourga, I used to be fond of "the friend of man;" but I had not been long in the sacred city before I got to hate the very sight of dogs. At night it was absolutely impossible to work owing to the incessant barking they kept up; at all times it was dangerous to venture out unless one was armed with a heavy stick. Although it would not be a difficult matter to exterminate these pests, they are left to increase unmolested; so it is not to be wondered at that every street is blocked with them, to the great danger of passengers.

These dogs do not confine their attentions entirely to strangers, the inhabitants themselves fearing them as much as the Europeans do. It will give some idea of the size and ferocity of the brutes when I add that only a short time ago an old woman, passing through a by-street, was set upon by a pack of them, and actually torn to pieces and devoured, in broad daylight, before any assistance could reach her. Nor is this an isolated instance, for not many years since an old Lama was riding through the city late at night, when he was literally dragged off his horse and killed. Very few of the inhabitants think of going out in the streets at night, unless they have very important business, and then very seldom alone.

One of the worst *mauvais quarts-d'heure* I think

I ever had was one afternoon here, when, accompanied by a Russian friend, who spoke a little English, I was returning from a stroll around. In order to make a short cut, we passed through a number of narrow back streets, and while going along the very narrowest of these we suddenly heard a sort of hoarse murmur behind us, which was quickly getting nearer. On looking back to see what it was, we saw a big cloud of dust, and in the midst of it a huge crowd of dogs, coming towards us at full speed, with one wretched-looking brute on ahead of them, which they were evidently chivying. The few people in the street made a rush for their doors, and got inside their enclosure without much hesitation. "It is a mad dog!" exclaimed my companion, at the same time pulling me close to the palisade behind us, which was flush with the road. We stood with our backs to it, as flat as we could make ourselves, and in less time than it takes to tell it the whole pack were abreast of us, with the poor hunted beast, covered with blood and dirt, snapping and biting viciously right and left at his tormentors as he flew past. Fortunately for us, they were too occupied to direct their energies in our direction, though they actually had to squeeze by us, so narrow was the street. I did not feel comfortable again until some little time after they were out of sight.

The savage nature of these brutes will be more readily understood when it is remembered that the

Mongols, in accordance with their creed, literally throw their dead to their dogs, and never bury them. Old or young, rich or poor, the custom is universal, forming as it does part and parcel of their religion. When a Mongol dies, the body is wrapped up in an old coat and is taken a short distance outside the city on to the hills, where it is placed on the ground, with only a "prayer-flag" over it to protect it, and is then abandoned, not to the mercy of the elements, but to the hundreds of dogs who have already scented their feast and are waiting patiently by. No sooner are the mourners out of sight than the dreadful repast commences, and in an incredibly short time nothing remains of the lifeless body but a few scraps of the covering it was rolled in. A general battle usually takes place over the body among the savage brutes, with the result that human remains are soon strewed over the ground, and the scene is too ghastly for description. As there is no cemetery or particular spot for depositing the dead, one not infrequently comes across a stray bone or a skull which has escaped those hungry canine sextons, and these poor vestiges of frail humanity certainly add to the desolate surroundings of the desert city. Such a wonderful instinct have the Ourga dogs, that I am told they will often wait for days outside a yourt where a person is dying.

The currency of Mongolia is peculiar, and takes a lot of getting used to. On one occasion I bought some trifling article and paid for it in Russian money, which the Mongols are, at any rate, shrewd enough never to refuse. Imagine my surprise when, for the change, I was handed a small slab of brick-tea and two dirty little bits of floss silk, which I should have passed unnoticed in the gutter. These rags, which intrinsically were probably worth less than a farthing, represented twenty kopeks (sixpence), as I was informed, while the tea was equivalent to thirty kopeks. This tea, by the way, is the only real currency throughout Mongolia; the silk is becoming gradually obsolete, probably because it wears out too soon, whereas the tea will stand almost any amount of hard wear. A "brick" of tea, sixteen inches long by eight wide and about one and a half thick, represents sixty kopeks, equal to one shilling and sixpence. If a smaller sum is necessary, the brick is cut up into sections, say, six of ten kopeks each, and even these are again subdivided by the poorer Mongols.

It is curious to note that, although Mongolia is really Chinese territory, everything is Russian, so to speak; and even the tea and silk represent an equivalent in Russian and not Chinese money. Some of the Russian merchants in Ourga have even adopted a sort of private bank-note system, so as to do away with the bother of having to keep a large stock of loose cash—that is, of "bricks"—always handy. These notes represent so many bricks each, and are redeemable on demand; but I hear that the Mongols prefer the bulky article to the flimsy paper substitute. When, after a time, this currency becomes injured by hard usage, and chipped round the edges, it is used for the usual purposes of tea, and it may be imagined what a delightful beverage it makes after it has been passing from hand to hand for some months among the dirty Mongols! However, these children of the desert are not fastidious, and the greasy-looking stuff is broken up and literally put to stew in the common cauldron of the yourt, where, eaten with millet seed, it makes a dish much appreciated for some days.

This dish is to the Mongol what the samovar is to the Russian, and if one is on intimate terms enough to visit a "big man" in his yourt, almost the first thing he offers you is a basin of tea, which is usually poured out of a metal jug begrimed with the dirt of generations. I remember on one occasion, accompanied by a friend who spoke Mongolian, visiting a Mongol who was rather a swell in his way, for his yourt, which I had been anxious to see, was fitted up with some pretension to "style." We seated ourselves in the usual manner, on the floor, and our host, after a few minutes of conversation, of course offered us the inevitable tea. This was what I wanted particularly to avoid, but there was no getting out of it this time. A particularly unwholesome-looking old hag then dived into the gloomy recesses of a sort of cupboard, and produced three wooden bowls containing some greasy-looking compound, which she forthwith proceeded to clean out with her grimy fingers, finishing up by polishing them vigorously with the tail of her gown; these tasty receptacles were then placed before us on the ground, and filled with some vile liquid which bore no more resemblance to the "cup which cheers but does not inebriate" than does the proverbial chalk to the proverbial cheese. It would have been an insult to the man to have refused his hospitality, so for the next five minutes I was racking my brain how to get out of even sipping the awful stuff. My companion, who was used to Mongolian customs, was not so delicate in his tastes, and managed to get through his bowl all right, at the same time advising me to try and do likewise, so as not to offend the man. Providentially at this moment some one came to the door of the yourt to speak to our host, and we all got up, I immediately taking advantage of the opportunity to quietly empty the contents of my bowl into a dark corner near me. We shortly after took our leave, in spite of the old Mongol's pressing invitation to stay and have a drop more tea; and when we got outside the yourt, my companion, who had not noticed my manœuvres, but had observed the empty bowl, remarked that he knew I should like Mongol tea if I once tried it!

It was fortunate I had plenty of work to occupy me, for there was little or nothing to do but to stroll round about a sort of market-place, where a bazaar

was daily held, and where everything almost could be bought—Mongolian, of course. This market alone offered almost endless scope for my pencil, for it always presented interesting scenes. One part was devoted to camels and ponies, and it was amusing to watch the zeal displayed by the owners of some promising lot when a likely purchaser appeared. When I was at Ourga one could get a very decent-looking pony for about two pounds (sixteen roubles), which was not dear, considering; for I don't think it is possible to get anything really good for less anywhere—this, I believe, will be conceded. In Southern Mongolia, in the district bordering on China, these serviceable little animals fetch much higher prices, especially if they show any sign of speed; and the district at certain times of the year is overrun with agents from Shanghai and Tientsin racing-men on the look-out for promising "griffins," * and comparatively big sums of money are paid for them. Apart from racing purposes, the Mongolian ponies make capital hacks when trimmed up a bit and knocked into shape. I could hardly believe that the smart, well-fed, carefully groomed animals I saw in Peking, Tientsin, and Shanghai were originally rough, unkempt brutes of the desert, so great was the transformation.

Another part of the market would be occupied by

* A "griffin" is a young untrained horse which shows signs of "speed."

vendors of saddlery, an important and flourishing
department, as well it might be, considering what
indefatigable horsemen the Mongols are. But what
always struck me as being the most unique part of
the motley gathering, and a sight almost worth going
to Ourga to see, was the hat-bazaar, a department
entirely in the hands of the fair sex. A Mongol's
hat is, perhaps, the most striking feature of his
toilet; and a rich man will often spend a large sum
on his fur-trimmed head-gear. There is very little
to distinguish a lady's from a gentleman's, only a
tassel or two behind, and as, owing to their peculiar
shape, no particular difference in size is necessary,
there is any number to select from. The noisy
crowd of chattering females, dressed in their quaint
costume, with their multi-coloured stock-in-trade,
was undoubtedly one of the most interesting sights
of Ourga; and often did I hover around them with
my sketch-book in hand. But although it was a
quiet and inoffensive crowd in the bazaar, it was
certainly a very curious and inquisitive one; and at
first it was very trying to my temper to find myself
suddenly the centre of a group of dirty, evil-smelling
Mongols, who were not satisfied with mere observa-
tion of my movements, but would actually maul me
all over with their hot grimy fingers to ascertain of
what stuff my clothes were made, my corduroy coat
especially coming in for the largest share of public
attention. After a time, however, I got used to these

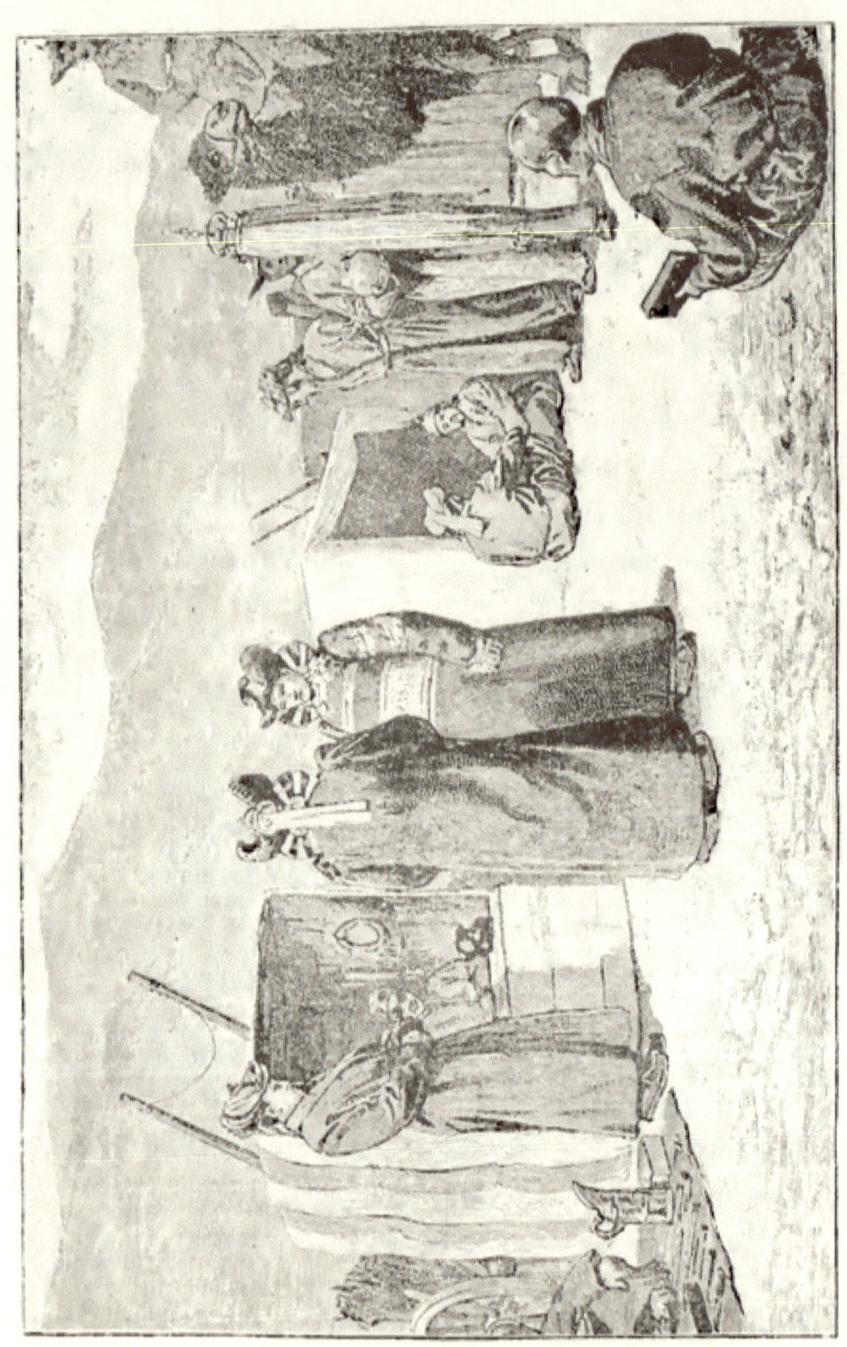

IN THE BAZAAR, URGA.

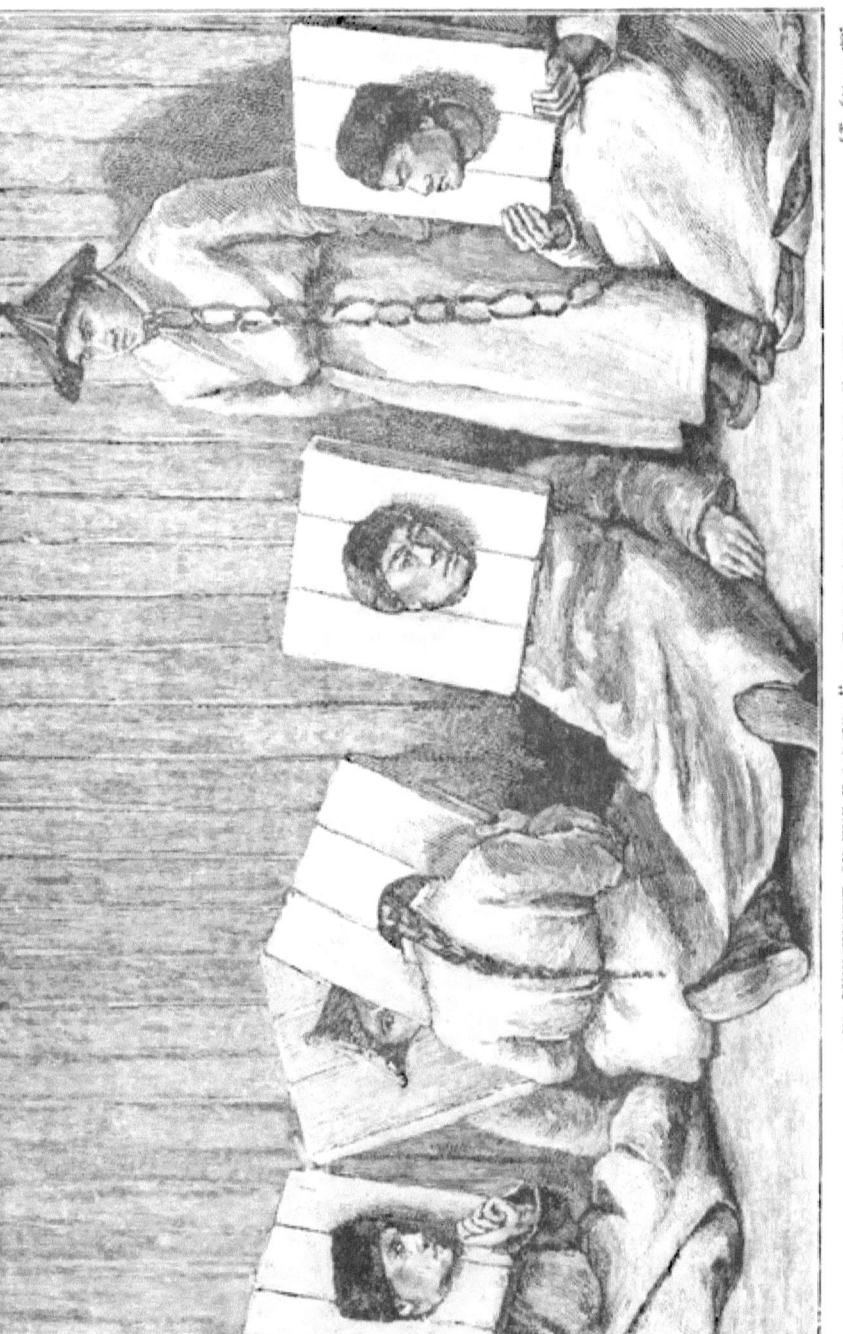

THE PUNISHMENT OF THE "CARGUE;" A SKETCH OUTSIDE THE PRISON, OUIDA.

practices, and usually found that the best way to put a stop to them was to catch hold of the man nearest me, and to begin turning him about, as I was being treated myself, and to examine him as though he were for sale. This nearly always raised a good-humoured laugh. If, however, it did not succeed in so doing, I had another plan, which I reserved as my *grande finale*, and which rarely failed, for the time, to rid me of the unpleasant crowd. I would take out my pipe and slowly fill it, every movement I made being watched with rapt attention by the bystanders; then I would produce a small magnifying-glass I always carried about me and proceed to light up with the aid of the sun—no difficult or lengthy an operation on a hot morning. This seemingly mysterious feat would simply strike the onlookers dumb with amazement, and they would generally draw back instinctively a few paces. I would then walk quietly away, leaving them to unravel the mystery as best they could.

Still, in spite of its uncivilized condition, there is yet some show of keeping order in the city, although the poor, inoffensive Mongols never struck me as having it in them to be guilty of any big acts of violence; petty larceny maybe, but nothing more than that, for they don't seem to have pluck enough left to do anything really bad. There is, however, a fairly large body of police to represent law and public authority; these look after the place by day, and during the dark hours watchmen with gongs parade the street, and combine with the dogs to make night hideous. Besides these varied arrangements, there is a regiment of Chinese soldiers quartered on the outskirts of the town, forming a sort of body-guard to the Chinese resident general, who represents the suzerainty of the First Cousin of the Moon over the Mongol Tartars, and who, in conjunction with the Mongol prince, constitutes the Government of the whole territory, for the Bogdor's power is merely spiritual, and he has actually nothing to do with the management of State affairs.

Still, I could not help feeling how much more under Russian than Chinese influence everything was in Mongolia. For instance, the consul at Ourga was undoubtedly a far more important personage than even the Chinese general himself, and from what I learnt, I believe the late consul, M. Shismaroff, was practically the leading man of Ourga, for he was not only very much esteemed and looked up to by the Mongols, but was actually consulted by them in most State affairs. The fact of all the trade of the country being virtually in the hands of the Russians may to a certain extent account for this ascendancy; but be it what it may, one thing is certain, that a Cossack cap inspires an incredible amount of respect in these distant regions, not only among the Mongols, but also the Chinese themselves; for there seems to be, as far as I could make out, a pretty general apprehension, or rather conviction, of what would happen were a subject of the Czar to be offered any insult. During my subsequent journey through China I was much struck with the difference of the footing on which English and other nationalities are placed with regard to the Chinese.

The days in Ourga passed by very slowly indeed, and had it not been for the work I had laid myself out to get through, the month I spent in the sacred city would have been very dreary indeed, for the whole time I was there but one event occurred to break the eternal monotony of the stagnant existence.

This was the annual commemoration of the festival of the Maidha, on April 23, the most important of yearly celebrations among the Mongol Buddhists. For days beforehand the city was in the throes of preparation, the various markets were shifted to other temporary quarters, and the streets through which the procession was to pass were invaded by hordes of youngsters, whose mission was to clean up the roads as much as possible—and it was no easy matter, considering that they are all used as open sewers. The mode of procedure was certainly novel, if nothing else. The bulk of the filth was swept into big heaps, and shovelled into dried bullock-hides, to which ropes were fastened. A dreary sort of chorus was then started, and the load was dragged away and deposited on some other road, generally only a few yards distant.

The appointed day arrived, and from an early hour

the populace thronged the different open spaces
where the best view of the proceedings could be
obtained. Fortunately, the weather was fine, so the
*coup-d'œil* was very animated and interesting; the
procession—which was really three processions moving
abreast—was certainly most imposing in effect, and
quite Oriental in the brilliancy of the colours displayed. It was composed exclusively of Lamas, and,
from the length of it, gave me a fair idea how many
of these men there are in the capital alone. On all
sides were to be seen huge waving banners, with
strange devices on them, and surmounted by still
stranger carvings; immense coloured umbrellas, on
stands, each drawn by several men; also crowds
fantastically attired, marching along, beating large
drums shaped like big warming-pans, others blowing
musical instruments of forms and shapes impossible
to describe; while in the centre of this immense
moving crowd was a huge sort of trophy, on wheels,
and surmounted by a large wooden horse, painted
red, and sheltered from the rays of the sun by a big
multi-coloured umbrella fixed over it. This was
evidently the *pièce de résistance*, for it towered high
above all the rest. Close behind it, surrounded by
a crowd of the highest Lamas, was a bright yellow
sedan-chair, in which reclined the sacred Bogdor
himself.

The procession, making a tour of the city, with
certain halts at different spots, either for refreshment

AN OURGA BEAUTY.

or religious observance—I could not quite make out which, probably both—occupied the greater part of the day, many of the rests being for as long as an hour, all the men then squatting on the ground in lines round the centre trophy. I managed to get a very good view of the early part of these proceedings from the roof of a friend's house, and then took my horse, and rode through the crowd to inspect it more closely. I don't think I ever saw a more gorgeous display of costumes and jewellery. Some of the women were dressed in the richest of silks, and were literally one mass of silver decorations from head to foot; back and front, every available part was covered with the very quaintest ornaments imaginable, till they had the appearance of walking jewellery shops—and they seemed not the least afraid of being robbed while pushing their way through the crowd. Of course, most of the *élite* were on horseback, and it was curious to notice how, even in faraway Ourga, "the old, old story" is still the same; for I saw many really pretty girls surrounded by quite a little crowd of admirers, flirting away just like their sisters in the civilized world.

One touch of nature makes the whole world kin, and for a moment I felt quite lonely at not knowing any of them, and being able to join in the fun. The days following all this animation were very dull indeed, and I could not help thinking that even a few more religious processions would have helped to liven dreary Ourga up a bit. As it was, I found myself eagerly looking forward to my journey across the desert to the Great Wall; and had I been able to curtail my stay, I certainly should have done so, but——

IN THE GOBI DESERT.

## CHAPTER XXIV.

### FROM OURGA TO THE GREAT WALL.

My preparations for the journey across the Gobi Desert—The Russian Heavy Mail—My camel-cart—Good-bye to Ourga—The first few days out—Discomforts of the journey—The homeward-bound mail—The desert settlement of Tcho-Iyr.

It was one thing getting to Ourga, quite another getting out of it, as I found when I made inquiries as to the most expeditious way of crossing the immense waste which lay between me and the Great Wall of China; it was, in fact, mainly owing to this circumstance that I stayed so long in the dreary city, for when I spoke to my Russian friends on the subject, they shook their heads, and expressed an opinion that I would not find it an easy matter to make up so small a caravan as I should require for the journey. And so it proved. Moreover, much to my annoyance, I learnt that there was not one really reliable Mongol in Ourga at the time, and that to think of going alone with doubtful guides would have been to tempt Providence. I was, therefore, advised to make the best of it and postpone my departure for a while, on the chance of something turning up. At length the Russian postmaster, with whom I was on very friendly terms, came to my rescue, and kindly offered to let me accompany the caravan of the Russian Heavy Mail as far as Peking. This was indeed a bit of luck, for the convoy is not only always accompanied by two experienced Cossacks, but does the journey in considerably less time than any ordinary caravan, and my expenses would also be very much lessened.

As the time for my departure approached, my preparations for the long and tedious journey required a good deal of attention, for nothing can be purchased *en route*. Much to my disappointment, I learned that I should not be able to take my horse with me, as there would be no means of getting sufficient food for him, even if he could stand the long forced marches, for it is only by having relays of fresh camels that the mail can get across so quickly as it does. I had taken the precaution to bring out with me from England a sufficient quantity of tinned pro-

MY CAMEL-CART. [To face p. 303.

visions to last me right across Siberia and leave me enough for my desert journey. I had also a small American cooking-stove, which the makers (Messrs. Poore and Co., of Cheapside, London) guaranteed would work equally well with coal, wood, or *argol* (dried camel-dung, the fuel of the desert), and this portable kitchener proved absolutely invaluable; even in wind or rain it worked to perfection, and many were the delicacies it afforded me.

Having overhauled my stock of provisions, my next trouble was to get a cart to travel in, or rather to sleep in, for I was then under the illusion that I should spend the greater part of the daytime on the back of one of our "ships of the desert." I was soon, however, undeceived; I had forgotten what a bad sailor I am. A camel-cart, as will be seen from my sketch, is of peculiar construction, and I do not think it is possible accurately to describe one of these boxes of torture without going into profanity. No matter how smooth or level may be the road, the camel-cart bumps and jolts about as vigorously as when it is passing over rocks, and the smallest pebble under the wheels will send a spasm through the whole vehicle like an electric shock; in fact, I could not help coming to the conclusion that, were a camel-cart to pass over the smoothest asphalt road, it would be affected by the geological sub-strata and jolt accordingly. There was one thing I discovered beyond a question of a doubt whilst crossing the Gobi in this camel-cart, and that was, that I possessed, under certain conditions, a thorough command of my mother tongue. I managed to hire one of these conveyances, for to have one built expressly is a very expensive affair, and would have taken some little time. I also had to hire an extra camel from the Mongol who runs the mail, for the postmaster only undertook to provide me with one for my baggage, so I had to get another expressly to draw my cart—no easy matter, as I soon found out, for it is not every one of these brutes that will allow himself to be harnessed; and when they don't at once condescend to walk between the shafts, no manner of persuasion will ever induce them to do so. With a camel whipping is simply out of the question; for, immediately one attempts to chastise him, he either lies down, and refuses to get up, or else starts kicking. Till I went to Mongolia I had always thought that the camel was the most patient and docile of animals. I soon, however, saw that for absolute bad temper and stubbornness he has not his equal anywhere; and, as added to these gentle traits of character, nature has also provided him with a unique and disgusting means of defence, in the form of a power to spit, or rather eject, almost on the slightest provocation, a mass of undigested food, at any one who may be unlucky enough to incur his displeasure, it may be imagined that he is seldom interfered with by strangers, owing to the risk of receiving one of these odoriferous discharges. No less than six camels were tried before one could be found which was deemed reliable enough to draw the cart, and this had to be bought for the purpose. The value of these brutes varies according to their age; full-grown ones generally average from 160 to 200 roubles (£20 to £25).

The Mongolian dromedary, or rather camel—for it has two humps—is a very different-looking animal to its Arabian cousin, for it is very much smaller, and in winter covered with a long and shaggy coat of hair. During the summer months this coat comes off, and the animal then presents an even more unpleasant appearance than usual, which, however, in summer or winter, is thoroughly in harmony with that of the Mongol attendants.

The caravan of the Russian Heavy Mail usually consists of the two Cossacks in charge of it, three Mongols, and six camels. If the mail be an exceptionally heavy one, an extra camel is perhaps added; but this occurs very seldom. It is, in reality, the Parcel Post, for only heavy matter is sent by it. Letters are conveyed across the Gobi by horse post, which goes three times a month both ways, on a system not unlike the old pony express in America, the distance of one thousand miles, from Kiakhta to Kalgan, being covered in the short time of nine days by five consecutive riders and nine relays of horses. Only Mongols are employed on this arduous task, and night and day, in all weathers and seasons, these

x

hardy sons of the desert do their monotonous and lonely journey, keeping their time with almost the regularity of clockwork, so well is the system organized. They go at a hard gallop the whole way, the mail being carried in saddle-bags, slung over a second horse, which they lead with them. The difference in the time occupied by the heavy and the light posts is naturally very considerable, the caravans taking as much as seventeen and eighteen days to do the distance from Ourga to Kalgan, and this even with four different relays of camels on the way. Still, this is very much quicker than the ordinary tea-caravans can do it, for it is no unusual occurrence for twenty-five, thirty, or even as much as forty days to be spent on the journey across. The great difference, of course, between the mail and the private caravan is that the latter has the same camels to go the whole way; so a road has to be taken which passes through the district most likely to afford pasturage to the animals. As, owing to the number of caravans passing, these pastures are yearly becoming more remote, the roads, in consequence, are getting longer for the ordinary caravans, for they have to go further afield in search of grass. The two Cossacks who went in charge of the mail I accompanied were both men who had had much experience on the road, the leader, Nicolaieff, having been eleven years continually passing to and fro across the Gobi, so he knew almost every inch of the ground.

MONGOL CONVEYING THE RUSSIAN LIGHT MAIL ACROSS THE GOBI DESERT.

I could not help wondering what inducement the dreary Mongolian waste could offer to any young and active man, for him to elect to pass his life in it, so to speak; for, although the same Cossacks accompany the mail right across China, as far even as Tientsin, they only stay long enough there for the contrast of the life in the busy town to appear even more marked in comparison with their own monotonous existence. Yet there are men, in most cases married, who actually give up the best years of their lives in this obscure and remote postal service—and for what? The Cossack Nicolaieff received, I learnt, the munificent sum of twenty roubles (£2 10s.) per month, out of which he had to keep himself and family! Stepanoff, who was his junior, received somewhat less. Of course, it must not be forgotten that living is cheap in these parts. Still, 12s. 6d. per week is not a big sum to keep a large family on.

It has seldom been my luck to come across two such thoroughly good fellows as these humble Cossacks, and it was with a real feeling of regret that I separated from them at the end of the journey; for I don't think that I ever met two men working together in more absolute harmony of friendship. There was none of the effusiveness one sees in the higher walks of life, but there was, I noticed, a certain quiet and unobtrusive steadfastness between them which meant volumes more than all the "old chap" this or "old man" that could ever convey.

Duty bound them together, and with the implicit obedience to it which is an instinctive quality in the character of the Russian soldier, they did their work together like men and brothers.

It was with a feeling of relief that on May 7 I left the dreary desert city of Ourga, though certainly not without some forebodings of the hardships which would have to be endured before I reached civilization. Eight hundred miles of sandy waste lay between me and the Great Wall of China—a sandy waste which, for utter desolation and monotony, is probably without an equal in the world. I do not propose to give a chronological account of the tedious journey; events were so few and far between during the long and tiresome marches that a description of the routine of one day will suffice for all. The start for the day's journey was usually made at daybreak, when in a few seconds the sleeping encampment would become a scene of bustle and movement. The dawn was scarcely visible in a faint streak of rosy red on the horizon, when the drivers would be awakened by the leader, and preparations at once made for the start. All had to be repacked on the camels, and mine reharnessed to my cart, everything being finished and ready to proceed in an incredibly short space of time. No time whatever was wasted in toilet arrangements or even refreshing the inner man, and, although I would often have given anything for a cup of hot coffee or Bouillon Fleet before starting, I did not like to disarrange the evidently invariable custom of making an early start, by delaying the caravan for the preparation which the making of such a beverage would have involved.

Long shall I remember those dreary, weary hours which always preceded our first stoppage, for no halt was ever made until close on noon. A bite of biscuit, perhaps some preserved icy-cold tinned meat, washed down by a limited quantity of stale water sucked through a pocket-filter, was my only breakfast—a

THE MIDDAY HALT IN THE DESERT.

breakfast so complete in its discomfort as to require the very keenest appetite to do justice to it. The appetite I fortunately usually possessed, for the bracing air of the desert acted on one like the strongest tonic. The noonday halt after seven or eight hours of incessant jolting in the cart was a veritable oasis in the discomfort of the day, as at this time I could make at least some attempt at an imitation of a civilized meal. At this time also the benefit of my little portable stove was simply inestimable; it fairly astonished the simple Mongol. Still, even this attempt at a square meal was never unattended by discomfort, for in the middle of the day a cold piercing easterly wind was invariably blowing, and, although the Cossacks always pitched their tent, the open air was preferable to its smoky, malodorous interior with a fire in the centre. Two hours and a half were usually the limit of time allowed for the midday rest; then the boys would be sent off to fetch back the camels, which would often stray far away from the encampment in search of pasturage. Then the tent was struck, loads readjusted, the caravan marshalled into its usual order, with my cart leading, and once more we started on another dreary and monotonous spell, which only terminated late at night.

Our rate of progression, even under the most favourable conditions, never exceeded three and a half miles an hour. It was usually managed so that we should have reached a well when we halted; still, the precaution was always taken of filling our waterbarrels whenever the opportunity offered, so as not to have to rely on doing the exact distances between the wells. These distances varied very considerably from fifteen up to even thirty miles; but the water varied still more. I thought, when I was up-country in Africa, that I had drunk the most repulsive water it would ever be my lot to have to put up with, but I had not then been in the Gobi Desert. Even my pocket-filter on one or two occasions gave it up as a bad job, for it got so clogged with dirt that it would not act, so I had then to throw aside the remains of my fastidiousness and drink the awful liquid in its natural state, which in appearance and consistency was a cut between chocolate paste and coffee and milk; for *il y avait de quoi boire et manger*. I could not help noticing how very slightly the Cossacks were affected by these nasty incidents.

Long habit had acclimatized them, so to speak, to living in dirt, and eating and drinking it also; they were quite Mongolized, in fact. On one occasion, at the commencement of the journey, I remember going into the tent when their dinner, a quantity of meat, was stewing, or rather boiling, in the large iron pan over the open fire. The preparation was a simple one, for the meat had been merely cut into chunks and thrown into the pot and covered with water. As the mess boiled, a nasty scum, consisting of all the dirt in the water and the meat, rose to the surface. This filth was eagerly scooped up by both the Cossacks and the Mongols, and swallowed with much avidity; in fact, I learned they look upon it as the best part of the food, for when I expressed my astonishment at their even leaving it in the stew, as it would be better and cleaner if it were removed, they stared in blank surprise at what they probably considered my ignorance. I was much surprised to notice how very little water a camel requires when on the road, and how little he gets given to him; even when there was an abundance they never received it more often than once every two days, so as not to accustom them to luxuries, and they did not seem to be very keen for it even then.

The first day after leaving Ourga was uneventful enough, the track offering little or nothing of interest, though the actual flat sandy expanse of desert had not yet commenced. The surrounding hills were bare and desolate-looking, and the dreary aspect was a fitting prelude to the unutterable solitude and desolation farther on. A few miles out from the capital we crossed the broad, swiftly running Tola River. Our camels were quite girth-deep in its waters, for there had been rain up in the mountains recently; still, the animals did not seem much to mind crossing it, breasting the current as unconcernedly as though they liked it. This was the last water of any importance we saw until we reached Kalgan, nearly three weeks after.

As we slowly advanced we gradually left the hills behind, till at last, three days out, we reached the actual commencement of the great desert; and I saw stretched out before me a vast, limitless waste, so flat and unbroken that it looked exactly like the sea. A quiet, as though of death, reigned over it, for not even the slightest sign of life broke the oppressive stillness of the scene. Neither the Karoo or the Kalahari deserts in South Africa ever produced on me an impression so weird and indescribable as did that first glimpse of the awful Gobi, "The Great Hungry Desert." The mere look of the dreary waste recalled all I had ever read of the horrors of a lingering death, by thirst or starvation, which has so often befallen travellers who have been

MY CARAVAN IN THE DESERT.
(From a Kodak photograph.)

unfortunate enough to lose themselves on its almost trackless surface. Nothing, in fact, was wanting to complete the gloomy picture. Even the faintly marked trail before us was rendered more easily discernable by the bleached bones of camels lying here and there on either side.

Our fourth day out was marked by an event—for

the slightest incident in that weary, uneventful journey magnified itself into an important occurrence. During the afternoon we met the caravan of the homeward-bound Russian mail, and, considering we had not seen a living soul, except each other, for more than forty-eight hours, it may be imagined how pleasurable was the meeting. The two convoys halted for a time; our Cossacks exchanged news with the other Cossacks, and even the Mongols hobnobbed together; the inevitable vodka was pro-

WE MEET THE HOMEWARD-BOUND MAIL.

duced, and, under its genial influence, for a few moments the weariness of the journey was forgotten; then, with many final shakes of the hand and friendly wishes, we were under way, and in a short time were once more alone on the boundless waste. It was on this occasion that I first heard of the attempted assassination of the Czarewitch.

The next day we reached a range of rocky hills—great heaps of huge boulders lay piled around in picturesque confusion, and, altogether, the scene was a welcome change after the flatness of the plains. Right in the very midst of these hills, nestling as it were under their shelter, to my surprise we came upon a miniature town, which I had never even heard of before. This, I learned, was Tcho-Iyr, a Lama settlement, entirely inhabited by Mongols who are devoting their lives to religion.

It was a lovely day, the finest one we had had as yet, and in the still air and the eternal silence of

THE LAMA SETTLEMENT OF TCHO-IYR IN THE GOBI DESERT.

the surroundings the effect was very impressive, for it was indeed "asleep in the sunshine of the East," and "far from the busy haunts of men." I therefore persuaded Nicolaieff to halt the caravan for a short time, so that I could have a stroll around the quaint little place, with my sketch-book and camera; and very pleased was I afterwards that I had done so, for it was one of the prettiest spots I saw in Mongolia. On a nearer inspection it turned out to be larger than I had first taken it to be, and absolutely different from what I expected to find, for the quiet pervading the streets was quite in keeping with the proximity to the vast desert—there was, in fact, quite the atmosphere of religious seclusion which one feels in a monastery. But what struck me most was the wonderful cleanliness I saw everywhere, and I don't think that, for its size, I ever saw its equal. Everything looked spick and span, as though it were cleaned carefully every day. There was also a striking absence of dogs, those pests of Mongolia. One could stroll about without being continually on the *qui vive*, as in Ourga. Instead of a conglomeration of dirty yourts, there were trim, neatly built, whitewashed cottages, of absolutely the same outward appearance as English ones, not so large perhaps, but still strangely reminding one of far-away England. Curiously enough, I did not see anything at all similar to them anywhere else, either in Mongolia or China; nor could I find out why this style of building was exclusively confined to the pretty little desert settlement.

My appearance naturally created quite an excitement, for I was probably the first Englishman that has ever visited the place, which is, I believe, out of the usual caravan route; and the appearance of a stranger in their midst will doubtless form the subject of conversation for a long time to come. Still, I was in no way annoyed—a little crowded in, perhaps, but that I was beginning to get accustomed to, and

I TAKE TEA WITH A LAMA IN THE GOBI DESERT.

[To face p. 30.

the half-hour I spent there was so pleasant that I really regretted having to hurry away. Either there were no women in the place, or at least very few, for I never saw them; the inhabitants appeared to be entirely of the sterner sex, and all of them, from the very youngest, Lamas or Lama students. The effect of the entire population being dressed in red and yellow was very curious. Many of the older men wore massive gold-rimmed spectacles, which gave them a very learned appearance. A couple of large temples of Tibetan architecture, in excellent preservation, seemed the most important buildings in the town, and, besides these, I learned, there was a monastery. When I got back to the caravan, I found it quite surrounded by visitors, for the news of our arrival had by this time spread all over the place, and evidently a general half-holiday had been taken in consequence.

THE RUSSIAN POST-STATION IN MID-DESERT.

## CHAPTER XXV.

### THE GOBI DESERT—*continued*.

Sport in the desert—The "post-station" at Oud-en—The last of the desert—Saham-Balhousar—First impressions of China—Chinese women—Returning to sea-level—Curious experience—The eclipse of the moon—Arrival at Kalgan.

NOTHING of particular interest occurred during the next few days after leaving Tcho-lyr. To the low range of rocky hills surrounding it succeeded a monotonous expanse of endless gravel-coloured plain, which was positively depressing to one's spirits. Day after day would find us surrounded by the same unbroken horizon, while, with the regularity of clockwork, at eleven o'clock every morning the piercing cold north-easterly wind would commence blowing, and continue until late in the afternoon, very often with the force of a strong gale. Owing, I believe, to its being some four thousand feet above the sea-level, the temperature of the great plateau of Mongolia is never high, even in summer; but in winter the cold is excessive, almost as great as in any part of Siberia, and the desert is covered with several feet of snow.

Although I had a Winchester rifle and a fowling-piece with me, and a store of ammunition, the sport I managed to get never compensated me for the bother of carting the heavy load about. During the whole time I was in the desert I did not fire off more than one hundred rounds, and these with but a very poor result; still, what I did get was large, and helped to increase our larder. From what I saw, it struck me that there is really very little sport to be got in the Gobi. It is true one often saw in the distance many herds of antelope, but, owing to the flatness of the country and the entire absence of cover, it was almost impossible to get even within range of them. If I had been a dead shot at, say, eight hundred or nine hundred yards, I might perhaps have done some execution, but, unfortunately, I am not. There was also a species of bird something like a very large wild goose, which the Cossacks called "Kuritze," which was splendid eating, not unlike venison. I managed to get some of these with my rifle, as they were not so shy —one in particular must have weighed twenty or thirty pounds, and it lasted us several days. Some districts abounded with a curious animal not unlike a rabbit, which the Mongols called "Tarbargan." These were easily got, probably because they were no good for eating purposes, even the Mongols refusing a couple I shot. Other parts of the desert were simply covered with large mounds, which the Cossacks told me were made by "Koshki," a sort of wild cat which burrows in the ground. I never, however, saw any of the animals, though we were passing through their haunts for days. Small green

IN THE GOBI DESERT—A TEA CARAVAN ON ITS WAY TO SIBERIA.
(From a Kodak photograph.)

lizards seemed to thrive everywhere, even in the most arid places; in fact, I don't think I ever saw so many before. A peculiar kind of beetle, which covered the ground in great numbers, seemed confined to a certain district or undefined zone, for once out of it they disappeared. Often in the early morning, when the sleeping caravan was aroused to prepare for the start, wolves would be seen prowling around at a short distance from us; but they always got away before I could get the sleep out of my eyes and my rifle ready. So it cannot be said that animal life in the Gobi is extensive enough to be considered good sport, or sufficient to enliven the monotony of travelling across it. Of course, I am speaking only from my experience on the caravan route; possibly in the more remote districts of the vast waste, on the Manchurian side, are animals in abundance, but they are too far away to be "get-at-able."

On May 15 we reached a post-station which stands at a place called "Oud-en," exactly in mid-desert, consisting of a couple of yourts in charge of a Russian. It would be impossible to imagine anything more unutterably lonely and dreary than this little station. For miles before we reached it the desert was simply a vast expanse of bare rocks, without the slightest sign of vegetation to break the monotony of their dull muddy-grey colour. It almost appeared as if the most bleak and wretched spot had been purposely chosen for the "post-station," for there was not even a Mongolian yourt within miles, and even the nearest water was some distance away. I could not help thinking that exile to the most far-away Siberian villages would be

Y

preferable to the awful existence here, while the life of the Cossacks in charge of the mail, continually on the march, was one of positive gaiety compared to it. Still, the man living thus, of his own free will, was no old, broken-down individual, looking as though he were sick of the world, but a smart young fellow, with very little of the hermit in his outward appearance; yet this is what to all intents and purposes he is, and for the wretchedly small pay of thirty roubles (£3 10s.) per month, out of which he had to keep himself! I learned that, with the exception of a Mongolian servant, he was quite alone, and never saw a soul except when the homeward or outward-bound mail passed once a month. He had not got even a horse or a gun to help while away the time, and his stock of books, the poor fellow told me, he had read through and through many times during the three years he had spent in the station.

What an existence! It has often struck me that there are certain types of men whose intelligence is so little above that of animals that, so long as they can manage to exist somehow and without too much exertion, it is all they require; to them, such words as discontent or ambition are unknown; like the blind horse turning a wheel, they plod on day after day in the same well-worn groove, with no other prospect but the respites for food or sleep. And it is, doubtless, fortunate it is so, for these are the men who uncomplainingly pass away their lives in distant

IN THE GOBI DESERT: LADY VISITORS TO OUR ENCAMPMENT.

[*To face p. 324.*]

lighthouses and other lonely and far-off places where other men would simply go raving mad in a short time. We stayed the night here, for our fresh camels had not arrived, and did our best to make a merry time of it, the postmaster giving us quite a feast, and producing a large bottle of some awful stuff, which I learned was "Chinese vodka," to wash it down with. Somehow, though, laughter seemed out of place in this remote solitude; for, to me at any rate, the death-like silence outside seemed as if endeavouring to reassert itself during every pause in the conversation. The Gobi is no place for frivolity.

We were astir betimes the following morning, and after a hasty breakfast and a final stirrup-cup with our host, the caravan was fairly got under way, and we were once more *en route* for the Celestial Empire. We were now over the top of the hill, so to speak, and every step brought us nearer our destination, though we still had many weary days before us. So few incidents worthy of note occurred during the next week that I will pass over the remainder of the journey through the Gobi itself. Suffice it to say that from one side to the other of it, with the exception of an occasional oasis, its desolate aspect remained unchanged. I might here mention how curiously everything in the desert became charged with electricity; my furs simply crackled like biscuits when touched.

At length, on May 23, there were signs that we

were at last reaching vegetation once more, for grass began to show itself, and in a short time, as though we had passed an invisible line, we were crossing rolling prairies, which were an agreeable change after the stony waste. Just on the confines of the desert we passed the Mongol Monastery of Holfer-Sum, a curious-looking group of buildings of Thibetan architecture; we were, however, too far away for me to be able to pay it a visit. This was my last glimpse of Mongolia; and it was certainly with no feelings of regret that I bid adieu to the most dreary and wearisome country I have ever visited.

Early the next morning we were in sight of the little Chinese frontier town of Saham-Balhousar, and shortly after drew up outside the station, where we had to change our camels for mules. The long and tedious desert journey was over at last, a journey on which I had anticipated meeting with difficulties, not to say dangers, considering I was quite alone; but the whole time I was in Mongolia I never had any serious molestation—as a matter of fact, I can only recall one incident which might have had an unpleasant ending, and that was the adventure on the road to Ourga.

Saham-Balhousar is quite a rising little place, and, although only called a village, is of very respectable dimensions. It was my first glimpse at China proper, for, though some distance from the Great Wall, it is thoroughly Chinese in character. As a matter of

YE GENTLE SHEPHERDESS OF YE STEPPE. [*To face p.* 324.

fact, it impressed me much more favourably than many places I passed through after; the style of its buildings also struck me very much, for they were quite distinct from anything I had as yet seen, and had an almost Egyptian appearance in the bright sunlight.

It was here that I first saw that most hideous of mutilations, the small foot of the Chinese women. The custom of crippling their female infants is, I believe, gradually dying out, and slowly but surely the Manchurian shoe is coming more into use. To see the wretched women hobbling about on their high heels is, I fancy, more painful to the European beholder than it is to the victims themselves, who have doubtless become quite accustomed to their crippled condition. I have a pair of shoes belonging to a full-grown woman, and they only measure three inches in length! The highest class of Chinese ladies are absolutely unable to walk about at all on account of the smallness of their feet.

It was in Saham-Balhousar that I had for the first time a real glimpse of what over-population means. Although I had, of course, often heard of the teeming millions of China, I had never until then really formed any accurate idea of what that meant. This first Chinese town I visited opened my eyes, for I saw everywhere such crowds of people and children that I could not help wondering where they all managed to live in the place, and the curious part of it was, how much they all resembled one another; they all seemed part of one huge family. The children throughout China were simply stunning, and quite pictures in themselves.

Our caravan drew up in the courtyard of the house, and the baggage was transferred from the camels to several curious-looking carts, built expressly for the road through the mountain-pass to Kalgan, a distance of some sixty miles. It was well on in the afternoon by the time our preparations were complete and we were ready to start again. I forgot to mention that my cart still remained with us, though it was now only a camel telega in name, for, instead of a "ship of the desert," two diminutive mules were harnessed tandem fashion in the shafts. The mail-carts were drawn by mules and donkeys, harnessed together anyhow, driven by Chinese "boys." It was certainly a grotesque procession, and one scarcely worthy of so high sounding an appellation as the "Russian Heavy Mail," and very out of place did the Cossacks with their official caps look, seated on the top of the heap of heterogeneous baggage.

Although there is no visible boundary-line between Mongolia and China, the difference was manifest immediately we left Saham-Balhousar. On all sides were small hamlets scattered about the plain, whilst the country was laid out in plantations and fields, which were simply teeming with industrious peasants.

It was a very different scene from anything met with over the border amongst the lazy Mongols.

Towards the evening the plains ahead of us were walled in by what appeared to be a line of low rocky hills. In vain I looked for the magnificent mountain range which I had been told encompasses Kalgan, and over the summit of which the Great Wall winds its immense length; yet we were certainly near enough, I thought, for any really high mountains to be visible by now, but nothing at all like a mountain was in sight. It was getting dusk, and the moon rising, when we reached the confines of the plain and began to descend a hill, or rather a steep rocky road leading right into the hills themselves, and which at every instant grew steeper and rougher.

After proceeding for some little time I noticed quite by accident that the moon, which was at its full and shining gloriously in a cloudless sky, was becoming gradually obscured; we were evidently going to witness an eclipse, and just at a time when we wanted as much light as possible to help us pick our way amongst the boulders with which the track was encumbered. Much to the dismay of our drivers, it grew darker and darker, until at last not a speck of light was left even to indicate where the brilliant orb had recently been, and our boys of their own accord halted the caravan and bowed themselves repeatedly to the earth, muttering prayers and incantations. It was so weird and supernatural an effect,

that it made me almost think I was in a dream. This
idea was, however, soon dispelled, for the road was
realistic and material enough, for it had meanwhile
been getting so steep and rocky, and the path so
narrow, that we all had to walk and lend a hand at
getting the waggons through.

I then suddenly remembered that the whole plateau
of Mongolia is more than five thousand feet above
the sea, so we were almost level before with the tops
of the mountains which form the northern boundary
of China. This, then, was the rocky range of hills
we had been approaching during the evening; we
were now, therefore, on our way down into the
Celestial Empire. As we gradually descended, the
granite cliffs and peaks loomed up higher and higher
around us, and so dark was the night, that at times
it became positively dangerous to advance owing to
the obscurity and the numerous precipices along the
edge of which the track lay. The moon remained
hidden for nearly two hours, till just as dawn showed
signs of breaking, when she began to appear once
more, to the evident relief of our followers. Half-
way down, at the end of the worst bit, we halted for
a couple of hours to have a rest and feed the animals,
and I felt so knocked up after my long and rough
walk, or rather climb, that I immediately fell into a
deep sleep, from which I only woke just as we were
starting again.

It was now broad daylight and a lovely morning—

so lovely, in fact, that it would require the pen of a poet to convey any idea of the glorious sunrise in that remote mountain-pass. We were now but a short distance from Kalgan, but the track was so rough that our progress was very slow, for we were still descending through a sort of gorge which looked like the old bed of a river. The scenery at times appeared magnificent; still, even in these wild and uninviting surroundings, the ever-energetic Celestials had seized on every available spot, and high up the almost precipitous sides of the mountains one could see here and there little patches of cultivation, which in places were so numerous as to form what looked like terraces on the side of the precipices, each plot being surrounded by a miniature wall. Certainly, one's first impressions of the Chinese, especially when coming from Mongolia, are such as to make one absolutely admire their marvellous energy and industry; this impression is, however, somewhat modified later by more intimate knowledge of the people.

One of the quaintest sights I think I have ever seen was in this pass, when we reached a little village (of which I forget the name), and which was built right on the face of the mountain itself. The effect of the tiny houses perched right away up in mid-air, and the glimpse of its blue-coated inhabitants dotted here and there like dolls, was quite unique. The awful state of the road over which I was being bumped to pieces somewhat marred, however, my appreciation of the scenery through which we were passing.

We were now quite close to our destination, and the traffic around us increased every moment; in a short time, a turn in the road showed me the welcome sight of a big cluster of houses. This was Yambooshan, a suburb of Kalgan, where lived the Russian tea merchants, and to one of whom I had a letter of introduction. My journey across the "Great Hungry Desert" was accomplished, and I was once more within touch of civilization.

## CHAPTER XXVI.

### KALGAN TO PEKING.

A hearty welcome—Yambooshan—The Great Wall of China—American missionaries — My mule-litter—From Kalgan to Peking—Scenery on the road—Chinese inn—First experience of a Chinese dinner—Amusing *rencontre*—The Nankaou Pass—The Second Parallel of the Great Wall—First impressions of Peking—The entrance to the city.

THE town of Kalgan stands at the very entrance to China proper, for one enters it through an archway in the Great Wall itself, and it is only, therefore, when the venerable portals are passed that one is really in the Celestial Empire. The suburb of Yambooshan, where the Russian postmaster and tea merchants live, is quite a little town in itself, outside the wall. As I had a letter of credit on one of these gentlemen, a M. Bassoff, of the firm of Kargovine and Bassoff, I went straight to his house, in order to get some Chinese money and to exchange the brick tea I still had left, for this ponderous currency was now of no further use to me. It is almost unnecessary for me to state, that I was received with the usual Russian courtesy and hospitality. M. Bassoff was away, I was informed by his representative, a gentleman clad

in white silk, who came out to meet me ; but a letter
had been received announcing my probable arrival, so
a room in the house had been prepared for me. Had
I been an old friend of the family it would have
been impossible to do more for me; and it may be
imagined how welcome all this was after the hardships I had just gone through. Nor was there in my
mind any pang of regret at saying good-bye to my
camel-cart which had brought me so many weary
miles, safely, it is true, but shaken to pieces almost.
My one hope was that I should never set eyes on its
like again. To have a good warm bath, to get rid
of the dust with which I felt literally saturated, was
my next move, and I then sat down with my host
to the best meal I had tasted since I left Irkutsk,
and washed down by a capital bottle of Burgundy.
"Roughing it" has its charms, but after all commend
me to the comforts of civilization. My friends, the
Cossacks, came in shortly after, and I learnt from
them that I should be able to spend two days in
Kalgan, as the mail would not be ready to start for
Peking sooner. So I was to be in clover for the
next forty-eight hours.

Yambooshan is one of the quaintest little places I
was ever in. It looks more like some little far-away
village nestling under the Alps in Northern Italy
than a Chinese settlement, the high mountains
which surround it, and amongst which the houses
are perched here and there, helping to carry out the

STREET SCENE, YAMBOOSHAN; SHOWING THE "GREAT WALL" ON MOUNTAIN IN THE BACKGROUND.

[*To face p.* 332.

illusion. It is so completely encircled, in fact, by the mountains, that the cold wind from the desert but rarely reaches it, and the temperature when I was there was simply delightful. As I smoked my cigar while strolling round the garden of the house in the genial sunshine after lunch, I felt a sense of enjoyment and physical repose such as can only be experienced after a long spell of discomfort has been endured. It was almost sufficient to compensate me for the wearisome journey I had just finished.

During the afternoon, accompanied by a Chinaman as guide, I went for a ride round the city. Before, however, describing Kalgan itself, I suppose I ought to give my "impressions" of the Great Wall, this huge and indelible record of a nation's panic, and which is often spoken of as one of the Seven Wonders of the World.

Although there are really two great walls, the one at Kalgan—the "First Parallel," as it is called—is, I believe, the only real and original one. The other, at the top of the Nankaou Pass, which I shall have occasion to describe later on, though in reality far and away finer, was evidently of much later construction, and possesses real architectural beauty; whereas the one at Kalgan looks at first sight more like an Irish stone fence than anything else. I could hardly realize, on first being shown it from the valley, that this almost shapeless mass of rubble, looking not unlike some huge fossilized serpent, winding away over the tops even of the highest mountains, had been raised as a serious defence of the empire in bygone days. However, I took the trouble to climb up the mountain to it, and it was only when I found how long it took to reach it that I began to realize its size. Of course it is so dilapidated that one can only conjecture what its original appearance was like; but although undoubtedly big, its dimensions were, to me, very disappointing. The base, of course, one cannot measure, as it follows the sinuosities of the ground, and in some places, therefore, is much wider than in others. The height also varies considerably from the same cause, but I should think, at a rough guess, it averaged twelve feet on the inside; on the outside it is in many places à pic with the sides of the mountain. I found I could sit astride the top, so it is not very wide. In shape the Kalgan Wall is conical, its base being formed of huge boulders loosely heaped together; at intervals of half a mile or so are rough towers, each capable of containing a few soldiers.

I found Kalgan even more curious and interesting than I anticipated it would be; in fact, I could never have imagined such a sight as met my eyes. The streets were well-nigh impassable, not only on account of their fearfully badly paved state, but on account of the immense amount of traffic of all sorts. I don't think I ever saw such a busy or novel scene as presented itself to me on passing through the ponderous gateway, with its huge paper lanterns swinging overhead. The principal street was simply blocked, and I had to wait some little time before I could advance my horse a step. My appearance attracted little or no attention, for I was in a Russian costume, and my Cossack cap was alone sufficient to guarantee me respect—such a wholesome dread have the Celestials of interfering with a subject of the czar. I have not been able to get any reliable figures as to the actual population of this frontier town, but there seemed to be positively myriads of people about, and the first impression was of being in some immense fair, the low-built houses, or rather open booths, on all sides adding considerably to this appearance. However interesting, though, the first visit to Kalgan was, the novel impression caused by the strangeness of the surroundings soon wore off, and then the dirt and abominations of the evil-smelling place were apparent in all their barbarous hideousness. As a matter of fact, this was my subsequent impression of all Chinese cities without any exception, and I believe most travellers will agree with me.

I had learnt that there were two mission-houses in Kalgan, one English, the other American. So I thought I would pay these gentlemen a visit, if only to have a chat, for I had not spoken English for some months. I therefore got my guide to take me first to the *envoyés* of Uncle Sam. The mission station was a large brick building, standing in its own grounds, which were laid out as an attempt at a garden, and surrounded by a high wall. I was received by a Mr. —— in the usual cold, distant, narrow-minded manner which, so far as my own experiences are concerned, seems peculiar to this particular profession; and after a few trivial remarks about the weather and other everyday topics (for my arrival seemed quite an ordinary occurrence to him), I was asked into the house and introduced to Mrs. ——, and we made some further attempts at a conversation. It was scarcely more than an attempt, however, for my visit did not appear to gratify these worthy people over-much. After about ten minutes of digging out syllables on my part, the gentleman left the room, apologizing for having to get on with his work, or something of the sort; and I took the hint, and my departure also. It is almost needless to add they did not press me to remain or to call again. As I rode away from this inhospitable abode I could not help mentally contrasting the reception I had just received with the hearty welcome I had invariably been shown throughout my travels amongst the Russians, who never can do enough for the stranger within their gates.

A couple of days in dirty Kalgan were more than sufficient to see all there was to see; therefore I was not at all sorry when Nicolaieff came in the next afternoon and announced the departure of the mail for Peking on the following morning; so I had to set to and make my further preparations for the four days' novel journey to the capital.

The Russian Heavy Mail is conveyed from Kalgan to Peking by donkeys and mules, carts being almost impracticable owing to the mountainous districts to be passed over. Travellers who do not care to ride the whole distance have to provide themselves with what is known as a "mule-litter." This is not only a novel conveyance to the average European, but owing to its subtle peculiarities affords also a continuous vein of excitement, which is a great change after the monotony of the bumping and shaking of a camel-cart. If the mules behave themselves and don't walk in step, the motion is simply delightful; but this state of beatitude is unfortunately the exception, and the bad qualities of the mule seem to develop themselves to an exasperating degree as soon as the animals find themselves attached to one of these litters; and as the occupant is completely at the mercy of the two animals carrying him, it may be imagined what an exciting time he has of it. Before travelling in a mule-litter I had always imagined, from what I had read, that the mule was the most surefooted of animals, and that he was more at home, so to speak, when passing along the very verge of a yawning precipice or crossing the frailest of bridges than on a level track. I was not long, however, in my litter before I was completely undeceived on this point, for we had not proceeded many miles when down fell the leader on a perfectly smooth road, and for a few seconds I had an uncomfortable time of it, as it was quite an open question what would have happened if he had started kicking, for I should not have had time to get out. Fortunately for me, he was got on his feet pretty easily. Still, the incident opened my eyes, and I realized long before we reached the mountains that travelling in a mule-litter is not all "beer and skittles." What struck me particularly was the wonderful intelligence of the mules, as they have no reins to guide them by, but are simply directed occasionally by a word or two from the boy in charge, and are, as a rule, allowed to pick their own way. I should certainly in many cases have preferred their being led, more especially when we reached the precipitous mountain-pass shown in my sketch; but such a procedure would have been against all precedent, and the mules would probably have resented any such implied doubt of their surefootedness, so used are they to being left entirely to themselves on the most dangerous parts of the road. Still, it was giddy work, for often on one side of the narrow path the rocks rose precipitously as a wall, whilst on the other was a sheer precipice, without the slightest rail to protect one. It was a magnificent bit of scenery, but one which

MY MULE-LITTER.                    [To face p. 338.

I felt could be appreciated better when seen in a photograph than from the insecure position of a mule-litter balanced on the very edge of the yawning gulf itself.

However, to return to my departure from Kalgan. Punctually at the appointed time our *cortége* assembled at the postmaster's house, and without unnecessary delay a start was made. It makes me smile even now to think what a grotesque procession it was. No saddles are provided with the donkeys or mules, so the Cossacks have to make themselves as comfortable as possible sitting astride the luggage the animals carry pack-wise, so the effect may be imagined. It is simply astounding the amount of weight they can carry; even the smallest donkey would jog gaily along under a big camel-load, and a man seated on the top of that. It took quite an hour to get through Kalgan from one side to the other, so this will give a slight idea of the size of the place. Once past the town, we pushed on without any halts at a good smart pace, for we had a considerable way to go before we should reach the town of Siu Fou Fou, our halting-place for the night.

The country we were passing through offered no particular interest, as it differed but slightly from what I have previously described. Village followed village so closely at times as to give the road the appearance of passing through an immense street, whilst everywhere was the same teaming population of blue-coated Celestials. Night was on us long before we reached the crenelated walls of the city where we were to put up till morning, and for miles and miles we had to skirt them till we reached the entrance gateway.

There was something indescribably weird and uncanny in these seemingly endless battlements, standing out in black and forbidding relief against the starlit sky; and this gloomy impression was in no degree lessened when we at length reached the frowning archway from which issued the hoarse murmur of the congested barbaric life within its precincts, and immediately after our entrance the iron-bound gates were closed with a clattering and clanging which reminded me that the civilized world was thus completely shut off from us till the next morning. Knowing what I did of the uncertainty of the Chinese character, I could not help feeling that in the event of any hostile feeling arising against the "white devils" during the night, our chances of getting out of the place were positively *nil*.

It took some little time to reach the "inn," for the streets were, as usual, crowded—at times even quite blocked with traffic, and in the uncertain flickering light of the paper lanterns presented a scene not easily to be forgotten. At last, however, we reached our destination, and I was able to form some idea of what a Chinese inn is like. I fancy I do not run much chance of being contradicted by any one who has travelled in these parts when I say that for filth and general discomfort the average Chinese inn is probably without its equal in the world. As a rule it consists of a dirty courtyard, surrounded by tumble-down, dilapidated outhouses, some of which are partitioned off as "rooms," whilst the others are

THE COURTYARD OF A CHINESE INN.

reserved for the mules and other animals. The place shown in my sketch is a fair sample of its kind. Unfortunately one cannot produce the smell pervading the place, without which no really accurate idea can be formed of it, a smell which, as far as I could guess, seemed a conglomeration of sewage, garlic, decomposed animal matter, and general human uncleanliness all mixed up together. In my many and varied travels I have always noticed how characteristic of the countries the different smells were; and even now, after a lapse of many years, I feel sure I could recognize a place I had visited long ago if its characteristic odour were put under my nostrils. But of all the "perfumes," the memory of which still lingers in my olfactory organs, that of a Chinese inn will, I feel sure, remain long after the others have vanished, for it is the most pungent and unpleasant I ever experienced.

A description of one "room" in these inns will suffice for all, as the difference was simply in the amount of dirt about them. The windows—if the tissue-paper-covered apertures in the walls can be so called—usually stretch the whole width of the room, and beyond preventing the full light of day from coming in, were of no earthly use as a rule, for the paper was generally hanging in shreds; so there was no privacy to be obtained. Along one side also was the *kang*, or raised platform, covered with matting, which serves as a sleeping-place, and under which, in winter, is lighted a fire. A small table is placed on the kang, round which visitors squat, tailor-fashion, to take their meals. There was seldom any other furniture in the place.

With regard to the food in these inns, for those whose stomachs are equal to Chinese cooking there is plenty

of choice, and the stuff they give you is plentiful
and cheap at the price. I tried one meal, but the
experiment made me so ill for several days after,
that I never desired to repeat it. Till I had tasted
Chinese cooking I had fondly imagined that I had

A "ROOM" IN A CHINESE INN.

a "gem" of a digestion, and could eat almost anything. I was, however, undeceived in North China.
The mere recollection of that awful, interminable
dinner, washed down with a vile, lukewarm con-
coction, which the Cossacks called "Chinese vodka,"
and which had a taste like what I imagine would be

tepid methylated spirits, makes me shudder even now to think of.

One look at the interior of our room decided me to sleep in my mule-litter out in the yard, which, although it was crowded with all sorts of vehicles and people, would be preferable to voluntarily surrendering myself to the enemy, as I knew would be the case if I slept on the dirty *kang*; and although my cramped bed was anything but luxurious, owing to the fact that my legs, from the knees downwards, protruded out into the cold night air, still, somehow I managed to sleep as soundly as usual, and did not wake up till I was disturbed in the early morning with the noise and bustle occasioned by the departure of some of the many travellers who had stopped at the place over-night. Sleep after this was impossible, so there was nothing for it but to get out and while away the time as best I could with my sketch-book till we were ready to start, after a makeshift sort of breakfast.

By the way, a rather amusing incident occurred one morning at one of these inns. I was busy repacking my litter, when Nicolaieff came up and told me, to my no little surprise, that an English gentleman and lady had arrived during the night, and pointed out to me an individual who was standing in a doorway close by as the *Angliski Gospodin* in question. This was quite an event for me, after not having seen any English people for so long, so to go up and ascertain whether he really did hail from the old country was naturally the impulse of the moment. His surprise at meeting an Englishman in such an out-of-the-way place was equal to mine at meeting him, for he had taken me for one of the Cossacks in charge of the mail, he told me laughingly. I then learnt he was travelling through with his wife to visit some missionary friends in North China, and intended spending the summer there. I was then introduced to the lady, who came out at that moment, on hearing English spoken. They both naturally wanted to know what brought me in such outlandish parts alone, and where I had come from (for they had not taken me for a missionary, so they said—and I believed them!), and seemed much astonished when I told them that I had just come from Siberia, and across the Gobi desert.

"I suppose you have not seen any of the London papers recently, then?" said the gentleman; and, on my replying that it was many months since I last saw one, he added that as I had just come through Siberia, it would doubtless interest me very much to see a lot of pictures of prison life in that country, which had been appearing for some time past in the *Illustrated London News;* so many, in fact, that the paper seemed to have devoted itself to Siberia, for some reason or other. It may be imagined how this information tickled me; for it was positively the first intimation I had got that my numerous batches of prison sketches and manuscript had got through the Russian post-office, and reached England safely. Without, however, giving my name or saying what I was, I asked, as unconcernedly as I could, if he knew who they were by, as I might, perhaps, have met the artist whilst in Siberia. "Price," was the name, he thought. With that I took out one of my cards, and presented it to him, and we had a hearty laugh at the incident.

After leaving Sin Fou Fou, the road passed through some really magnificent mountain scenery, the wildest and grandest, I think, I have ever seen. At times the track passed right along the very edge of awful precipices, which made me feel quite sick to look down into, for one false step of either of my mules would have been fatal. Yet the brutes somehow would persist in keeping as near the edge as it was absolutely possible to go, in spite of the endeavours of the boy to hold them back. Knowing, from personal experience, that they were not so surefooted as they seem to imagine they are, I felt anything but comfortable. However, not the slightest incident of any kind occurred worth mentioning. To the mountain passes succeeded valleys covered with rich plantations of rice, their submerged state giving a curious and inundated appearance to the landscape. Everywhere the industrious Celestials were hard at work as though there was not a moment

to lose. The whole scene was one of great and incessant animation; in fact, I never saw anything to equal the sight. The traffic along the road, which was of enormous width, seemed simply endless, and resembled a continuous caravan of camels, donkeys, and mules, and immense flocks of sheep, and the noise at times was deafening.

Many of the towns we passed through were evidently very old, and in most cases their venerable crenelated walls showed signs of great antiquity. One place in particular, Tchai Dar, the entrance to which was through a sort of double archway in splendid preservation, was very fine, and doubtless dating back very many hundreds of years. Once, however, inside these magnificent relics, all illusion vanished; it was almost like going behind the scenes of a theatre, for the cities were invariably squalid in the extreme, and offered a striking and disappointing contrast to their outer mediaeval appearance.

On Friday, May 29, we reached the famous Nankaou Pass, and a little before we reached the town of that name, the road passed under an archway through what is generally known as the "Great Wall of China." Some time before reaching it, I could distinguish the mighty structure standing out in bold relief against the sky, where in places it actually crossed the very tops of the highest mountains. I had fully prepared myself for something wonderful, but this marvellous work more than realized my expectations, and fairly held me spellbound for a few minutes. One can form some idea of the panic the Celestials must have been in when they undertook such a gigantic barrier. The Kalgan wall, in my opinion, is not worthy of being mentioned in the same breath even, and any one who first saw this one, and then fancied he would find something finer at Kalgan, would be grievously disappointed. What struck me most about it was its wonderful state of preservation, the symmetrically hewn stones of which it is composed showing but few signs of the ravages of time. I persuaded Nicolaieff to halt the caravan long enough for me to make a rough sketch; but it is too overpowering and colossal for an ordinary pencil to be able to do justice to. How it could have ever been defended is a mystery, for it would undoubtedly have been as difficult to hold as to attack. The Nankaou Pass is very beautiful, and reminded me not a little of parts of Wales or Ireland. Through the rocky gorge ran a sparkling torrent, and the boulders on either side were clothed with the most brilliant lichen.

The town itself, where we arrived in time for our mid-day halt, offered but little of particular interest, as it was very like all the others we had passed through, except that it was market day, and the narrow streets were, if possible, more crowded. I noticed here more women walking about than hitherto, many of them not crippled with the hideous

THE GREAT WALL OF CHINA AT THE ENTRANCE TO NANKAW PASS.

[To face p. 38.

Chinese foot, but wearing the more sensible Manchurian shoe.

Nankaou also impressed itself on my memory on account of the awful amount of flies everywhere; in fact, they were positively maddening, as there was no getting away from them. One's food, if left exposed for only a few seconds, became covered with what resembled a moving mass of jet. Up till then I had been enjoying a comparative immunity from insect pests, but I should now have to pay the penalty of having continuous warm weather and sunshine. These flies were, however, insignificant, compared with what I had to endure later on, when the mosquitoes and sandflies never for a moment left me alone night or day.

We were now rapidly nearing the end of our long journey, and evidently beginning to get in touch, so to speak, with the capital, the country becoming if possible even more cultivated, and the stream of traffic along the road more and more congested. I now began to get a slight foretaste of what heat and dust in China really mean; for at times everything within a few yards on either side was lost in a dense sort of fog, through which the moving, perspiring masses of people appeared to be groping their way tediously. At last on the horizon, not very far ahead, I made out a long dark line just visible above the surrounding trees. At the same moment Nicolaieff, who was riding close to my litter, pointed to it, and, with a smile of satisfaction on his sunburnt face, informed me that the walls of Peking were before us.

Our goal once in sight, the time did not seem so long in reaching it, and in less than half an hour we were advancing in the midst of a dense crowd, under the shadow of the massive crenelated battlements, towards the entrance of the immense city. In comparison to its size, there are but few entrances, and these far apart, and we had to follow the walls quite a long way before we reached an archway, but not the entrance to the city itself, for on the other side of the vast walls were the inner walls enclosing the Tartar city, our destination, a wide expanse of waste ground separating them from the outer *enceinte*. Along this dusty, stony waste hundreds of caravans and vehicles and passengers were passing to and fro. It was a strange scene, and rendered doubly so by the weird hoarse murmur of the great city so close. The venerable walls seemed almost endless, at any rate to me, for I was all impatience for the wonders which I felt sure were coming.

At last we reached the principal entrance, a huge tunnel-like archway through the thickness of the walls themselves. With difficulty, and advancing but very slowly through the throng of people, we made our way in, and I found myself in a vast open square paved with immense slabs of stone. This square was surrounded on all four sides by the city walls, archways through them leading to the different quarters—one to the Chinese city; another, which was closed, to the imperial city; and in front of me the principal entrance of all, the famous Tchien-Men gate, leading into the Tartar city. And what an entrance! I don't think I ever in my life saw anything which made a more overpowering and indescribable impression on me than did this huge archway, surmounted by its immense donjen-like temple; it was more like a vision of ancient Babylon than anything I had ever expected to see in the Celestial Empire. One seemed so absolutely insignificant in comparison to this vast monument of a so distant past, that it produced in me a feeling akin to awe as I passed under the walls which had witnessed so many wonderful scenes and echoed to so many hundreds of generations.

It would be almost impossible to describe the strange semi-barbaric crowd which I saw around me. Accustomed though I was beginning to get to the wonders of the Far East, I felt that Peking was the most wonderful of all. It was almost like stepping back into the Middle Ages to find one's self in such surroundings. The wonderful impression caused by the first view of the entrance to the Celestial city is, however, rudely dispelled as soon as its portals are passed, for all illusion immediately vanishes. The abominations of the northern cities are here magnified, for I don't think I was ever in a more hideously dirty place than Peking. In fact, to say it is dirty is but to describe it mildly, for I can safely assert that one does not know what dust and dirt really are unless one has been to Peking.

## CHAPTER XXVII.

### PEKING.

Exciting times—A chat with Sir John Walsham—The Chinese city—Horrible scenes—Social life at the Legations in Peking—Lady Walsham's "At homes"—The hardest-worked man in the East—Interesting evening with Sir Robert Hart—His account of his life.

PEKING, though perhaps from its general appearance the last place in the world where one would expect to find a good European hotel, can boast of a really fair *hostellerie*—fortunately for such travellers as find their way to this out-of-the-way city; and after the long and dusty ride through the crowded streets, it may be imagined what a relief it is to find one's self in this welcome oasis. The Hotel de Pékin, as it is somewhat humorously called, is part of a large general store kept by a genial Frenchman, M. Taillieu, who many years ago came out to the Far East to make his fortune, and has ended by settling down in the Celestial capital as a sort of purveyor to the different Legations. Travellers are not numerous here, so the hotel is but a sort of *annexe* of the store; still, the accommodation was all that could be desired, and the living, which was a kind of

2 A

family *table-d'hôte*, was excellent, and fairly cheap considering.

I happened to arrive in the city at a particularly exciting time, just after the anti-European riots and murders on the Yangste, and the air was full of disquieting rumours of approaching troubles. In fact, on the very day I reached Peking the walls of the various European compounds had been covered with placards calling on the people to rise that night and exterminate the "foreign devils." Nothing, however, came of it, fortunately, and the night passed without the slightest indication of any hostile feeling on the part of the inhabitants. As a matter of fact, had anything occurred I should probably not now be writing this, for the Europeans in Peking are in the unenviable position of the proverbial "rat in a hole;" as, whatever resistance they might offer were they attacked after nightfall, the result would be absolutely inevitable, as no outer help could reach them. At eight every night the city gates are closed, and as the telegraph wires are outside the walls, all communication with civilization is thus completely severed.

Of course my first duty was to call at the British Legation and pay my respects to Sir John Walsham, our Minister to the Court of Peking. I had already heard a lot about the magnificence of the palace which represents Great Britain in the capital of the Celestial Empire, but I was unprepared for the gorgeous temple-like structure standing in a spacious compound into which I was ushered. It was like a big work of art, and in no way spoilt by the evidences of female taste and handiwork I saw on all sides in the luxurious reception-rooms.

Although, beyond my credentials as correspondent of the *Illustrated London News*, I was unprovided with any letter of introduction, I was immediately received in a most friendly and informal manner by courteous Sir John Walsham, and we had quite a long chat together. Sir John seemed somewhat surprised at my having been permitted to come through China from Kalgan, and still more so when I informed him I had accompanied the Russian mail. The reason of his surprise I could only conjecture. One subject led to another, and I gradually learnt a lot of interesting particulars about the position of European Ministers in Peking. Although I was already somewhat *au courant* with the state of affairs, I must confess I was fairly astounded when I was informed that beyond being, as it were, tolerated, they never have any communication with Celestial officials except on business matters, and there was absolutely no friendship lost between them; that their position was always, as it were, on a volcano, and often almost insupportable. This remarkable *status quo*, Sir John added, would doubtless have to be rectified one day, for China is an important country from many points of view. For the moment, however, Europe had her hands full. I could not help mentioning that I had already heard of all this, and that it was always a source of wonderment to me that the great Powers had so long stood this sort of arrogant insolence on the part of a semi-barbaric nation.

It is only my intention to attempt to describe

STREET SCENE, TARTAR CITY, PEKING.

Peking in a very superficial manner; for, although I spent a month in it, I felt that it would require a much longer stay in the place, and a much abler pen than mine, to do even scanty justice to its many curiosities and the historical souvenirs it recalls, or to give even a slight idea of the many horrible and strange sights to be witnessed in its crowded, evil-smelling streets, where one cannot take a step without having one's eyes or nostrils shocked by some abomination or other. I have heard Canton described as the most hideous city in the Far East, but I fancy Peking runs it pretty closely. It will give some idea of its horrors when I state that I don't think I ever went through the Chinese city without seeing the dead body of a beggar lying about somewhere. I well remember my astonishment on the first of these occasions. Accompanied by a friend and a guide, I was passing along a very crowded thoroughfare called the "Beggars' Bridge," when I espied a poor emaciated wretch in a state of absolute nudity, lying in the centre of the pathway right out in the broiling sun. He was in such a twisted, contorted position, that I remarked to my boy—

"That's a queer place for a man to sleep, Joe."

"He no belong sleep, sir; he belong dead man," replied Joe in his quaint "pigeon English."

It might have been a dead dog for all the notice the body attracted. The busy crowds passed to and fro, evidently so used to such sights that they never even thought of moving it on one side, or even of covering it up.

It is to live in the midst of such barbaric surroundings that civilized nations have sent their representative ministers with their families.

Still, in spite of the many inevitable discomforts,

social life amongst the Europeans in Peking seemed to me pleasant enough in its way, for there was always plenty to do; and when I was not working, the time never hung heavily on my hands, for the hospitality I was shown whilst there was quite equal to anything I had experienced in Siberia, and that is saying a good deal.

With such a charming and hospitable an ambassadress, it may be imagined that the life of the little colony centred itself, so to speak, round the British Legation, and Lady Walsham's "At home" days were events to be looked forward to; and the *coup d'œil* during the afternoon, when tennis and tea were in full swing and the gardens crowded, was as pretty as it was unique, the temple-like buildings in the background forming a telling contrast to the white-clad figures under the trees or on the lawn.

I was particularly fortunate in arriving in Peking during the "season," for towards the end of June, when the heat and dust become insupportable, its European residents betake themselves up into the hills, where many disused temples are annually converted into temporary country-houses, and, from all accounts, very charming places they make.

No description of European life in Peking would be complete without some reference to that most striking personality of the East, Sir Robert Hart, the Inspector-General of the Chinese Imperial Customs, so a brief *résumé* of an extremely interesting evening I had the pleasure of spending with the great man will doubtless be of interest.

It was Sir Robert's "At home" day, for every Wednesday afternoon he receives his numerous friends in the beautiful grounds surrounding his house, and from six till eight there is tennis and dancing on the spacious lawns. A delightful sense of calm prevailed in this snug and cool retreat, which was a great relief after the continual turmoil and dust outside, a sense of relief in no way marred by the distant strains of the excellent band playing on the lawn— not a Chinese band, thank goodness, but thoroughly European in all but its musicians, who are Chinese boys in the Customs service, and who look strikingly quaint in their national costumes, with their pigtails rolled round their heads like chignons under their straw hats.

The entertainment was concluded, and I was about to take my leave, when Sir Robert whispered in my ear, "Don't run away, but stay and have a bit of dinner with me *en tête-à-tête*." I naturally jumped at the chance of a quiet and informal chat with the great man, so accepted the invitation without hesitation. By-and-by the company gradually left, and we had the beautiful gardens to ourselves. It was such a calm and lovely evening that I could not help remarking to Sir Robert as we strolled up and down, that life in Peking would not be so bad after all if every European had such a beautiful place to live in, so entirely isolated from the foul smells and sights of the native city outside.

"Yes," replied Sir Robert, "it certainly is a very pleasant retreat, and it is very seldom indeed that I ever leave it to go into the city. My work occupies so much of my time that I have little inclination after it is over of a day to go out visiting, so I live here almost like a hermit. My Wednesday garden-parties are my sole relaxation, and I have only had eighteen months' holiday in all since I joined the Chinese Customs Service in 1859. Lady Hart left China for England some ten years ago, and I had arranged to join her there in a few months, but every time I commenced making arrangements to leave Peking something turned up to prevent me, and I am even now uncertain when I shall be able to get away, but when I do, it will certainly be for good, for I have had enough of it."

At this moment dinner was announced, so we adjourned to the house, which is a very large bungalow-built structure, which reminded me very much of the houses to be seen in the newer suburbs of London. Everything inside was about as English-looking as it could well have been. They were huge bachelor quarters, such as, barring their size, could be found anywhere in England, and the resemblance was heightened by the fact of all the rooms being lighted by gas—made on the premises, I learnt.

The dinner was excellent, and would not have

disgraced a Parisian *chef*, and although the *menu* was written in Chinese, and I therefore did not always know what I was eating, I appreciated it none the less. We dined positively in Oriental magnificence, no less than eight men-servants waiting on us; for the high position which Sir Robert holds in China forces him to keep up a style on a footing with his rank, and he told me that even when he is alone the same ceremony has to be observed. It was one of the penalties of greatness, I remarked. To me, however, unused to such splendour, there was something particularly jarring in feeling myself thus surrounded, and every mouthful I took watched by the many and observant eyes, so I felt quite a sense of relief when the banquet was concluded, and we were left alone with our cigars and coffee, and could talk unrestrained.

Reverting to the length of time he had been in China, I remarked to Sir Robert that he must have come out as a mere youth, for he does not look a very old man now.

"Why, how old do you think I am?" he asked.

As I hesitated to give a direct answer to this question, he proceeded to inform me, to my surprise, that he joined her Majesty's Consular service in Hong Kong in 1854, just one year before reaching his majority. (He was born in Belfast in 1834.)

"Well, you have had a wonderful time of it since then, Sir Robert," said I, "and could doubtless write a book of reminiscences which would be of thrilling interest."

"Yes," replied my genial host; "but although it has often been suggested to me to publish such a book, I shall probably never carry it into effect, for once I commenced there would be no end to my souvenirs."

"But how did you come to attain the wonderfully influential position you now hold?"

"Oh, it was simple enough," replied Sir Robert. "It came about somewhat in this fashion. After I had been in the Consular service five years, I was invited to join the Chinese Customs. This was shortly after Lord Elgin's treaty, when certain ports were to be opened to Europeans. Something inspired me to accept the offer; one thing led to another, and in 1861 I was made Acting Inspector-General, in the place of Mr. Lay, who was going home on leave for two years. A few months after his return to China he was compelled to resign, and I was appointed Inspector-General in his stead. So in four years I had risen to the highest post in the service. In those days the position was not nearly so important as it is now, for the Chinese Customs Service was in its infancy. It has since grown to such huge dimensions that the work it entails is something incredible. In 1861 there were only three ports open to Europeans, whereas there are now thirty; the ramifications of the system extend as far south as Tonkin, and in

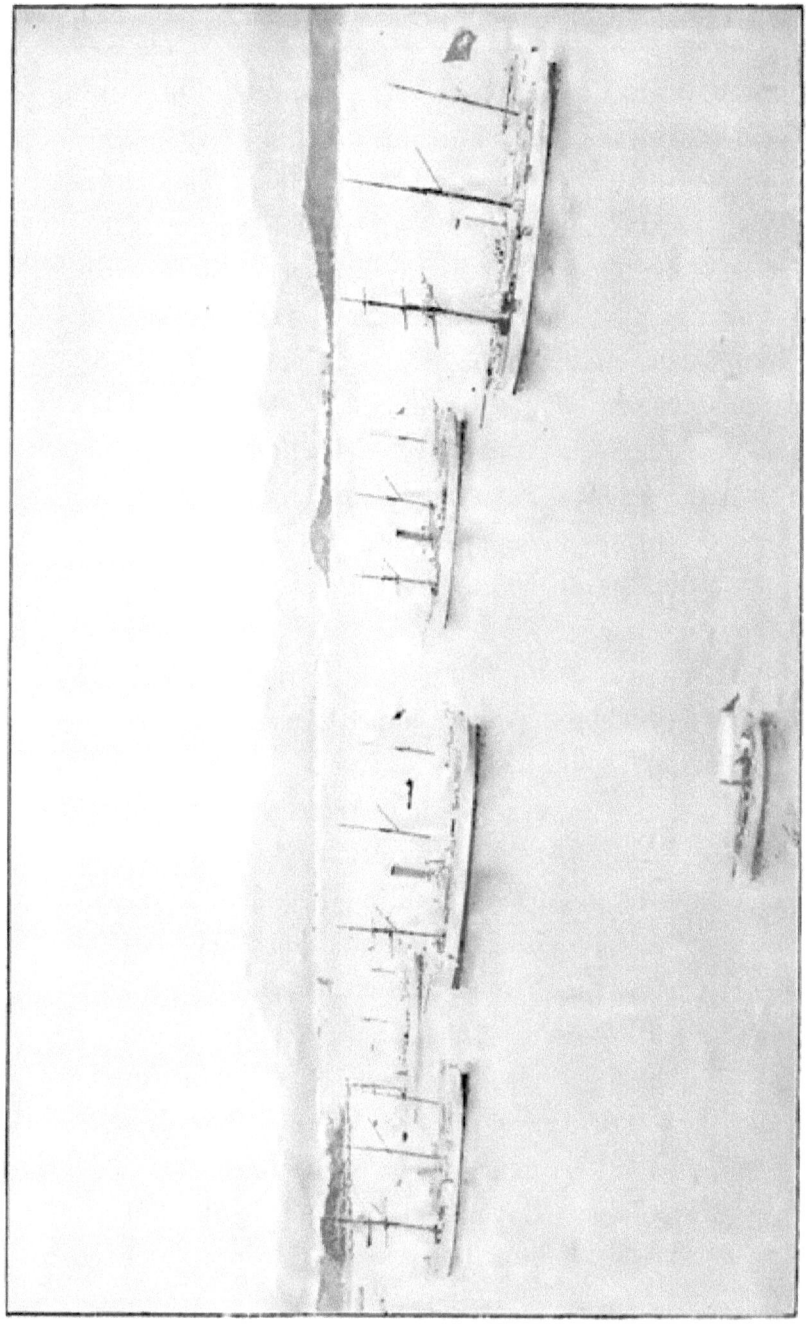

CHINESE REVENUE CRUISERS IN HONG KONG ROADSTEAD.

the north to Corea. Over seven hundred Europeans and three thousand Chinamen, of all classes, are employed in the land service alone. The entire coast-line is guarded by twenty armed cruisers of the very latest types, built in England, most of them by Armstrong. These cruisers are commanded by Europeans and manned by Chinese. There is, besides, quite a flotilla of armed steam-launches used in the various harbours. The lighthouses along the coast are also under my jurisdiction. Each port has its European commissioner, who has acting under him a Chinese official and staff of assistants, European and otherwise."

"How do you admit Europeans into the service?" I asked. "Have you a competitive examination, or are special qualifications necessary?"

"Well, it is very seldom there is a vacancy," replied Sir Robert, "but when there is, there are so many candidates on the waiting list that my agent in London has a sort of examination held; but, of course, a man with some knowledge, however slight, of Chinese has the best chance of getting the berth."

"But how is all this supported?" I naturally asked, though aware that the Chinese Government got a splendid revenue out of the Customs service.

"The Chinese Government," replied Sir Robert, "allows about £400,000 a year for the support of the service. This is absolutely under my control; also the appointment or dismissal of all officials. The

Chinese Customs are assuming bigger proportions every year, and are an ever-increasing source of revenue to the State. The great mistake that foreigners make with regard to China is to imagine that she is in want of extraneous pecuniary assistance —that she is bordering on a state of insolvency. Nothing could be more erroneous; it is rather the other way. If the Chinese monied men only trusted their own Government a little more, China would undoubtedly soon be in the position of being able to lend money to other countries. Putting this aside, China is not trying, nor has she ever been trying, to borrow money, though many German, French, and other syndicates have been doing their utmost to lend her some."

I could not help remarking that this was a very enviable position for a country to be in.

"Besides," continued Sir Robert, "the system of such loans is contrary to Chinese ideas; for a Chinaman prefers a short loan at a high rate of interest to a long one at a low rate. I have been much amused, knowing what I do, to hear of agents of syndicates stopping in Peking for months at a time on the chance of floating a loan. In several cases, in their anxiety to do business, they were on the point of doing so with the wrong people. After all, the Chinamen are no better than they ought to be; and as it takes so little to make the average European believe that every well-dressed Celestial is an official mandarin, they often took advantage of this simplicity of the Western barbarian. There were some extraordinary cases, a few years ago, of people being introduced to these agents as the Grand Chamberlain of the Court, or some other high dignitary, empowered to negotiate a loan. They were absolutely nothing of the sort, but were perhaps connected with officialism in the remotest and obscurest way. In some instances, however, though not what they pretended to be, they were actually connected with the big officials. This was proved by the fact of the Government, though not officially recognizing the loan thus obtained, still assuming to a certain extent the responsibility of it, as it had been used partially for official purposes. Very little, however, has transpired of these curious transactions.

"As it has been with loans, so it is with railways. Undoubtedly China will one day have her railways, but though she has for years past been pestered with offers by foreign capitalists to help her start them, so far the reply has always been that when the time comes the engineers, the capital, all, in fact, that is needful, will be found by China—a strong hint, which has not, however, been taken, that no foreigners need apply. Of one thing I feel convinced," continued Sir Robert, "that China, though certainly very many years behindhand, is undoubtedly going ahead—advancing slowly, it is true, but still advancing, and every step she takes forward is a certain one. In spite of sarcasm and adverse criticism, she adheres to her slow, steady pace, and, so far, has never receded a single step. As compared with Japan, she reminds me always of the old adage of the hare and the tortoise."

Having finished our coffee, we rose from the table and had a stroll through the suite of rooms in which Sir Robert dwells in solitary grandeur. There was a striking absence of the curios which one would have expected to find in the quarters of a man who had passed so many years in the Far East. Beyond his work Sir Robert had evidently but few hobbies. In one corner of the drawing-room was a large table covered with the Christmas cards which my host received last year from his many friends all over the world, whilst on the walls were a few very ordinary pictures. The whole place, even to the large bare-looking ballroom with two pianos in it, was very comfortless in appearance, and I could not help thinking that it must be very trying to one's nerves to have such a big bare place all to one's self. However, *chacun à son goût!* Sir Robert's office, or rather his "den," as he called it, was very characteristic of the man, and showed evident signs of being more used than any other room in the house, for here Sir Robert spends the greater part of his day. His writing-table particularly struck me as being very unusual, for he informed me he never sits down to his work, but always stands and does his writing at the tall desk in the centre of the room.

SIR ROBERT HART, G.C.M.G., IN HIS "DEN" AT PEKING.

[*To face p.* 366.

"The air of Peking," said Sir Robert laughingly, "has a very somniferous effect, and I feel I should instantly fall asleep if I were to sit down of an afternoon to do my work."

A quotation written on a small discoloured piece of paper stuck over the desk attracted my attention.

"That," said my host, "is a verse I copied very many years ago out of Dickens's *Household Words*. It appealed to me very strangely, so I stuck it up over my desk, and it has been there ever since."

The lines were the following, and may be of interest :—

> "If thou hast yesterday thy duty done,
>   And thereby found firm footing for to-day,
>   Whatever clouds may dark to-morrow's sun
>   Thou shalt not miss thy solitary way."

"By the way, Sir Robert," said I, "before dinner you were speaking of going home for good. Have you any immediate prospect of seeing the old country? For I am sure you must be anxious to do so after so many years' absence."

"Well, there's nothing definite fixed at present, anyhow," he replied.

"And your successor—have you any idea who he will be?" I hinted.

"No. No suggestion has yet been made of even my probable successor, but so far as I can judge, seeing the way Chinese views are tending, my idea is that it will be a Chinaman who will take up my work, for the Chinese seem particularly anxious to take the foreign customs under their own control."

I could not help remarking on the immense collection of books and papers which encumbered the room, and added that doubtless Sir Robert felt quite in his element amongst this accumulation of statistical matter.

"Well, curiously enough," replied the inspector-general laughingly, "although I have been mixed up with it for so many years, there is no work I have disliked more all my life than statistics; but, forming as it does part of my daily routine, I have become so accustomed to it that, though I can never like it, it has ceased to be irksome to me."

Leading out of the "den" was a room which Sir Robert told me he uses as his audience chamber, and where he receives all Chinese officials. The place was furnished in a sort of semi-Chinese fashion, with the indispensable raised platform for sitting on, and the usual small table in the centre. There was nothing particularly striking about it except a huge Chinese inscription stuck over the door, which, in reply to my inquiry, Sir Robert informed me was a proverb, and meant, "Like a bird on a twig," which simile, he further added, is, according to the Chinese, supposed to convey the idea of how insecure one's footing is in this weary world of ours. I did not like to ask whether this motto had been given to Sir Robert by his Chinese friends to stick up over the door, or whether it was a pet proverb of his, for I was not very certain as to what it really meant.

We then strolled out into the verandah, and as I was lighting another cheroot preparatory to taking my ease in one of the two long chairs which lay so invitingly handy, with a small table between with the materials on it for whiskey and seltzer, I turned to my host and remarked that I had often heard how difficult foreigners usually found it to get on with the Chinese officials owing to the contempt in which the latter hold any rank but their own, and asked him how he managed, having to deal with such a high class of mandarin.

"Well," replied Sir Robert, "owing to the favour of the emperor, there are but few with whom I am brought into contact who hold a higher rank than mine; for I am the happy possessor of almost all the distinctions—a Red Button of the First Class, a Peacock's Feather, and the First Class of the Second Division of the Double Dragon. But the honour recently bestowed upon me is the highest that it is possible to confer on even a most distinguished Chinese subject: my family was ennobled by imperial decree, to three generations back; that is to say, 'Ancestral rank of the first class of the first order for three generations, with letters patent.' The value of this decree may be estimated from the fact that at the same time the emperor ennobled his own grandmother in like fashion, she having been an inferior wife of the Emperor Taou Kwang, in whose reign took place the first opium war."

Although Sir Robert was too modest to refer to them, most people are aware that he holds also many of the most coveted of European decorations also, such as the Knight Grand Cross of St. Michael and St. George, and Grand Officer of the Legion of Honour, etc.

I was on the point of asking further questions, when I noticed my host glancing surreptitiously at his watch. Mechanically I followed suit, and found that, absorbed in such an interesting conversation, the hours had flown by, and it was already past midnight, an unprecedented hour for Peking; so without delay and with hearty thanks to my kind entertainer I took my leave.

While returning to my hotel I could not help pondering on the wonderful career of the man, and his devotion to the nation which has done so much for him, as is shown by his refusal in 1885 of the post of British minister to China, which was offered him. Nevertheless, he still keeps a warm corner in his heart for the country of his birth, as is shown by the fact, according to what one generally hears in China, that an Irishman in his service has better chance of quick advancement than any other nationality.

## CHAPTER XXVIII.

### PEKING (*continued*)—AND HOME.

Difficulty of sketching in the streets—My journey from Peking to Tientsin—A Chinese house-boat—The Peiho River—Tientsin—From Tientsin to Shanghai—And home.

I DON'T think I was ever in a place where it was more difficult to sketch out in the open than Peking. I tried it on several occasions, and nearly always had to abandon my intention, for almost immediately I produced my sketch-book, and before even I had time to commence operations, I would be absolutely hemmed in on all sides by a dense crowd of dirty insolent rascals, who, as a rule, seemed far more interested in me than in what I was sketching. It was absolutely useless getting my "boy" to ask them civilly to move on one side, as this only appeared to cause greater amusement among them, and, of course, it would have been absolute madness to lose one's temper, so I generally gave in, and beat a retreat. Naturally there were a few quiet spots where one could work undisturbed, such as on the city walls, but the *coup d'œil* one got from such an elevated position was not to be compared with that in the midst of the busy throngs. As ill luck would have it, I had run short of photographic films, so my Kodak was useless.

There was so much to see in the various quarters of Peking that one could spend hours simply roaming about looking at the shops, or rather open booths. The Chinese city was far and away the most interesting. Its narrow streets, which were darkened by the immense number of sign-boards hanging overhead, resembled an immense bazaar where everything conceivable almost could be purchased. The "curio-hunting" fever came over me like it does over all new-comers to the Far East, and many were the good bargains I imagined I had made, although, doubtless, I shall find that most of the things could have been bought cheaper in London.

Of course I did the "lions" as completely as possible, and visited the theatres and the opium dens, and saw enough temples and monuments to last me for many years, and witnessed scenes which made it hard to realize that all these relics of the barbarism of the Middle Ages were within touch of the civilization of the nineteenth century. Still, I could not help coming to the same conclusion as Sir Mackenzie Wallace, and thoroughly agree with him that "sight-seeing is the weariness of the flesh;" so at last I made up my mind to bid adieu to all my hospitable friends and make another move on my homeward journey, for I still had many weary miles to traverse before I reached Old England again.

There are two ways of getting to Tientsin, the port of Peking, where one embarks for Shanghai—either in what is known as a Peking cart, or by house-boat. Having already had some not altogether delightful experiences of these native carts, it did not take me long to decide which mode of conveyance to use, and although I learnt that the river route was considerably longer I settled at once to go by it.

As luck would have it, just as I had made all my arrangements to start, I managed to find a very genial companion for the journey in Mr. Savage Landor, a traveller and roving artist, whose acquaintance I had made whilst in Peking. This gentleman, who had just returned from Japan, was on his way to Australia, so we arranged to go as far as Shanghai together. Travelling in company is undoubtedly more pleasant than alone, more especially if one's companion has tastes at all in sympathy with one's own, and in this particular instance it was especially so, for the three days' uneventful journey to Tientsin passed away very agreeably. We had taken the precaution of providing ourselves with a "boy" to act as servant and cook; and a very excellent *chef* did he make, the little dinners he gave us being quite works of art in their way, considering his limited culinary arrangements. *Il va sans dire* that we had stocked our larder before starting with a plentiful supply of delicacies, as we had been informed that nothing except nameless Chinese abominations could be purchased *en route*.

The house-boat, which we had previously secured, was lying in the river Peiho at Tungchow, the nearest point to Peking, and to reach it we had a six hours' journey before us down the canal, in a small open boat. Our baggage we sent on ahead of us by cart.

It was on an absolutely perfect day in June, with the sun shining in a cloudless sky, that I bid a fond (and I hope last) farewell to dirty Peking, and started on the final stage of my journey towards the Yellow Sea. After a not unpleasant, though somewhat tedious journey down the canal, we eventually reached Tungchow, and went on board the "yacht," where we found that Joe, our boy, had got quite a nice little supper ready for us.

A Chinese native house-boat, though undoubtedly admirably adapted for its purposes, is certainly not what one would term a luxurious craft, nor one in which I should care to linger longer than was absolutely necessary. It is a very long vessel, partially decked over, with the saloon amidships, the galley aft, and the men's quarters "up for'ard." Its rig consists of one mast, with the usual Chinese picturesque mat-sail. The crew is usually composed of five men and the master.

Although perhaps not scrupulously clean, the cabin, by candlelight at any rate, looked all right, and for

MY HOUSE-BOAT.

a wonder did not smell over-stuffy, as such places usually do; so as we sat down to supper we congratulated ourselves on at least having decent quarters for the next two days. While we were eating our meal, talking of one thing and another, I happened to remark that we were doubtless fortunate in getting this particular house-boat, for I had heard that as a rule these craft simply swarmed with vermin of all sorts, whereas this one seemed absolutely free from them, as I had not detected any sign of "life" about the place. The words were scarcely out of my mouth when I noticed Landor, who was seated opposite me, smile and look at the wall behind me. I glanced round, when to my horror I saw coming towards us what looked like a long procession of positively the biggest blackbeetles and cockroaches I ever set eyes on, and which, doubtless attracted by the food, were making for the table. I have such a natural loathing of these filthy creatures that I cleared out on to the deck in no time, and, as may be imagined, my supper was abruptly ended. We then discovered that the saloon was simply infested with all sorts of playful creatures, which, though perhaps presenting some interest to the entymological student, certainly offered no attraction from an artistic point of view. I decided without much hesitation that sleeping on deck in the open air under the canopy of the stars would be preferable to an unconditional surrender of my person during the dark hours to this watchful enemy; so when "sweet slumber beckoned us to her arms," I betook myself to a downy couch, consisting of an old sail thrown over two packing cases on the fore-deck, whilst Landor, relying on the merits of Keating's powder, retired to the sleeping-apartment of the cabin, and barricaded himself inside quite a magic circle of "vermin-killer."

These trivial discomforts did not, however, interfere with our enjoyment of the trip and the novel scenes around us, for from the time we left Tungchow till we reached Tientsin the winding river was one continuous and ever-changing panorama of life and movement. I don't think I ever before saw such an immense number of boats on any river as we passed during that journey, all apparently of the same size and pattern, and as usual positively crowded with human beings. As far as the eye could see on either side, owing to the flatness of the scenery and the many turns in the river, the country seemed absolutely planted, so to speak, with huge mat sails, and the effect was indescribably strange. All this, added to the teeming crowds at work in the fields, presented a scene of population the like of which I imagine could not be witnessed anywhere but in China.

We reached the last village before Tientsin too late for the boat to be able to proceed that evening, as the river, we learnt, was closed after a certain hour; so, rather than spend another night on board when so close to a decent hotel, we decided to leave the boy in charge of our belongings, with instructions to bring them on the first thing in the morning, and to go across country to the town in some conveyance.

With some difficulty two jinrickshas were procured, and with two boys in the shafts of each, we started off at a good pace for our goal. This was my first experience of these convenient little carriages with their apparently indefatigable human steeds in the shafts, and very pleasant did I find the motion, more especially with the recollection of my recent travels fresh in my memory.

We had about six miles to go, and the whole way the two boys went at a quick run, only stopping once or twice to change places between the shafts. Gradually the native houses on either side of the broad road began to get more numerous. On the horizon in front I could make out that indefinable sort of glare which by night seems to hang over all large towns, whilst, as though to assure me that my long journey was at length over, the distant sound of the whistle of some large steamer in the river came wafted to my ears on the calm evening air; and when shortly after I found myself passing through fine well-arranged avenues and streets lighted by gas, I felt this really was the end of my discomforts, the fact of our finding excellent accommodation and a most obliging landlord at the Globe Hotel, where we put up, helping not a little to increase this pleasurable feeling.

We found we had about twenty-four hours before the steamer started for Shanghai, so had ample time to look round and see all there was to be seen of this busy place. The next day, therefore, passed rapidly enough, and after a delightful little dinner at the British Consulate with Mr. and Mrs. Brennan, we went on board the s.s. *Hsin-Yu* in the very best possible spirits ; in fact, I don't remember ever feeling happier than I did when I found myself once more on a well-appointed ship, and with the feeling that I had safely accomplished the greater part of my self-imposed task.

The trip to Shanghai occupied three and a half days, the weather being so delightful that it was quite like yachting in the Channel. The *Hsin-Yu* was a fine steamer of some 1500 tons, belonging to the China Merchants Company, manned by Chinese, but officered entirely by Europeans. She had, I learnt, the proud privilege of flying the "Greyhound" flag of the East. We called in at Chefoo, and remained there long enough to have a hasty look round this quaint little semi-English village. Then on again to Shanghai, where I arrived on June 26, 1891.

And here I will leave you, kind reader, for my long and arduous ten months' pilgrimage across the vast Continent of Asia was thus complete—a pilgrimage which, although full of hardships and discomforts, was fully compensated by my strange and delightful experiences, so much so that in spite of all I should be glad of an opportunity to do many parts of it over again.

Nought remained for me now but to choose my route home. This I eventually decided to make *viâ* Japan and America, thus completing a circuit of the globe by an entirely novel route.

SHANGHAI.

# INDEX.

## A

Aalesund, 6
Accident on Great Post Road, 176
Angara river, 178, 224
——, navigation of, 227
——, Siberiakoff's scheme for its navigation, 226
"*Angliske Boxe*," 268
April 8, 1891
"At homes" at Lady Walsham's, 358

## B

Bear-hunting, 95
*Biscaya*, the steamship, 2
——, good-bye to the, 59
——, in the ice, 16
——, our party on board, 3
—— and *Thule*, departure of, 60
Botoiskaya, 158
Bradiagga, 170
"Brick" tea, 290

## C

Camel-cart, 303
Camels, 304
Cape Flyaway, 11
Capital punishment, 144
"Chaman" stone, the, 228
China, over-population, 325
Chinese cities, 340
—— cooking, 343
—— house-boat, 374
—— inns, 340
—— inn, room in, 342
—— vodka, 343
—— women, small feet of, 325
Cold, 161
Cold, first touch of, 96
"Convict's word," 199
Crowther, our ice-master, 12
Czar's birthday, celebration of, in Irkutsk, 219

## D

Dogger Bank, 4
Dogs, native, 79
Dudinskoi, 64

## E

Eclipse of the moon, 327
Englishman in North China, 345
Exciting incident, 264

## F

Flies, 349
Forest track, 167
Forests of Northern Siberia, 69
Foxes, white, 64

## G

Gobi Desert, early morning in, 308
——, first glimpse of, 313
——, Holfer-Sum, 324
——, meets homeward-bound mail in, 314
——, Lama settlement of Tcho-Iyr, 315
——, Mongol food, 311
——, my American cooking-stove, 303
——, post-station in mid-desert, 321
——, preparations for, 302
——, prevalent wind in, 318
——, sport in, 319
——, the noon-day halt, 309

382 INDEX.

Gobi Desert, Tola river, 312
——, water in, 310
Golchika, 32
—— to Karaoul, 34
Great Wall of China, 347
——, the "First Parallel," 333

H

Hart, Sir Robert, interview with, 359
Highway robbery, 160
Holidays in Siberia, 217

I

Inquest, 84
Irkutsk, arrival at, 179
——, a ball at M. de Sievers, 187
——, amusements, 217
——, cost of living in, 219
——, fire brigade, 215
——, foundling hospital, 212
——, garrison of, 190
——, Moskovskaia Podvorié, 180
——, museum, 216
——, police, 190
——, prison, 192
—— ——, artists, 196
—— ——, criminal madhouse, 203
—— ——, incongruities of, 194
—— ——, internal arrangements of, 193
—— ——, I paint a picture in, 206
—— ——, political prisoners, 205
—— ——, solitary cells, 204
—— ——, the baroness, 200
—— ——, ——, last interview with, 207
—— ——, workshops, 194
——, prisoners, outdoor employment of, 198
——, public institutions, 188
—— society, 184
——, telephones and telegraphs, 216
——, the Bolshoi Oulitza, 183
——, the gold industry, 209
—— to Kiakhta, my preparation for journey, 223
——, unpleasant experiences, 181

K

Kalgan, 334
——, American missionaries, 335
——, impressions of, 334
Kamin pass, 88
Kansk, 165
Karaoul, 35
——, the chief inhabitant of, 37
Kara Sea, curio-hunting, 21
——, entrance to, 15
——, ice-bound in the, 24
——, icefields in, 17
——, its deadly silence, 27
——, seal-shooting, 25
——, the captain's polar bear in the, 29
——, the walrus-hunters, 20
——, thickness of the ice, 28
——, twilight in, 20
Kasanskoi, my first visit to, 49
——, trader's house at, 50
——, departure from, 61
Khabarova, the hamlet of, 14
Kiakhta, arrival at, 244
——, departure for, 223
——, departure from, 250
—— to Ourga, my preparations for journey, 249
Kolguier Island, 11
Koutoulik, 165
——, waiting-room in post-house, 175
Krasnoiarsk, departure for, 124
——, a convoy of prisoners on the road to, 138
——, a *Priviligiert* prisoner, 148
——, arrival at, 130
——, cigarette-making in, prison, 149
——, courtyard of perasilny, 146
——, criminal exiles, 134
——, fire-towers, 155
——, hotel at, 130
——, incident at fancy dress ball, 152
——, interior of perasilny, 147
——, Jewish and Mohammedan prisoners, 140
——, local malefactors, 153
——, married prisoners' quarters in perasilny, 147
——, political exiles, 151
——, *Priviligierts* criminals, 136

Krasnoiarsk, scene outside prison, 149
—— society, 132
——, the market place, 134
——, the night refuge, 153
——, the perasilny of, 141
——, the theatre, 155
——, verification of prisoners, 145
——, departure from, 157
"Kupetski track," 236
——, incidents on, 237

## L

Lake Baikal, 230
——, first view of, 229
——, the road across, on the ice, 232
——, transparency of ice, 233
Landor, Mr. Savage, 373
Lee, Mr. Charles, 182, 227
——, Mr. George, death of, 71
Lhassa, 277
Liestvinitz, 230
Lofoden Islands, 7

## M

Mail courier, 173
Manhati Pass, 266
Matwieff, my servant, 157
Miamachin, 250
Midnight sun, 8
Mirage on the Yenisei river, 46
Mongol farmyard, 258
—— hair-dressing, 255
Mongolia, currency of, 289
——, Russian influence in, 296
Mongolian camels, 305
Mongols, 255
Moufshkaya, 234
Mountains of North China, 328
Mule-litter, 357
Mules, 337

## N

Nankaou Pass, 347
Nasymoro, 95
Nijui Udinsk, 165
North Cape, 8

## O

Official Russia, first visit from, 83
Oka river, 175

Ostiaks, 77
Ourga, my arrival at, 271
——, absence of beggars, 286
——, a mad dog, 288
——, an impromptu "interview," 279
——, disposal of the dead, 289
—— dogs, 286
——, festival of the Maidha, 297
——, first impressions of, 273
——, Lamas, 281
——, Mr. Feodroff, 274
——, prayer-boards, 284
——, prayer-flags, 285
——, prayer-wheels, 282
——, religious fervour of the Mongols, 282
——, the bazaar, 292
——, the "Bogdor," 275
——, the figure of the Maidha, 276
——, the "old, old story," 299
——, the pony and camel market, 293
——, the Russian Consulate, 273
—— watchmen, 295
——, departure from, 308

## P

Peiho river, 374
Peking, departure from, 374
——, entrance to, 354
——, exciting times, 354
——, sketching in, 371
——, street scenes, 357
——, the British Legation, 354
——, the hotel, 353
*Phœnix*, arrival of, 42
——, cabin of, 45
——, her crew, 43
—— springs a leak, 67
Political exiles at Kiakhta, 247

## R

Russian cooking, our first taste of, 11
—— custom-house officer, 48
—— heavy mail, caravan of, 305
——, the two Cossacks with, 306
—— hospitality, my first experience of, 54
—— Imperial Mail, 173
—— light mail in the Gobi, 305

Russian police officer, 84
Russo-Chinese frontier, 250

S

Sabam Balhousar, 324
———, departure from, 326
Samovars, 168
Samoyede grave, 38
——— hut, 40
Samoyedes at Golchika, 33
Seagulls, 77
Selenga river, 242
———, exciting incident on, 243
Selivanaka, 77
Shanghai, arrival at, 379
———, Tientsin to, 379
Siberia, first glimpse of, 12
Sin Fou Fou, 339
Sketching at Kasanskoi, 52
Skopti, 77
Snow ridges, 159
Sotnikoff, Mr., a visit to, 75
Sledge-travelling, novelty of, 162
Sledging, 124
———, first experiences of, 129
——— on Great Post Road, 156
———, the cold, 129
———, the *padarojou*, 127
———, the post houses, 128
———, the widow, 125
Staroster of prisoners, 142
Steam-launch, expedition of our, 41

T

Tarantass, 239
Tchai Dar 347
Tchien-Men gate, Peking, 351
Tea caravans, 160
——— with a Lama, 294
*Thale*, arrival of the, 56
Tientsin, arrival at, 378
Tiretskaya, 175
Touloung, 165, 174
Travellers, scarcity of, in Siberia, 173
Trees, northern limit of, 64

Troitzkosavsk, 245
Tundras, 38
——— of Northern Siberia, 17
Tungchow, 374
Turuchansk, 80
———, visit to the monastery, 81

V

Ventilation, 165
Village communes, 164
——— priest, 85

W

Walsham, Sir John, interview with, 355
Waygatch, the Straits of, 14
Werchneimbackskoi, 83
Wiggins's expedition, 63
Wood, fuel on the Yenisei, 66
Worogovo, 90
———, the Tartar at, 91

Y

Yenisei river, proportions of, 62
Yeniseisk, arrival at, 96
——— amusements, 104
———, a visit to the men's prison, 107
———, a visit to the women's prison, 112
———, chat with political exile, 115
———, custom-house officials, 101
———, departure of criminals, 113
———, fire brigade, 118
———, first impressions of, 98
——— gold fields, 103
———, High Street, 120
———, houses, 119
———, my lodgings, 102
———, political exiles at, 114
———, shops, 101
——— society, 105
———, the hospital, 117
———, the market, 101
Yamboushan, arrival at, 330
Yourts, 252

www.ingramcontent.com/pod-product-compliance
Lightning Source LLC
Chambersburg PA
CBHW051157300426
44116CB00006B/346